Economic Statecraft and US Foreign Policy

Explaining the connection between economics and violent extremism, this book argues that American foreign policy must be rebalanced with a greater emphasis on social inclusion and shared prosperity in order to mitigate the root causes of conflict.

Rosenberger argues that economic coercion has usually proven counter-productive, and that a militarized American foreign policy too often results in frustration and strategic failure. He analyses this theory through a number of case studies, from the Treaty of Versailles to the more recent issues of Israel in Gaza, US sanctions against Iran, the US-backed, Saudi-led boycott of Qatar and Donald Trump's trade war against China. He concludes that the economic logic of social inclusion and shared prosperity demonstrated in Jean Monnet's European Coal and Steel Community would be a more successful strategy in reducing the demand for violence in the civil wars in Afghanistan, Iraq, Yemen and Syria.

This book will be of particular relevance for courses on American Foreign Policy, International Relations and International Political Economy and seminars on the Near East and South Asia. Professional economists, diplomats and military officers in America and in the Near East and South Asia will also find the argument useful.

Dr. Leif Rosenberger retired from the US government in March 2016 after a 35-year career as a practitioner, scholar and educator. He was a Full Professor of Economics at the US Army War College, where he also held the General Douglas MacArthur Academic Chair of Research in the Strategic Studies Institute.

Routledge Studies in US Foreign Policy
Edited by Inderjeet Parmar, City University, and John Dumbrell, University of Durham

This new series sets out to publish high-quality works by leading and emerging scholars critically engaging with United States Foreign Policy. The series welcomes a variety of approaches to the subject and draws on scholarship from international relations, security studies, international political economy, foreign policy analysis and contemporary international history.

Subjects covered include the role of administrations and institutions, the media, think tanks, ideologues and intellectuals, elites, transnational corporations, public opinion, and pressure groups in shaping foreign policy, US relations with individual nations, with global regions and global institutions and America's evolving strategic and military policies.

The series aims to provide a range of books – from individual research monographs and edited collections to textbooks and supplemental reading for scholars, researchers, policy analysts and students.

US Democracy Promotion after the Cold War
Stability, Basic Premises, and Policy towards Egypt
Annika Elena Poppe

Kissinger, Angola and US-African Foreign Policy
The Unintentional Realist
Steven O'Sullivan

North Korea – US Relations
From Kim Jong-il to Kim Jong-un, 2nd edition
Ramon Pacheco Pardo

Economic Statecraft and US Foreign Policy
Reducing the Demand for Violence
Leif Rosenberger

For more information about this series, please visit: www.routledge.com/series/RSUSFP

Economic Statecraft and US Foreign Policy

Reducing the Demand for Violence

Leif Rosenberger

LONDON AND NEW YORK

First published 2020
by Routledge
2 Park Square, Milton Park, Abingdon, Oxon OX14 4RN

and by Routledge
52 Vanderbilt Avenue, New York, NY 10017

Routledge is an imprint of the Taylor & Francis Group, an informa business

© 2020 Leif Rosenberger

The right of Leif Rosenberger to be identified as author of this work has been asserted by him in accordance with sections 77 and 78 of the Copyright, Designs and Patents Act 1988.

All rights reserved. No part of this book may be reprinted or reproduced or utilised in any form or by any electronic, mechanical, or other means, now known or hereafter invented, including photocopying and recording, or in any information storage or retrieval system, without permission in writing from the publishers.

Trademark notice: Product or corporate names may be trademarks or registered trademarks, and are used only for identification and explanation without intent to infringe.

British Library Cataloguing-in-Publication Data
A catalogue record for this book is available from the British Library

Library of Congress Cataloging-in-Publication Data
Names: Rosenberger, Leif, author.
Title: Economic statecraft and US foreign policy : reducing the demand for violence / Leif Rosenberger.
Other titles: Economic statecraft and United States foreign policy
Description: Abingdon, Oxon ; New York, NY : Routledge, 2020. | Series: Routledge studies in US foreign policy | Includes bibliographical references and index.
Identifiers: LCCN 2019028171 (print) | LCCN 2019028172 (ebook) | ISBN 9780367134204 (hardback) | ISBN 9780429026362 (ebook)
Subjects: LCSH: United States—Foreign relations—Middle East. | Middle East—Foreign relations—United States. | United States—Foreign relations—China. | China—Foreign relations—United States. | Middle East—Economic conditions—21st century. | China—Economic conditions—21st century. | Security, International—Economic aspects. | Political violence—Economic aspects.
Classification: LCC JZ1480.A55 R67 2020 (print) | LCC JZ1480.A55 (ebook) | DDC 327.1/110973—dc23
LC record available at https://lccn.loc.gov/2019028171
LC ebook record available at https://lccn.loc.gov/2019028172

ISBN: 978-0-367-13420-4 (hbk)
ISBN: 978-0-429-02636-2 (ebk)

Typeset in Times New Roman
by codeMantra

This book is dedicated to my wife Regina, the love of my life. Her patience and understanding made this book possible. In addition, I was fortunate along the way to be part of wonderful learning communities consisting of the brave military officers and civilians I had the honor of teaching at the US Army War College and serving with at the Strategic Studies Institute, the US Central Command, the US Pacific Command, the US Central Intelligence Agency and the US Defense Intelligence Agency for 35 years in the US Civil Service.

Contents

About the author		ix
1	Introduction	1
2	Iraq	11
3	Afghanistan	25
4	Yemen	42
5	Syria	53
6	Gaza	68
7	Iran	78
8	Qatar	89
9	Lebanon	96
10	Turkey	103
11	Trump and China	111
12	Taiwan	120
13	Bangladesh	133
	Conclusion	138
	Index	157

About the author

Dr. Leif Rosenberger retired from US government in March 2016 after a 35-year career as a practitioner, scholar and educator. He was a Full Professor of Economics at the US Army War College, where he also held the General Douglas MacArthur Academic Chair of Research in the Strategic Studies Institute. In addition, he was the Chief Economist at the US Pacific Command (PACOM) and the US Central Command (CENTCOM) and an analyst at the US Central Intelligence Agency (CIA) and the US Defense Intelligence Agency (DIA).

In February 2018, Dr. Rosenberger was promoted to Chief Economist at ACERTAS, a think tank in Los Angeles that performs economic, political and military risk assessments. His services are also in demand as the Head of the Global Division at the Global Economic Institute in Ottawa; as Editor and Contributor at Roubini Global Economics in New York; as an Executive Director at Paragon Worldwide Group in Gig Harbor, Washington and as a Director at Think Renewables Group and Thank-Biz Africa in Toronto.

Dr. Rosenberger holds a BA with honors from Harvard University, a masters from Boston University and a PhD in International Relations from Claremont Graduate University.

1 Introduction

A few years back, Robert Zoellick, former President of the World Bank, wrote an article that became a classic, praising a US foreign policy tradition which had been deeply infused with economic logic for its first 150 years.[1] Zoellick then argued that after the start of the Cold War, Washington marginalized economics in the global war against communism. In the process, Robert D. Blackwill and Jennifer M. Harris note, Washington too often reached for the "gun instead of the purse." Not surprisingly, the systematic use of economic instruments to accomplish geopolitical objectives (or what Blackwill and Harris call "geo-economics") became a lost art.[2]

The attacks on the World Trade Center in New York City and the Pentagon in Washington, D.C. on 11 September 2001 triggered another global war, this time against terrorism. Would Washington keep marginalizing economics? To answer this question, one needs to separate thoughtful discussion from foreign policy action.

In terms of thoughtful discussion, the answer is clear. Three years after the 2001 attacks, the 9/11 Commission issued a report which underscored the need to address the negative underlying economic conditions that fostered violent extremism. In fact, of the 27 recommendations of the report, only one can be seen as advocating the use of military force. Former Deputy Secretary of State Richard Armitage notes that the US has exported the anger and fear of their citizens, not their vision of hope and opportunity. He suggests that the US needs to foster economic opportunity and hope for a better life if the global war on terrorism is to achieve anything but tactical successes.[3]

The 9/11 Commission's Report says that

> When people lose hope, when societies break down, when countries fragment, the breeding grounds for terrorism are created... Backward economic policies and repressive political regimes slip into societies that are without hope, where ambition and passions have no constructive outlet.[4]

2 Introduction

Spreading prosperity, while not a silver bullet, does help in combating violent extremism. Conversely, poverty and illiteracy are easy prey for violent extremists to exploit.

But terrorism was not the only cause for concern back then: Full blown wars were also breaking out, most of them were civil wars. In academe, speculative political debates broke out regarding the root causes of civil wars.[5] Thankfully, a definitive World Bank statistical study came out in 2003, with the finding that civil wars were heavily concentrated in the poorest countries. It therefore follows that poverty increases the likelihood of civil war. In other words, elevating economics in American foreign policy would be a logical approach in reducing the number of civil wars globally.[6]

Thus, the World Bank and the 9/11 Commission were mutually supportive of one another. The World Bank research showed that the root cause of civil wars was the failure of economic development. The 9/11 Commission Report recommended addressing the economic conditions that fostered violent extremism. But this was rhetoric, not action. American foreign policy was still militarized and out of balance. Douglas Lovelace, former Director of the Strategic Studies Institute at the US Army War College, notes that "The administration of President George W. Bush was frequently accused of favoring the use of unilateral military power over multilateral diplomacy and development as the primary tool of American national security."[7] And when Donald Trump became president, former General Martin Dempsey and former Admiral Michael Mullen, two former chairmen of the Joint Chiefs of Staff, voiced their concern that having too many generals and admirals in the highest US national security positions could lead to the over-militarization of US national security policy.[8]

President Obama took office in 2009 with a different mindset from President Bush. He said he wanted to rebalance American foreign policy, away from what he felt was an over-reliance on the military toward greater reliance on diplomacy and development. If one looks at his rhetoric and National Security Strategy documents from 2010 and 2015, it's clear that the Obama administration favored diplomatic solutions over military ones. For instance, years of negotiations between the US and Iran resulted in both sides signing an agreement in July 2015 to restrict Iran's nuclear program. President Trump, however, subsequently withdrew from the agreement in 2018.

While President Obama deserves some credit for his rhetoric in his speeches about the need to rebalance American foreign policy, US Army War College Professor John Deni says the tragedy of the Obama administration is that Obama failed to rebalance American foreign policy. Deni says there is plenty of evidence showing that US foreign policy remained militarized. The most obvious indicator was federal spending. Deni's research indicates that the international affairs expenditure (which includes money for diplomacy and development) remained a small fraction of what the Pentagon was spending throughout the eight years of the Obama administration.[9]

Introduction   3

What is the effect of marginalizing diplomacy and development? As the Chief Economist at the US Central Command (CENTCOM) and the US Pacific Command (PACOM) for almost two decades, I too often saw the White House (regardless of party) squandering peaceful foreign policy opportunities. I saw the US stuck in its economic coercion mindset, never seriously considering creative opportunities to use diplomacy and economic actions to mitigate the risk of drought, migration and social unrest, which ultimately led to humanitarian crises and civil war in places like Syria. As US Major General John Campbell, the top Commander of US military forces in Afghanistan, said in 2011, "We can't kill our way out of Afghanistan."[10] In other words, a militarist approach won't work as a way to produce peace and stability in Afghanistan. In essence, the militarized approach simply counters violent extremism with more violence. It deals with the symptoms of conflict rather than the economic root causes. At best, it produces short-lived tactical and operational military victories, ultimately leading to frustration and strategic failure.

We should always honor the sacrifices that US military members make to keep America free. Unfortunately, I will argue that civilian hawks in Washington too often rush to judgment and needlessly put our brave men and women in harm's way. Members of the Army National Guard and Reserves are redeployed over and over again. Later, we will see how the creative economic statecraft and efforts at creating shared prosperity of the Marshall Plan and the European Coal and Steel Community would help prevent unnecessary US military casualties and deaths.

The top positions in the US national security arena need to be filled by people who can connect the dots. We need generals and admirals who already understand the social, economic and political conditions that have an impact on the demand for violence. Too often, generals and admirals only consider kinetic solutions. Instead, they must understand the importance of social and political inclusion and shared prosperity.

One of the few generals I worked for who can do this superbly is David Petraeus. Petraeus is one of the most decorated US generals since World War II, but what makes him different is that he holds a PhD in International Relations from Princeton University, and he taught economics at West Point.

His ability to connect all the socio-economic, political and military dots opens his eyes to non-violent ways in which to resolve conflicts. He was the author of the US counterinsurgency doctrine that advocated living with the locals and winning hearts and minds.[11] Petraeus does believe that there is a time and place for kinetic courses of action, but thankfully, to him, endangering the lives of his troops was an option of last resort.

The time has come for Washington to seriously consider rebalancing American foreign policy. This book asks the questions: What if America pursued a rebalanced foreign policy? What if it actually tried to address the negative underlying socio-economic conditions which increase the demand for violence, terrorism and civil wars? What if it put more emphasis on

4 *Introduction*

social inclusion, which, in turn, tracks with what Martin Dempsey, former Chairman of the US Joint Chiefs of Staff, and Berkeley Professor Ori Brafman talk about in their book *Radical Inclusion: What the Post-9/11World Should Have Taught us About Leadership.*[12]

Too idealistic? President Harry S. Truman once said, "The only thing new in the world is the history you do not know." If we think back to the Treaty of Versailles, it's clear that victors of World War I came up with a punitive peace. French Prime Minister George Clemenceau wanted revenge, to make Germany pay for the wartime damage it (and the Central Powers) had done against Allied Powers, like France, during the war. Clemenceau got his economic coercion. Heavy reparations were used to keep the German economy down and punish Germany for its bad behavior. Clemenceau assumed that a weak economy would also keep the German military weak. How did Clemenceau's economic coercion work? A collective German resentment of these economic sanctions arguably aided the increase in the socio-economic demand for violence and, in turn, contributed to the rise of Hitler and World War II.[13]

Professor Ulrich Krotz at the European University Institute in Italy points out that relations between France and Germany have gone through three grand periods since 1871: "hereditary enmity" (up to 1945), "reconciliation" (1945–63) and the "special relationship" embodied in a cooperation called Franco-German Friendship (since 1963). Given the fact that the French and Germans had fought each other for centuries and had developed this hereditary enmity towards each other,[14] was Clemenceau's economic coercion against Germany inevitable? After World War II, the statesman Jean Monnet argued that it was not. Jon Meacham, author of *The Soul of America*, would argue that people can and do change if you give them a chance to find their better angels.[15]

In this regard, Monnet looked for common ground and social inclusion between the French and German people. In his strategic vision, French and German businessmen would work together and build a European Coal and Steel Community. Common bonds among businessmen would spread to the rest of the French and German populations, and help turn longstanding enemies into friends.

Did Monnet appear naïve and hopelessly idealistic? Possibly. But appearances can be deceiving. Monnet showed that a web of economic interdependence and social inclusion could lead to shared prosperity and a more durable peace than more short-sighted economic coercion. In other words, shared prosperity would reduce the demand for violence and thus lower mutual threat perceptions – not a bad way to keep the peace in Europe for 70 years.

Like Monnet, US Secretary of State George Marshall felt it was important to help Germany and the rest of Western Europe rebuild their factories and enjoy shared prosperity with America, rather than resorting to the ill-fated Clemenceau's economic coercion of Germany.

Of course, World War I and World War II were wars fought among nation states. That raises the question: Are the approaches of Monnet and

Introduction 5

Marshall regarding shared prosperity rather than economic coercion, still relevant when it comes to ending civil wars in more recent times?

This book says yes. A good place to find lessons learned would be in the 1990s, when there were numerous civil wars (in places like Angola, Rwanda, Cambodia, Liberia, Bosnia, Croatia, Nicaragua, El Salvador, Guatemala, Namibia and Mozambique). In his book *At War's End*, University of Ottawa Professor Roland Paris talks about the liberalism of President Wilson (or Wilsonialism). Paris notes that peacebuilding missions in the 1990s generally followed the Wilsonian notion that promoting "liberalization" in countries that had recently experienced civil war would help to create the conditions for a stable and lasting peace. In the political realm, liberalization means democratization. In the economic realm, liberalization means movement toward a market-oriented economic model (or marketization). Although the 14 peacebuilding operations launched in the 1990s varied in many respects, their common characteristic was to try to transform war-shattered states into "liberal market economies" as quickly as possible.[16]

Paris notes that those who designed these peacebuilding operations hoped and expected that democratization would shift societal conflicts away from the battlefield and into the peaceful arena of electoral politics, thereby replacing violent warfare. Similarly, Paris notes that those who designed these peacebuilding operations also hoped and expected that marketization would promote sustainable economic growth, which, in turn, would reduce tensions.[17] Paris notes that there is a large body of empirical scholarship (dating back to John Locke) that partially supports this "liberal peace thesis."[18]

However, Paris notes that the transition from civil conflict to a market democracy is full of pitfalls: Promoting democratization and marketization has the potential to stimulate higher levels of societal competition at the very moment when states are least equipped to contain such tensions within peaceful bounds. In other words, the Wilsonian goals of democratization and marketization are still valid. The problem is the method used to effect this change. If you try Colombia University Professor Jeffrey Sachs' shock treatment, competition quickly turns to conflict, and civil war is resumed.[19] In *At War's End*, Paris recommends building "institutions before liberalization" (IBL), much as Monnet helped to build the European Coal and Steel Community, and Marshall helped to create the Marshall Plan.[20] In other words, institutions soften the blows of the transition.

This book builds on the research that Paris conducted on civil wars taking place in the 1990s. It looks at the militarization of conflict and marginalization of shared prosperity.

Chapter 2 looks at the civil war in Iraq from the perspective of the American war plan. From an operational perspective, the combat arms phases of the war plans went reasonably well, but the US never bothered to implement phases 3 and 4 of the war plan (stabilization and reconstruction) in Iraq. ISIS filled the gap left behind. So, the US had to go back and try another costly military intervention. How is it that America and its coalition

6   *Introduction*

partners can win the combat arms phases but lose the peace? If the US got serious about stabilization and reconstruction in Iraq, what would need to be done? What are the opportunities and challenges of Iraqi reconstruction? Why is implementation of reconstruction so difficult?

Chapter 3 looks at the war in Afghanistan. General David Petraeus, our Commander at CENTCOM, asked us to design and then implement the New Silk Road Initiative for Afghanistan. Our design was promising, but some say no good deed goes unpunished. Others say the profit is never honored in his own country. In any event, funding dried up at CENTCOM. Why? What did we do right, and what did we do wrong? How did China turn the tables on the US? Did the US make a mistake in not implementing a New Silk Road? Why do so many countries in the world like China's version of the New Silk Road, the so-called Belt and Road Initiative (BRI)? Why did nobody else in the US government replace CENTCOM in implementing the New Silk Road? Should the US keep retreating from South and Central Asia? What if the US got serious about the New Silk Road again? Should it compete or collaborate with China on a new and better version of the New Silk Road? Or is retreat to Fortress America our fate in the Great Power Competition with China? Is the Taliban ready for a settlement in Afghanistan? After 18 years of war, why is a settlement in Afghanistan so difficult to reach?[21]

Chapter 4 looks at Yemen. US military involvement was more indirect here. There was and is no significant US troop presence on the ground in Yemen.[22] That said, the US has provided military assistance for the Saudi bombing campaign in the country. Despite the overwhelming Saudi military involvement, Saudi Arabia has been losing the peace as well. Why did America once again militarize this conflict and marginalize shared prosperity? Why do the Democrats want to cut off military assistance to Saudi military activities in Yemen? Why does President Trump say no?

Chapter 5 looks at the Syrian civil war. America put Syria on the back burner.[23] When the US military did enter Syria, it was only marginally involved. President Obama repeated the political rhetoric that Syrian President Bashar al-Assad had to abnegate his leadership and kept encouraging opposition to Assad. However, Assad showed no sign of giving up power. Given Obama's stated goals of regime change, why was the US military so unsuccessful in Syria? What economic windows of opportunity for shared prosperity were squandered along the way?[24]

Could the humanitarian crisis and ensuing civil war have been prevented? International security experts said that Syria was stable and immune to Arab Spring the day before the civil war began in 2011. What did they miss? Was the extreme drought a key underlying root cause of the tragedy? Does Syria need to be more resilient? Do the Syrian people deserve the right to be protected (R2P)? Is outside economic intervention needed if the Syrian government lacks the capacity?

Chapter 6 looks at Gaza, our last civil war case study. This case study is a hybrid, considering Israeli military actions against Palestinians in Gaza as well as Israeli economic coercion of the enclave. The Norwegian Refugee

Introduction 7

Council (NRC) called Gaza the world's largest open-air prison for Palestinians in April 2018.[25] The Israelis have also won clear-cut military victories in wars against the Palestinians. If this is true, why does Israel keep losing the peace and experiencing strategic failure?[26]

The book continues to focus on economic coercion in trouble spots in the Middle East and parts of Asia. That raises the question: How is economic coercion working in modern times?

Chapter 7 looks at the international community's nuclear agreement with Iran. The International Atomic Energy Agency (IAEA) said that Iran was still abiding by the nuclear agreement in April 2019.[27] However, President Trump decertified the nuclear deal in December 2017.[28] He returned to a systematic imposition of severe sanctions on Iran. Is this economic coercion a good idea? Is it likely to be any more successful than the sanctions against Castro in Cuba in terms of changing the behavior of the country targeted?

Chapter 8 looks at the boycott of the quartet (Saudi Arabia, the United Arab Emirates (UAE) Bahrain and Egypt) against Qatar, which was successful in the short run.[29] However, the boycott appears to be failing in the long run.[30] If this is the case, why is economic coercion failing once more?

Chapter 9 looks at Lebanon, a country with a stormy past of sectarian conflict. Lebanon was finally able to put its volatile history behind it. The politicians were somehow able to craft a delicate power sharing agreement. They now value social inclusion and diversity because it helps them to reduce the demand for violence inside Lebanon. To be sure, it has been a long and rocky road. But on 6 May 2018, Lebanon held its first parliamentary election in 9 years. It also had its first budget in 12 years. The big question was: How would President Trump respond? Would he praise and celebrate their successful democratic process and pursue shared prosperity with them? Or would he use US economic coercion to divide them and destabilize the country?

Chapter 10 looks at Turkey. In the recent past, its economy appeared to be on a roll. In 2017, it grew 7.4%, and the Organization for Economic Cooperation and Development (OECD) expected it to be one of the fastest growing economies among OECD members from 2015 to 2025.[31] But in economics, things can and often do change quickly. The country is now in recession, not aided by the US sanctions that slammed Turkey's economy in November 2018, following the country's purchase of oil from Iran, just a few months after the US' withdrawal from the Iran Deal. The timing of this US economic coercion against Turkey was therefore not helpful to a NATO country struggling to keep its economy afloat.

That said, US troops were essential to filling the gap between the combat arms phases of war plans and finishing the stabilization and reconstruction phases of the war plan in Syria. The Turkish military filled the gap with violence against the Kurds in October 2019 when President Trump made a strategic mistake when he told US soldiers to cut and run from Syria. Once again, ISIS was free to begin another resurgence of global terrorism.

Chapter 11 looks at Trump's "America First" (or America Alone) economic nationalism and his trade war with China. His economic statecraft,

8   Introduction

which blames China for the high US trade deficit against the US, plays well with folks in his rust-belt base, which is angry and afraid China is stealing their jobs. But his policies reflect economic misconceptions about US productivity and the role technology plays in job losses, and an important omission in the dispersion of global production. The days of goods being made in one factory and one country are long over. The chapter addresses the correlation between free trade and reducing the demand for violence.

Chapter 12 looks at the historically strong economic growth of "Greater China," which includes Mainland China, Hong Kong and Taiwan, until the slowdown during the recent trade war.[32] That said, a counter trend in Taiwanese identity is easily identified.[33] Can these two trends co-exist? Some argue that Beijing is guilty of the economic coercion in Taiwan. Is this true? Are we more likely to see peaceful Chinese unification, Taiwanese political independence (and war) or an uneasy *status quo ante*? Taiwan is also carefully monitoring how China deals with protesters in Hong Kong.[34]

Chapter 13 looks at head to head competition between China and Bangladesh in the global garment industry. The question of fairness is important to consider here, given the fact that President Trump accuses China of "raping" the US with unfair trade policy.[35] Is China breaking international business rules and competing unfairly in the global garment industry? If so, it would seem logical that China would try to cheat in the cut-throat competition of the global garment market. This case study explores whether it cheats in order to corner the market or should receive kudos for shared prosperity. It also vividly shows the connection between shared prosperity and reducing the demand for violence.

One final thought regarding my research and methodology. This study reflects the insights I have drawn from working for 35 years as a practitioner at CENTCOM and PACOM, as a scholar in two think tanks and as an educator in the school house at the US Army War College. I did not try to standardize into a model or mathematical equation the militarization of American foreign policy, the marginalization of economics and the urge to opt for economic coercion instead of shared prosperity. Quantifying this study is difficult because each case study has a different context. For instance, sometimes, the US government itself is the main actor. At other times, it supports a close ally, such as Israel, which takes on the role of main actor. That said, I see important common characteristics and themes which quantitative scholars in academe may find useful.

Notes

1 Robert Zoellick, "The Currency of Power", *Foreign Policy*, 8 October 2012.
2 Robert D. Blackwill and Jennifer M. Harris, *War by Other Means: Geoeconomics and Statecraft*, Harvard University Press, Cambridge, MA, 2016.
3 See 9/11 Commission, *What to do? A Global Strategy, the 9/11 Commission Report*, Norton, W. W. & Company, Inc., New York, NY, 22 July 2004.
4 Ibid.

Introduction 9

5 In these speculative debates, the political right claimed that civil wars happened because of longstanding ethnic and religious conflicts. The political left said that civil wars were due to economic inequalities and a deep-rooted legacy of colonialism. The political center said that civil war occurred where opportunities were lacking for the peaceful resolution of political disputes (i.e. a lack of democracy). Paul Collier et al., *Breaking the Conflict Trap: Civil War and Development Policy*, Oxford University Press, Washington, DC, 2003, p. 53. In the subsequent discussion of reconciliation in Afghanistan in this book, much of the assessment is based on the excellent research of Paul Collier and his colleagues at the World Bank.

6 Ibid.

7 John R. Deni, *The Real Rebalancing: American Diplomacy and the Tragedy of President Obama's Foreign Policy*, Strategic Studies Institute, US Army War College Press, Carlisle, PA, 2015, p. ix.

8 See Leif Rosenberger, "The US National Security Arena Needs More Than Warriors", *Financial Times*, 12 December 2016.

9 Ibid.

10 General: We Can't Kill Our Way Out of Afghanistan, NPR, 28 May 2011.

11 The Field Manual of Counterinsurgency Operations, Joint Chiefs of Staff Joint Publication 3–24, 5 October 2009.

12 Martin Dempsey and Ori Brafman, *Radical Inclusion: What the Post-9/11World Should Have Taught Us About Leadership*, Missionday, Berkeley, CA, 2017.

13 See Robert Wilde, "How the Treaty of Versailles Contributed to Hitler's Rise", *Thought Company*, 10 July 2019.

14 The relationship between France and Germany, since 1871, according to Ulrich Krotz[1], has three grand periods: "hereditary enmity" (up to 1945), "reconciliation" (1945–63) and the "special relationship" embodied in a cooperation called Franco-German Friendship (since 1963). See Ulrich Krotz.

15 Jon Meacham, *The Soul of America: The Battle for Our Better Angels*, Random House, New York, NY, 2018.

16 The case studies Roland Paris looks at include Angola and Rwanda, Cambodia and Liberia, Bosnia and Croatia, Nicaragua, El Salvador, Guatemala, Namibia and Mozambique, and Kosovo and Sierra Leone. See Roland Paris, *At War's End: Building Peace after Civil Conflict*, Cambridge University Press, Cambridge, 2004, p. 5.

17 Ibid., p. 5.

18 Ibid., p. 6.

19 See Jeffrey D. Sachs, "Twentieth Century Political Economy", *Oxford Review of Economic Policy* (Winter), vol. 15, no. 4, pp. 90–101, 1999.

20 Roland Paris, *At War's End*, Cambridge University Press, New York, NY, p. 7.

21 For historical documentation concerning the rise of the New Silk Road Initiative at CENTCOM, see the following video comments from Vice Admiral Mark Fox, Deputy Commander at CENTCOM until April of 2016. www.youtube.com/watch?v=AKRb9397pmE&list=PLma-pJGyyfBblagn1uoUaSI0obyRumymE&index=3&t=0s

22 See Leo Shane III and Joe Gould, "Should US Troops Be Involved in the Yemen Civil War?" *Military Times*, 13 February 2019.

23 See The Associated Press, "A Timeline of the US Involvement in Syria's Conflict", 11 January 2019.

24 See Carsten Wieland, *Syria: A Decade of Lost Chances*, Cune Press, Seattle, 2012; also see Myriam Ababsa, "The End of the World: Drought and Agrarian Transformation in Northeast Syria (2007–2010)", in Raymond Hinnebusch and Tina Zintl, ed., *Syria from Reform to Revolt*, Volume 1, Syracuse University

10 *Introduction*

Press, Syracuse, NY, 2015, for a lost opportunity for US agriculture strategists to engage their counterparts in order to mitigate a longstanding vulnerability to a scenario of drought, migration, social unrest and civil war.

25 Roald Hovring, "Gaza: The World's Largest Open-Air Prison", *Norwegian Refugee Council (NRC)*, 26 April 2018.

26 See Carl von Clausewitz, *On War*, Oxford University Press, Oxford, 2008.

27 Kelsey Davenport, "IAEA Says Iran Abiding by Nuclear Deal", *Arms Control Association*, April 2019.

28 Mahsa Rouhi, "Trump's Decertification Doesn't Mean the Death of the Iran Nuclear Deal", *Boston Globe*, 8 December 2017.

29 "Qatar Crisis: What You Need to Know", *BBC News*, 19 July 2017.

30 Steven Mufson, "How Qatar Is Learning to Beat the Saudi-led Boycott", *Washington Post*, 21 July 2019.

31 Hurriyet Daily News, "Turkish Economy Grows 7.4 Percent in 2017, Exceeds Forecast", 29 March 2018, and Hurriyet, "OECD Lifts Turkey's Growth Estimate", 13 March 2018.

32 James T. Areddy, "China's Economy Shows Fresh Signs of Weakness", *Wall Street Journal*, 16 June 2019.

33 Alice Su, "With Each Generation, the People of Taiwan Feel More Taiwanese – and Less Chinese", *Los Angeles Times*, 15 February 2019.

34 Julie, McCarthy, "Taiwan Monitors How China Deals with Hong Kong Protesters", *NPR*, 16 August 2019.

35 "Trump Accuses China of 'raping' US with Unfair Trade Policy", *BBC News*, 2 May 2016.

Bibliography

Blackwell, Robert D. and Harris, Jennifer M. *War by Other Means: Geo-economics and Statecraft*, Belknap Press, Cambridge, MA, 2016.

Gelvin, James L. *The New Middle East: What Everyone Needs to Know*, Oxford University Press, New York, NY, 2018.

Haas, Richard. *A World in Disarray: American Foreign Policy and the Crisis of the Old Order*, Penguin Books, New York, NY, 2017.

Hook, Steven W. and Spanier, John. *American Foreign Policy since World War II*, Sage Publications, London, 2016.

Keohane, Robert O. and Nye, Joseph S. *Power and Interdependence: World Politics in Transition*, Little, Brown and Company, Boston, MA, 1977.

Paris, Roland. *At War's End: Building Peace after Civil Conflict*, Cambridge University Press, Cambridge, 2003.

Ulrich Krotz, Three eras and possible futures: a long-term view on the Franco-German relationship a century after the First World War, International Affairs (March 2014) 90#2. pp. 337–350.

Woodward, Bob. *Obama's Wars*, Simon and Schuster, New York, NY, 2010.

World Bank. *Breaking the Conflict Trap: Civil War and Development Policy*, World Bank Press, Washington, DC, 2003.

2 Iraq

In November 2016, the Iraqi government started to celebrate its military victory over the Islamic State of Iraq and Syria (ISIS). Investors once again saw reasons for optimism about Iraq's economic prospects. The stock market was on the upswing. Fitch gave the economy another vote of confidence in March when it upgraded Iraq's economic outlook to stable, mostly based on the country's improving public finances. And its Gross Domestic Product (GDP) growth was also booming. The defeat of ISIS prompted rare optimism and a window of opportunity for social inclusion and shared prosperity among all Iraqis.[1]

But before long, that window of opportunity was squandered. Just eight months after Baghdad and the Western allies celebrated a hard-won victory over ISIS, the most serious anti-government protests to hit the country in years swept across its oil-rich south. Baghdad struggled to contain the protests. Demonstrators laid siege to government buildings, ports and oil companies.

The demonstrators faced serious electricity and water shortages as well as high unemployment. The demonstrators were fed up with their incompetent political leaders. They demanded sweeping reform to dismantle the corruption and mismanagement that has crippled the Iraqi economy, despite its oil wealth. The protests undermined hopes that elections in May 2018 would be a turning point and put the embattled country on the road to social inclusion and shared prosperity after decades of conflict.[2]

Interestingly enough, the Iraqi people have experienced this big build-up for the big let-down before. In 2014, it also seemed like the best of times. The war was over in Iraq, and investors were pouring money into its economy. Corporate earnings were booming. International investors were confident that economic rewards in Iraq outweighed any possible risks.

Iraq's economy looked promising in so many ways. In February 2014, its oil production surged to its highest level in over 30 years, and its oil exports hit a post-2003 high. It had one of the hottest commercial markets in the world. Asia Cell Communications had the biggest initial public offering (IPO) in the Middle East since 2008.[3]

12 *Iraq*

The future also looked bright. With the second-largest proven oil reserves in the Organization of the Petroleum Exporting Countries (OPEC), the International Energy Agency predicted Iraq's oil output would double by the end of the decade. Its oil output was expected to grow by 600–700%. The Economist Intelligence Unit (EIU) predicted that Iraq's GDP growth would reach 8% in 2014 and almost 9% by 2020. No other country in the world had this kind of growth trajectory.[4]

But this was all a false dawn.[5] What did the optimists miss? US military doctrine says that phase three in a campaign plan is civilian-led stabilization. It follows two combat arms phases (first, seize the initiative, and second, dominate the enemy). Stabilization "consolidates the gains achieved through offense and defense in order to achieve sustainable outcomes that align with US national interests and strategic goals. In other words, successful post-conflict stabilization assures that the US wins the war, rather than a series of battles."[6]

US military doctrine also includes Reconstruction (phase four).[7] Hans Binnendijk and Stuart Johnson correctly argue that there has been a widening gap between the scale-down of combat operations and the start of stabilization and reconstruction operations in US doctrine.[8] Bad things happen in this gap. The most dangerous events included ISIS filling the gap in Iraq. More recently, the Turkish military filled the gap against the Kurds in October 2019 when President Trump told US soldiers to cut and run from Syria. Once again, ISIS was free to begin another resurgence of terrorism.

Optimists thought that the fall of the divisive Prime Minister Maliki and the rise of a seemingly more inclusive Prime Minister Abadi was a hopeful sign. But it was too little, too late. Maliki's repression of the Sunnis was deep-rooted and contributed to the rapid expansion of ISIS. The initial ISIS military success and the subsequent and belated military response of the US and its allies are now well known.

However, what was not so well known at the time was the economic impact of ISIS. While the major oil fields in southern Iraq were located far away from the battle zones and not seriously affected, ISIS actions in northern Iraq occurred close to the Kurdish oil fields. In addition, ISIS-controlled areas in Iraq seriously hindered the routing of oil and gas beyond its borders. ISIS control of this area prevented Iraq's oil from being shipped via the Kirkuk-Ceyhan pipeline to Turkey and over highways to Jordan.[9]

As a result, Iraq's international trade took a big hit. It lost $1.5 billion a month due to an oil export pipeline under ISIS control that ran from Kirkuk to the Turkish port of Ceylon.[10] And of course, low oil prices also hit Iraq's exports. In addition, its imports fell 60–70%.[11] Foreign reserve levels also fell. On the domestic front, two million internally displaced people (IDP) lost their jobs. Investors were then understandably scared off. Farms and factories shut down, which, in turn, caused several domestic markets to collapse.[12]

The Iraqi economy went from boom to bust. The International Monetary Fund (IMF) announced that the Iraqi GDP was contracting. When an economy like Iraq's gets smaller, its revenues also shrink. This, in turn, caused the budget to run a large deficit. Not surprisingly, therefore, Iraq ran a budget deficit of 4% of GDP. The Maastricht criterion from the European Union (EU) says that any budget deficit over 3% of GDP is financially unstable. In short, Iraq suddenly found itself in a fiscal crisis.

What were the drivers of this fiscal crisis? Even before the war against ISIS, Iraq was struggling to finance the reconstruction of its armed forces, but the war meant that Iraqi military spending started to skyrocket. Iraq suddenly needed to train, feed and house tens of thousands of men who volunteered to fight ISIS. The associated costs of this fighting were also rising. In addition, Iraq had no productive industry or agriculture, so, it obviously couldn't tax farms and factories that no longer existed.

That left Iraq as a "one trick pony" economy that relied on high oil prices to make ends meet. This, in turn, made it extremely vulnerable to falling oil prices which hit Iraq's economy and budget hard. Oil prices fell from over $100 a barrel in May 2014 to about $50 a barrel by early January 2015. Additionally, Iraq could not increase southern oil production and exports because of poor infrastructure and a shortage of water.[13]

In addition to these unexpected costs, the Iraqi economy suffered from years of corruption and mismanagement, despite billions of dollars in US financing. As a result, the budget was full of structural problems. For instance, the government funded public payroll and food and energy subsidies equal to 70% of the budget. To make matters worse, the country was in arrears. Baghdad still owed the Kurdish Regional Government (KRG) billions of dollars.

Baghdad weighed its options: Due to a doubling its gold holdings in recent years and relatively large foreign reserves, Iraq could finance the current fiscal crisis, but this would reduce its ability to address the balance of payment crises and future financial crises.

Until oil prices fell, Iraq's dinar had been solidly pegged to the US dollar. Instead of reducing reserves, Baghdad could devalue its foreign exchange rate. However, this could cause a panic, destabilize Iraq's financial markets and trigger massive capital flight. It would also worsen Iraq's debt and increase inflation, the cruelest tax of all to Iraq's working poor.

Baghdad could also go to the IMF to finance its budget deficit, but the IMF wouldn't give Iraq loans to finance its budget deficit until a budget was in place. New Iraqi Prime Minister Haider-al-Abadi initially created a 2015 budget that was based on a "break even oil price" of $70 a barrel, but he had to scrap the budget once oil prices hit $60 a barrel.

Once Iraq decided on how to finance the budget deficit, it had to come up with a new, more realistic budget so that the fiscal crisis did not continue. In this regard, Iraqi Prime Minister Abadi decided to create an austerity budget that would safeguard against the war on ISIS while sharply cutting back on other spending. Under this plan, the Iraqi government proposed prioritizing public-sector salaries, security needs, the energy sector, humanitarian relief and provincial transfers. It would finance the projected 2015

14   *Iraq*

budget deficit of $40 billion by freezing development and reconstruction, and issuing domestic bonds and exploring efforts to generate additional revenue. In this regard, the austerity budget was a vital first step which, in turn, paved the way for future IMF financing.

On the kinetic side, the austerity budget showed that Prime Minister Abadi was serious about the war effort. For instance, $1.5 billion was transferred from the finance ministry to pay the remaining balance in the contract for 36 F-16 fighters. But instead of transferring money from wasteful subsidies or cutting bloated civil service salaries, Prime Minister Abadi postponed most of the spending on development and reconstruction. While breaking things and killing people is obviously a necessary part of the war effort against ISIS, there is also an important non-kinetic side to the war effort.

In this regard, Iraq needed to strike a balance. The Abadi government also needed to win the hearts and minds of all Iraqis, which wasn't easy. ISIS propaganda and recruitment were quick to criticize Abadi for using money to buy more F-16s that should have gone to Sunni economic development. In other words, he needed to make sure that his kinetic approach did not play into the hands of ISIS or another insurgent group.

During Arab Spring, oil prices were high, and Iraq was running a budget surplus. It was able to tap into this budget surplus and boost social spending to placate potentially rebellious Iraqis. But then oil prices fell, and it was faced with a large budget deficit. This meant that Abadi had to find creative ways to unify all Iraqis – Shia, Sunni and Kurds.[14] This wasn't easy.

It didn't take long for ISIS expansionism across a third of Iraq to turn an economic boom into economic contraction and a fiscal crisis. During this crisis, it was tempting for Baghdad to maximize military spending to crush ISIS and short-change socio-economic development for all Iraqis.

But that was a mistake. Although Iraq's economy was primarily a war economy, unity among all Iraqis in the war effort was essential to the recruitment of good soldiers to fight ISIS. In addition, Iraq struggled to sustain the costs and sacrifice of the war effort because there was not a unified effort against ISIS.

What did we learn from the false dawn of 2014? And what should we keep in mind now that the Iraqi military has almost won the operational war against ISIS? The short answer is that winning the operational war is not enough. Stabilization and reconstruction must happen immediately. If a gap widens between combat arms and stabilization/reconstruction, another insurgent group (like ISIS) will be able to fill the socio-economic gap. We saw this repeatedly in Iraq and we are seeing it again in October 2019 because President Trump told US soldiers to cut and run from Syria.

Iraqi Reconstruction

In March 2018, Kuwait hosted a conference on reconstruction for Iraq. The Iraqis argued that a failure to address the reconstruction needs of their country would add to its chronic instability. Their assessment focused on damage to the strategic infrastructure and the need to rebuild it. The government said it needed $88 billion for the reconstruction program. Foreign investors only pledged $30 billion.[15]

What went wrong? For years, high oil prices enabled Iraq's economy to muddle through. But in 2014, low oil prices and the rise of ISIS was a wake-up call that shattered its complacency. Iraq can no longer be a "one trick pony" oil economy. It must diversify.

That said, Iraq has still not come to grips with the scale of the reconstruction challenge. It has seriously underestimated the cost of rebuilding. It cannot just rebuild the infrastructure which ISIS destroyed; it must also rebuild the infrastructure left in tatters by almost 4 decades of conflict. In fact, the World Bank said that businesses in Iraq faced one of the worst logistical systems in the world (ranking 147 out of 160 nations evaluated).[16]

Iraq must also expand its oil industry and replace its non-oil sector, which has been distorted by mismanagement and market failure.[17]

Now let's look at Iraq's oil. At first glance, all is well. Iraq's proven oil and gas reserves are still huge, although there is an ongoing debate over the best metric to estimate exactly how big they are. According to the US Energy Information Agency (EIA), Iraq has about 143 billion barrels – giving it the 5th-largest proven reserves in the world. In 2017, Iraq was 7th-largest oil producer in the world and 3rd-largest oil producer in OPEC after Saudi Arabia and Iran.[18]

But all is not well in Iraq's oil industry. The problem is Iraqi gross inefficiency. If Iraq could improve efficiency, it could cover its extraction and transport costs at a world price of only $12 per barrel. Only 10% of the country has been explored for energy using modern techniques. So, it has outdated estimates of its energy reserves. In addition, it needs technical assistance to more accurately estimate the reserves in the other 90% of the country. With good advice, Iraq could produce a 50 to 250 billion-barrel increase in the country's proven reserves.[19] In addition to oil, Iraq also has the twelfth-largest natural gas reserves in the world.[20]

Now, let's turn to the two biggest areas of Iraq's current oil and gas exports. First, most of its current oil exports, about 85% in 2017, come from the fields in the southeast of the country and are pumped aboard crude carriers in the ports south of Basra to be shipped through the Persian Gulf. The second-highest export capacity is through the Kirkuk-Ceyhan pipeline from the Kirkuk supergiant field to Turkey. Both routes have little excess capacity. In the short term, the binding infrastructure constraint on increasing Iraqi oil exports is the limited capacity of oil pipelines, storage facilities and moorings for oil tankers in the Persian Gulf south of Basra.

That said, attempts to rapidly expand the oil infrastructure in the south have already created severe bottlenecks as sharp increases in the importation of equipment and supplies overwhelmed existing port facilities.

16   *Iraq*

In the long term, the most serious challenge to expanding oil production is the water shortage. In the southern oil fields, the viscosity of the oil and the nature of the oil reservoirs mean that rising quantities of water must be injected whenever more oil is produced.[21]

To recap, a key issue is the disposal of contaminated water. Water used in oil recovery is often severely contaminated and will pollute river or ground-water if it is dumped. This is a public health problem that may become an-other humanitarian crisis unless mitigated. Therefore, Iraq needs to create new facilities to deal with wastewater disposal, a problem that is generally ignored at lower levels of oil production.

There is a substantial decrease in the volume and quality of water in the Euphrates and Tigris Rivers. Why is this happening? Upstream, Turkey, Syria, and Iran are curbing water flow to Iraq. The reduction in available water has reduced hydroelectricity generation – which accounts for about 7% of Iraq's energy production – from the dams in Haditha and Mosul. When it comes to rebuilding infrastructure, nothing is easy. Take expanding facilities for seaborne trade. Admittedly, there is the need for deeper chan-nels and improved port facilities. The problem is that there are over 200 ves-sels sunk in or near Iraq's primary port of Umm Qasr and hundreds more in the channels from Umm Qasr north to Basra. These sunken vessels limit access to the port. They also leak hazardous chemicals from munitions, pes-ticides, refined fuels and unknown toxins.

Electricity: Most Critical Challenge

Providing reliable, quality, around-the-clock electricity is the most critical infrastructure challenge facing Iraq. Electricity is also the best example of new investment to compensate for maintenance failings. Despite govern-ment spending of $36 billion since 2003 as well as the hard work of many Iraqis, the gap between the demand and supply of electricity is greater than ever. The average Iraqi can only depend on the grid for 6–8 hours of electricity per day, while some households receive only a few hours.[22]

Iraq's electricity has been in near-constant crisis mode since the fall of Saddam Hussein. Blackouts and brownouts are common during its hot summers. Its aging and inefficient generation and transmission systems suf-fered $7 billion in damage at the hands of ISIS. But even before ISIS's push through Mosul in 2014, Iraq's electricity sector was struggling to keep up with demand.

Annual demand for electricity in Iraq, which hit a peak of 24,000 mega-watts (MW) in 2018, is climbing by about 7% a year, a pace expected to re-main steady for the foreseeable future. But since Iraq can only deliver 16,000 MW, there is a 30% gap between supply and demand for power.

Iraq's electricity problems begin with aging and inefficient physical in-frastructure. Most of its electricity is generated by old-style gas turbine and even older steam turbine power plants that use natural gas or diesel as a fuel

Iraq 17

source (steam turbine plants can also use crude oil and fuel oil). Once electricity is generated, it travels to the end user through a decrepit transmission and distribution system that suffers from 50% line loss (meaning half of the power sent out on the lines doesn't reach the customer). In a healthy electrical grid, line loss is typically between 5 and 15%.

The electricity sector has started to address the power plant issue by building plants that use combined-cycle generation, a highly efficient method of creating electricity. But their use is limited by insufficient supplies of natural gas for fuel and water to generate steam to drive the turbines. Although Iraq is rich in oil, it has a chronic shortage of natural gas production. Most of its natural gas is a byproduct of crude oil output, but it has not invested in ways to capture that gas. Instead, most of its natural gas is flared off, proving both an economic waste and environmentally damaging. Iraq only captured 10.4 billion cubic meters (bcm) of 28.2 bcm of gas from its wells, the rest being flared, in 2017.

Baghdad has recently made efforts to capture more gas at the wellhead. It struck a deal with the Basra Gas Company, a $17 billion joint venture set up in 2013 with Shell and Mitsubishi. But thus far, that venture is capturing only half of its goal of 57 million cubic meters per day.[23] Even if Iraq were able to capture all the natural gas it currently flares, it might still need to import natural gas. Currently, the power sector alone consumes 9.4 bcm annually, and the power plants that will come online over the next few years are expected to require an additional 15 bcm. Beyond flaring, Iraq has sought to import natural gas from Iran.

While Iraq can ultimately overcome some shortcomings, the power sector is beset with other economic and political problems. Finding financing for infrastructure improvements may be one of them. Iraq has spent much of this year trying, in a largely fruitless search, to attract enough investment to rebuild infrastructure left in tatters by years of war.

Iraq's power sector cannot break even financially, despite the high demand for electricity. The collection rates for electricity bills stood at just 28 percent in 2017. And even if customers actually paid their bills, power is being sold at a loss: Electricity rates are set too low to recover generation, transmission and distribution costs. The World Bank estimates that between collection shortfalls and poor infrastructure, the losses in the electricity sector reduce Iraq's annual GDP by 5.2%. Baghdad also operates at a loss on natural gas sales. It pays the Basra Gas Company $2.50 per one million British Thermal Units for captured natural gas and pays Iran a price indexed to 11 percent of that of Brent crude (currently around $6.75 per mmbtu). Baghdad turns around and sells that gas at around $1.20 per mmbtu.[24]

Given its inefficient and volatile political economy, it's difficult for Iraq to make the power sector solvent. Cutting off service for those who don't pay their electricity bills would quickly lead to street demonstrations. Iraq could further increase electricity rates, but that would also provoke unrest. Any attempt to reduce the size of the ministry's workforce would lead to

18   *Iraq*

protests as unemployment is a serious issue in the country. With no good choices, Iraq has had to maintain its focus on generating as much electricity as possible. That means setting aside a large chunk of the federal budget to provide investment and transfers to the power sector to make up for revenue shortfalls.

Even then, Iraq has fallen behind on its payments for energy imports from Iran. Over the summer, Tehran cut off electricity exports due to nonpayment, helping contribute to shortages that led to protests. In its 2019 budget, Iraq has set aside more than $1.2 billion to cover arrears in electricity and natural gas.

What should Iraq do? At this point, its electricity sector must swim at full speed just to tread water. Resolving its myriad issues is a difficult proposition. But considering that demand is projected to continue increasing by 7 to 10 percent annually, Baghdad will need to figure out how to increase generation capacity and efficiency at a faster rate just to keep up.

Over the past five years, Iraq has considered imports of electricity and natural gas from Iran as an easy, relatively cheap way to help shore up its electricity picture. And Tehran, always eager to deepen its influence with the Shiite-led Iraqi government, has been happy to oblige.

In 2013, Iraq signed a deal to import 25 million cubic meters (mcm) per day of Iranian natural gas – 9.1 bcm annually – to feed three Baghdad-area power plants. In total, the natural gas imports from Iran feed power plants with a capacity of about 5,000 MW. Adding in the direct electricity imports means that Baghdad depends on Tehran to fulfill about one-third of its peak demand.

But there's a problem. Even this incomplete solution to Iraq's power shortages could soon be coming to an end. Why? As the US continues its pressure campaign against Iran, Washington continues to demand that Baghdad come up with a plan to wean itself off Iranian energy supplies, which constitute a significant chunk of Iraq's electricity needs. At first, Trump gave Iraq a temporary exemption. But that respite is over.

The Trump administration is tightening the screws on Iraq, encouraging it to stop buying energy from its neighbor and sole foreign supplier, Iran. US sanctions would financially punish Iraq severely at a time when it can ill afford another economic setback. This unreasonable Trump demand has become a major point of conflict between Washington and Baghdad. Iraqi leaders, fearing that a further shortfall in power would lead to mass protests and political instability in their electricity-starved country, are understandably pushing back on this demand.[25] In the process, Trump is turning US military victory in Iraq into an economic/political defeat.

Can Iraq Replace Iranian Imports?

This US demand presents Prime Minister Adel Abdul-Mahdi with a formidable challenge. Replacing that amount of generation quickly will not be easy. Since Iraq would have to deal with sanctioned entities in Iran to pay for the imports, the Iraqi purchases of Iranian natural gas and electricity could run afoul of US sanctions. Would bartering work? Iraq has offered to set up a barter-like system that would give Iran credit for its gas exports that can be exchanged directly for Iraqi goods. But this does not look promising because Iraqi bilateral trade with Iran skews heavily toward Iranian exports. There are few Iraqi goods that Iran would desire, besides agricultural exports. The problem with this is that Iraqis consume most of what their country produces, leaving little for export to Iran.

Any Iraqi strategy to bolster its energy infrastructure and replace Iranian energy would necessarily center on various options. These include: a) increasing domestic infrastructure and power plant investment, b) securing more natural gas and electricity supplies and c) reforming the sector itself.

Regarding the first option, Iraq was negotiating with GE and Siemens over a potential $15 billion deal to boost its generation capacity. GE was working with Iraq to build power plants and rehabilitate older infrastructure to boost capacity by 14,000 MW. GE said that this plan would bring 1,500 MW online by 2019. Siemens also announced a possible agreement with Baghdad to increase Iraq's power generation capacity by 11,000 MW. But on 10 February 2019 the Financial Times said Iraq's Electricity Minister indicated that Iraq lacked the money to close any deals, one more warning not to expect a rapid transformation of Iraq's faltering electricity system.

The second option is to help Iraq secure more natural gas and electrical supplies (most likely via imports). Providing direct supplies of energy to Iraq would be a highly strategic move for Saudi Arabia and its allies, giving them an advantage in talks with Baghdad. Saudi Arabia already subsidizes energy supplies to countries like Egypt in exchange for political favors – and withholds subsidies and resources if those countries do not fall in line with Riyadh's wishes. Saudi electricity exports to Iraq could fulfill that role in a smaller but similar fashion, all while undercutting the kingdom's main rival, Iran. Saudi Arabia and the rest of the Gulf Cooperation Council (GCC) could also try to hook Iraq's transmission infrastructure into the GCC's electricity grid to directly export electricity. However, since the GCC and Iraqi grids do not operate at the same frequencies, the required interconnection infrastructure would be costly. Beyond the GCC, Iraq has proposed boosting electricity imports from Turkey and Jordan by 300 MW.

Baghdad hopes to eventually end dependence on electricity imports altogether. But if Iraq's thirst for electricity continues to increase as expected, its peak demand will grow to as much as 39,000 MW over the next five years.

Other Neighbors.

In the interim, Iraq could look to neighbors other than Iran to help it fill its short-term needs. Arab Gulf states, which are seeking to increase their own economic and political influence in Iraq, would jump at the chance – if

20 *Iraq*

certain conditions were met. In July, as protests erupted in Iraq over electricity shortages, Saudi Arabia proposed building a 3,000 MW solar power plant in northern Saudi Arabia that would export power to Iraq and sell it at a preferential rate to Iraq. Iraq has also proposed importing 300 MW from Kuwait.

Even if the Basra Gas Company realizes its goal of capturing 20.6 bcm of natural gas annually, this would still leave Iraq some 4 bcm short of meeting the demand for its power sector alone. However, of Iraq's immediate neighbors, only Iran is a net exporter of natural gas. Saudi Arabia has a long-term natural gas development plan, but that will initially serve the domestic market. Kuwait is a net importer of natural gas, as is Turkey, leaving Iraq with few good alternatives.

What about liquid natural gas (LNG)? In the short term, Iraq could import natural gas through Kuwait's liquid natural gas import terminal to Basra, although that would require them to build associated pumping stations and pipelines from the terminal. In the long term, Iraq could try to lease its own LNG import facility or piggyback on Kuwait's larger second LNG import terminal, slated to come online in 2021. Either solution would likely prove more expensive.

But beyond the expense, cultivating more economic ties with the GCC will be politically difficult for Iraq. While there has been a relative warming of relations between Iraqi Shiite leaders like Muqtada al-Sadr and the GCC, this expanding relationship is still in its early stages. Any quick expansion of GCC economic activity into southern Iraq could provoke Iran's allies as well as nationalist Iraqis who increasingly reject both Iranian and Gulf influence in internal Iraqi affairs. Abdul-Mahdi will also have to deal with Iran's allies pushing back against any plan to bring in substantial connections to Saudi Arabia and the GCC.

This leaves Iraq in a difficult position. The US has sought a long-term plan to reduce its energy imports from Iran, but because the US needs Baghdad in its fight against ISIS, it is not able to cut off waivers and sanction Baghdad. Nor is a collapse of the Iraqi economy in the US's best interest. This means that the US will likely continue issuing waivers when it comes to Iranian energy exports to Iraq. But it will still expect Baghdad to make progress in reducing its imports from Tehran. And more importantly, the US can use the promise of continuing to grant waivers as leverage to push Iraq to strengthen connections to Saudi Arabia and the GCC, which share the strategic goal of reducing Iranian influence over Baghdad.

Nevertheless, until Iraq's long-term plans to improve its electricity generation and transmission systems come to fruition, its power outlook will remain dim. The added sanctions pressure from the US and continued political and financial woes in the sector mean that electricity, or the shortage of it, will continue to drive unrest in Iraq, particularly in Basra, for the foreseeable future.

Iraq 21

Increasing energy capacity at home is by far the most popular electricity option among Iraqi politicians and bureaucrats. Why? Massive construction projects, especially with a large imported component, provide much greater opportunities for graft and favoritism than efforts to improve the efficiency of existing capacity.

However, adding substantial capacity is not only fraught with engineering challenges but is also expensive. Still, that doesn't faze Baghdad, which favors the first option: Building new power plants. To this end, the Ministry of Electricity has proposed spending $25 billion over the next 5 years – approximately 7% of total government expenditures.

The third option involves reforming the power sector. This would help grid operators to minimize unscheduled maintenance outages and ensure that the correct standard fuel was available in high enough quantities for existing generators. That, in turn, would help the existing electrical infrastructure produce an additional 20–30% MW. That additional 20–30% would close most of the gap between supply and demand for electricity. It would also do so without the addition of $25 billion in wasteful, unnecessary spending for more electricity generation capacity.

What should foreign investors do who want to help Iraq with its reconstruction?

Iraq needs help in more accurately estimating its reserves in the other 90% of the country. If foreign investors were to take the long view, Iraqi oil producers could potentially produce a 50 billion to 250 billion-barrel increase in the country's proven reserves. In addition, the Iraqis waste resources because they flare an estimated 60% of gas instead of reinjecting it into oil wells to maintain the pressure needed to force oil to the surface. Innovative technology could capture the natural gas that is currently wasted and put it to better use. Baghdad has made recent efforts to capture more gas at the wellhead.

Turning to oil infrastructure, Iraq could use an $8.4 billion project to build new storage facilities on the Faw Peninsula south of Basra, three new pipelines to the water's edge and four floating terminals in the Gulf to speed up the filling of large oil tankers. That said, attempts to rapidly expand the oil infrastructure in the south have already created severe bottlenecks as sharply increased imports of equipment and supplies overwhelmed existing port facilities. So, foreign investors could help Iraq increase capacity at the port facilities, which, in turn, would reduce the existing bottlenecks.

Due to falling water levels in the Euphrates and Tigris Rivers, foreign investors could work with Iraq to develop a $10 billion project that would help Iraq treat seawater from the Persian Gulf and transport it by pipeline to six southern oil fields. A related issue is the disposal of contaminated water. Water used in oil recovery is often severely contaminated and will pollute river or groundwater if it is dumped. This is a public health problem that may become another humanitarian crisis unless mitigated. Therefore,

22 *Iraq*

foreign investors could help facilitate mitigation required for the creation of new facilities to deal with wastewater disposal.

In addition, Iraq should seek to reduce its economic dependency on oil by reducing regulatory hostility towards private businesses. Instituting a more business-friendly commercial code does not have to be a long, drawn-out process. The World Bank has substantial experience in instituting regulatory "best practices." Why not have Iraq adapt the commercial code of the UAE, its neighbor on the Persian Gulf? The UAE is the 51st best place to start a business – compared to Iraq's 154th ranking – and its commercial code is consistent with Islamic principles.

Foreign investors could also encourage Iraq to imitate China and establish a special economic zone to experiment with rationalizing regulations before imposing them on the entire country. Regulatory reform would help diversify the Iraqi economy in two ways: By reducing its dependency on oil exports and by creating a more business-friendly regulatory environment, both of which will reduce incentives for corruption.

To sum up, the collapse of oil prices may provide strong incentives to improve the efficiency of public infrastructure investment by fighting corruption, reducing subsidies and deregulating private business.

But Baghdad must act quickly. As Henry Kissinger would say, "Opportunities can't be hoarded. Once past, they are usually irretrievable."

Notes

1 See Ancuta Hansen, "Turning Fragile Optimism into Stability in Iraq", *National Democratic Institute*, 7 June 2017 and Hardin Lang and Daniel Benaim, "Cautious optimism in Iraq", *US News and World Report*, 8 January 2017.
2 Andrew England, "Iraq's Political Unrest Stoke Instability Fears", *Financial Times*, 22 July 2018 and Simon Foltyn, "Iraq's Disillusioned Give Up on Political Leaders", *Financial Times*, 14 August 2018.
3 See Mark DeWraver and Ali Albazzaz, "Guest Post: Iraq on the Brink? Markets Tell a Different Story", *Financial Times*, 30 September 2013.
4 See Steve Johnson, "Iraq: Can a Dusty War Zone Become a Golden Opportunity?" *Financial Times*, 5 October 2013; Borzou Daragahi, "International Companies Aim to Set Up Shop in Iraq Despite Violence", *Financial Times*, 29 December 2013; and Chris Wright, "Investing in Iraq: A Frontier Too Far?" *Financial Times*, 7 March 2014.
5 For the end of optimism in 2014, see FT View: "The Nightmare Emerging in Iraq", *Financial Times*, 11 June 2014.
6 Bill Flavin, "Stabilization: A New Approach to Whole of Government Operational Planning and Execution", US Army Peacekeeping and Stability Operations Institute, June 2018.
7 See Stuart W. Brown, "Hard Lessons: The Iraq Reconstruction Experience", CreateSpace Independent Publishing Platform (2 February 2009); also see C. Alexander Ohlers, "A Revised Strategy for Post-War Stabilization and Reconstruction", *Orbis*, vol. 63, no. 1, 2019. US Department of Defense, Military Support to Stabilization, "Transition and Reconstruction Operations Joint Operations Concept", Version 2.0, December 2006.

Iraq 23

8 Hans Binnenddijk and Stuart E. Johnson, Editors. *Transforming for Stabilization and Reconstruction Operations*, NDU Press, Washington, DC, 2004.
9 "Iraq: Risk Assessment", *Coface*, www.coface.com/Economic-Studies-and-Country-Risks/Iraq.
10 Ibid.
11 AINA, "Iraq's Economy Collapsing under Pressure of Security Crisis", http://aina.org/news/20141004193538.htm.
12 Ibid.
13 Iraq had counted on producing 3.4 million barrels a day of oil in 2014, but output sagged to 2.3 million barrels a day in August (excluding Kurdish oil fields).
14 It's important to understand that 250,000 barrels a day would come from Kurdistan, and 300,000 barrels a day would come from oil fields near Kirkuk that the Peshmerga (Kurdish military) seized from the Islamic State of Iraq and the Levant (ISIL) in June 2014. Loveday Morris and Brian Murphy, "Baghdad and Kurds Reach 'Win-Win' Accord over Iraq's Oil Revenue", *Reuters*, 2 December 2014.
15 Dlawer Ala'Aldeen, "Reconstructing Iraq: Where Do We Stand? Italian Institute for International Political Studies", 8 March 2019; and Eugenio Dacrema and Valeria Talbot, "Rebuilding Syria: The Middle East's Next Power Game?" *Italian Institute for International Political Studies*, 9 September 2019.
16 World Bank, "Connecting to Compete: Iraq", 2018.
17 As with other discussions of Iraqi reconstruction in this book, much of the assessment in this section is based on the excellent fieldwork and analysis of Lehigh Professor Frank R. Gunter. See Frank R. Gunter, *The Political Economy of Iraq*, Edward Edgar, Northampton, MA, 2013.
18 See Anthony H. Cordesman and Khalid R. al-Rodhan, *The Changing Dynamics of Energy in the Middle East*, volume 2, Praeger Security International, Westport, CT, 2006, p. 229. At current rates of production, its oil will last over a century. Energy Information Administration, *Total Petroleum and Other Liquids Production*, EIA, Washington, DC, 2018.
19 Gunter Energy Information Administration, "Country Analysis Brief: Iraq", p. 12, Frank Gunter, *The Political Economy of Iraq*, Edward Edgar, Northampton, MA, 2013, pp. 90–91.
20 For Iraqi inefficiency in the oil and gas industry, see Frank R. Gunter, *The Political Economy of Iraq*, Edward Edgar, Northampton, MA, 2013, Chapter 6.
21 Energy Information Administration, "Country Analysis Brief: Iraq", p. 5.
22 Isabel Coles and Ali Nabhan, "Despite Its Oil Wealth, Iraq Can't Keep the Lights On", *Wall Street Journal*, 23 July 2018; and "Iraq to Rebuild Infrastructure through Five Year Plan Post ISIS", *Rudaw*, 1 May 2017.
23 Ibid.
24 Ibid., pp. 95–96
25 Edward Wong, "Trump Pushes Iraq to Stop Buying Energy from Iran", *The New York Times*, 11 February 2019.

Bibliography

Alkifaey, Hamid Jaber Ali. *The Failure of Democracy in Iraq: Religion, Ideology and Sectarianism* (Routledge Studies in Middle Eastern Democratization and Government), 8 April 2019.
Banco, Erin. *Pipe Dreams: The Plundering of Iraq's Oil Wealth, Colombia Global Reports*, New York, NY, 2018.
Dodge, Toby. *Iraq – From War to a New Authoritarianism* (Adelphi series), 1st Edition, Taylor and Francis, London, 2013.

24 *Iraq*

Harris, William. *Quicksilver War: Syria, Iraq and the Spiral of Conflict*, Oxford University Press, New York, NY, 2018.

Rayburn, Joel. *Iraq after America: Strongmen, Sectarians, Resistance* (The Great Unraveling: The Remaking of the Middle East: Hoover Institution Press Publication; No. 643), 1 August 2014.

Sky, Emma. *The Unraveling: High Hopes and Missed Opportunities in Iraq*, Public Affairs, New York, NY, 2015.

US Army. "United States Government, Hard Lessons: The Iraq Reconstruction Experience", A Report of SIGIR, the Special Inspector General for Iraq Reconstruction, 9 March 2013.

World Bank. *The Kurdistan Region of Iraq: Assessing the Economic and Social Impact of the Syrian Conflict and ISIS*, World Bank, Washington, DC, 2015.

Zaid, Al-Ali, *The Struggle for Iraq's Future: How Corruption, Incompetence and Sectarianism Have Undermined Democracy*, 18 February 2014.

3 Afghanistan

In late April 2019, the Chinese hosted their second international forum for their One Belt, One Road Initiative (BRI) – their version of the New Silk Road. 36 heads of state or government attended the forum. Enthusiasm was especially apparent in four regions of the world. In Southeast Asia, China secured the attendance of top leaders from 9 out of the 10 ASEAN member states. In Central Asia, four out of the five regional countries sent their top leaders. In Europe, 12 of the 36 heads of state or government attended, including those of Russia and Azerbaijan. And in Africa, the five top leaders of Djibouti, Egypt, Ethiopia, Kenya and Mozambique also attended.[1]

In the years ahead, historians may well ask: How was China able to turn the tables on America? Just 8 years earlier, Eurasian strategists had been bullish on America's New Silk Road strategy and plans. That perception was punctuated by US Secretary of State Hillary Clinton's "New Silk Road" speech on 20 July 2011 in Chennai, India.[2]

Back then, China was on the sidelines. In contrast, General Dave Petraeus and his interagency task force at the US Central Command (CENTCOM) were front and center, creating an inclusive New Silk Road strategy with plans for infrastructure that would go through Afghanistan and turn enemies into friends and aid into trade. All of this was intended to promote shared prosperity and collective security.

But behind the scenes, American foreign policy was starting to change. General Petraeus left CENTCOM and became the commander of the International Security Assistance Force (ISAF) in July 2010.[3] General James Mattis replaced Petraeus and was the CENTCOM Commander from August 2010 until March 2013. General Mattis felt that the US State Department should run the New Silk Road. So, by 2013, Mattis had zeroed out the funding for the New Silk Road Task Force which General Petraeus had successfully created at CENTCOM. China turned the tables on America by filling this gap with its own version of the New Silk Road, the BRI. In contrast to America, which surrendered its New Silk Road strategy, Beijing is serious. The World Economic Forum says China is committing itself to a $8 trillion BRI. In the so-called Great Power Competition with China, America is giving the Eurasian playing field to China and retreating to Fortress America.

26   *Afghanistan*

How was China so successful in turning the tables on America? And why is America so reluctant to implement its version of the New Silk Road plan? The short answer is that China understands how to connect economics and security in its foreign policy. In contrast, American foreign policy keeps economics and security in separate silos. For the most part, America waives the economic white flag and tries to solve conflicts in the world either militarily or with economic coercion. The Iranian nuclear agreement was an exception – but the Trump foreign policy team threw away all that brilliant work as well.[4]

Once in a blue moon and almost by mistake, someone like a George Marshall or a Dave Petraeus will come along to connect the economic and military dots at a high level. Unfortunately, the economic/security connection is not institutionalized. So, when the Dave Petraeus leaves the picture, foreign policy problems once again become militarized, and America looks for hammers to pound nails. In short, too many American strategists don't understand the importance of connecting economics and security.

Take Afghanistan, for instance. President Obama announced in 2011 that the lion's share of the 150,000 US troops would come home, leaving only about 10–15% of the troops behind.[5] There would also be a simultaneous and proportional 10–15% reduction of about 130,000 military contracts. US military doctrine says that civilians will take the lead in stabilization and reconstruction operations. But Hans Binnendijk and Stuart Johnson correctly argue that there is now a widening gap between the scale-down of combat operations and the start of stabilization and reconstruction operations.[6]

Bad things happen in this gap. So, when President Obama announced the US drawdown in Afghanistan, the US Treasury did a study that predicted how much of a negative impact there would be on the overall Afghan economy when 85–90% of the war economy went away. The best-case scenario was a 13% cut in Afghan Gross Domestic Product (GDP), which equates to the US Great Depression. The worst-case scenario was a 41% cut in Afghan GDP. Either way, the number of jobless people was expected to soar.[7]

So, what happens militarily if nothing is done to fill this gap between combat power and stabilization and reconstruction? In East Timor, violence rose when the United Nations (UN) peacekeepers played cut and run.[8]

In Iraq, we saw the rise of ISIS after the US played cut and run, leaving the country without making any serious stabilization and reconstruction efforts.[9] But, in Iraq, at least, oil production is not located near war zones, even if low oil prices recently reduced profit margins.

In Afghanistan, the good news is that there is lots of potential wealth. In fact, the US Geological Survey says that the country has a trillion dollars of potential mineral wealth.[10] Unfortunately, Afghanistan is struggling to turn this potential wealth into actual wealth. Former MIT Professor Walt Rostow would say that it lacks preconditions for economic takeoff.[11]

If land-locked Afghanistan had good infrastructure, it could still have market access. But Afghan infrastructure has been largely destroyed because of continuous wars. In this regard, only 7% of the roads are paved.

Therefore, this inadequate infrastructure equates to poor market access. When it rains, the roads turn to mud or flood. So, there is little incentive to increase production.

Therefore, Afghanistan faced a double whammy. On the cyclical side, the war economy was collapsing. On the structural side, it struggled with inadequate infrastructure and poor market access. With these combined, Afghanistan is faced depression economics. This is why it needed a Keynesian economic strategy to fill the gap in aggregate demand (or at least soften the blow).

Weak Trade Diversification

The International Monetary Fund (IMF) research shows that Afghanistan's external trade contributes little to economic growth. Its share of international trade is insignificant, and it has been running a trade deficit for the last two decades. Why the trade imbalance? IMF says that the country compares poorly with its neighbors, especially with respect to the low value of its official exports, which have remained below 10 percent of GDP since 2012, while imports are dominated by foreign-financed security spending and aid-related imports.[12]

In addition, IMF research highlights Afghanistan's low degree of trade diversification, which makes it more vulnerable to external shocks, like the current balance of payments crisis. Its external trade is over-concentrated in agricultural products (nearly 45 percent of exports). This reflects the small manufacturing base and a recent decline in specialized products, such as carpets and textiles, owing to global competition. And its heavy export concentration (to Pakistan and India) expose the country to demand shocks in those markets.[13]

IMF also cites several country-specific factors that have held back trade performance. Constant conflict over the last 35 years, a landlocked geography and infrastructure and institutional gaps have combined to thwart trade expansion. World Bank data documents the costs of Afghanistan's being landlocked. The World Bank's Logistics Performance Index (LPI) shows that on average, the delays and costs for both importing and exporting are far higher for landlocked countries than their coastal neighbors.[14]

Johns Hopkins Professor Fred Starr had been advocating a New Silk Road for decades.[15] His concept was transcontinental in scope and ran from China to Europe via Central and South Asia. But the US government did not push very hard for it. If they were going to support it, conventional wisdom says that the US State Department would be the logical place to do so, and the Policy Planning Council at there would ordinarily be the logical office in which to develop policy.

With this in mind, Mike Gfoeller (the Political Advisor), Lewis Elbinger (the Deputy Political Advisor) and I (the Chief Economist) at CENTCOM flew from Tampa to Washington, D.C. and met with the Policy Planning Council at STATE.[16] Unfortunately, the diplomats in policy planning

28   *Afghanistan*

wanted no part of the New Silk Road. It would be too difficult, with too many moving parts. Richard Holbrooke, the Special Representative for Afghanistan and Pakistan (SRAP), wanted no part of it either.

Since nobody else in Washington wanted to develop policy for a New Silk Road, General Petraeus signed off on CENTCOM doing policy formulation for a New Silk Road to close the gap in aggregate demand. A "tiger team" (or interagency task force) including Deputy CENTCOM Commander John Allen, Rear Admiral Jeffrey Harley, Ambassador Michael Gfoeller, myself, Dr. Adib Farhadi, Colonel Ted Hodgson, Dr. Martin Hanratty, Dr. Richard Ponzio, Lewis Elbinger and many other experts was created to develop a New Silk Road Strategy and Plan. Twenty economic development projects were designed and planned.[17] The hard infrastructure included transport, mining, energy and telecom projects. Transport included completing the Afghan Ring Road, the Afghan North-South Road Corridor, the Afghan East-West Road Corridor, the Kabul-Jalalabad-Peshawar Expressway, the Salang Tunnel, the Northern Rail Corridor and commercial aviation. Mining included the Aynak Copper Mine and the Hajigak Iron Ore Mine. Energy included the Turkmenistan, Afghanistan, Pakistan and India (TAPI) gas pipeline; the Central Asia-South Asia Electricity Project (CASA 1000); and the Sheberghan Gas Fired Thermal Power Facility. The Fiber Optic Ring was the telecom project.

Fortunately, interest rates had been low and negative in Germany and Japan. So, the time was right for public infrastructure. Harvard's Lawrence Summers notes that it's irresponsible not to invest in public infrastructure now. He explains that for every $1 in input, you get $3 in output.[18]

Public infrastructure is an indispensable input in the Afghan economy's production and arguably one that is highly complementary to other inputs, such as labor and private (non-infrastructure) capital. In fact, it is hard to imagine any new production process in any sector of the Afghan economy that would not rely on infrastructure. Conversely, the inadequacies in Afghan infrastructure – power outages, insufficient water supply and decrepit roads – adversely affect the quality of life in Afghanistan and present significant barriers to the operation of the private sector in Afghanistan. In this regard, there has been a significant decline in Afghan infrastructure since the Soviets seriously damaged it while occupying the country. Although some progress has been made since then, the gaps in the quantity of infrastructure provision in Afghanistan are still glaring. It's interesting to see the difference between the quality of infrastructure in advanced, emerging and low-income economies. Take power, for instance. Power generation capacity per person in emerging market economies is only one-fifth of the level it is in advanced economies, and in low income-countries, it is about one-eighth of the level it is in emerging market economies.

While the argument for investment in infrastructure applies almost everywhere, the role of China stands out in the world. China used public infrastructure investment to enjoy the fastest GDP growth in the history of the world. However, that internal infrastructure growth has arguably reached its limit inside China. Now, as part of its "go west" strategy, it has created an Asian Infrastructure Investment Bank (AIIB) to fund its own version of the New Silk Road.

While the US and the World Bank will probably not be competitive with China for public infrastructure investment in the New Silk Road, it is absolutely essential for US diplomats to make sure that it does not go around Afghanistan. China's New Silk Road needs to go through Afghanistan; Afghanistan needs to be the hub or "heart" of this commercial activity. If it is a beneficiary of this commercial activity, its stakeholders will arguably protect the New Silk Road.

What is the key assumption behind China's New Silk Road strategy and its AIIB? Perhaps Harvard's Lawrence Summers puts it best: "What is crucial everywhere is the recognition that in a time of economic shortfall and inadequate public investment, there is for once a free lunch – a way for governments to strengthen both the economy and their own financial positions."

Why does Lawrence Summers call public infrastructure investment a free lunch? A recent IMF study addresses this question. For starters, the IMF discusses the macroeconomic effects of public investment in infrastructure. In the short term, increasing public infrastructure investment raises output by boosting aggregate demand (which has been collapsing in the Afghan war economy). In the long term, increasing public infrastructure investment also raises aggregate supply. In countries with clear infrastructure needs (such as Afghanistan), the time is right for an infrastructure push for three compelling reasons: a) borrowing costs are low, b) aggregate demand is weak (from the collapse in the Afghan war economy) and c) there are significant infrastructure bottlenecks in a place like Afghanistan.

In addition, the IMF argues that increasing public infrastructure investment raises (GDP) output in the short and the long term. This is particularly so during periods of economic slack (such as the war economy collapse in Afghanistan) and when investment efficiency is high.

In addition, the IMF asserts that when unemployment is high, as it is in Afghanistan as the economy collapses, properly designed infrastructure investment will reduce rather than increase government debt burdens. Debt-financed kinds of New Silk Road projects could have large output effects without increasing the debt-to-GDP ratio, if clearly identified needs are met through efficient investment, as cited above. This is because the level of rising nominal debt grows slower than the boost to GDP, so, debt, as a percentage of GDP, falls. In this way, public infrastructure investment pays for itself, if done correctly. A dollar of spending on infrastructure increases output by nearly three dollars.

It follows that annual tax collections, adjusted for inflation, would increase by 1.5% of the amount invested since the government claims about 25 cents out of every additional dollar of income. That would certainly be a shot in the arm for an Afghan government presently struggling to balance its budget.

The good news is that we can also respond positively to the USCENTCOM Commander's request to find targets of opportunity for our strategists. The

30 *Afghanistan*

time is right for an infrastructure push in countries like Afghanistan, where conditions are right. For starters, the monetary policy environment was attractive. Real interest costs (i.e. interest costs less inflation) at US and advanced economy banks were below 1% over horizons of up to 30 years. This means that infrastructure investment makes it possible to reduce the real burdens on future generations.

Further good news is that earlier calculations understate the positive budgetary impact of well-designed infrastructure investment. For instance, public infrastructure would serve as a platform for boosting export industries. Lawrence Summers cites additional omissions in our earlier and simpler calculation which neglect key benefits. Our earlier calculation neglects tax revenue that comes from the simulative benefit of putting Afghan people to work constructing infrastructure. It neglects how public investment in infrastructure can contribute by supporting private investments in areas such as telecommunications and energy. In Afghanistan, there are long-run benefits that come from combating the collapse of the war economy by boosting jobs and curbing insurgency. And by increasing the economy's capacity, infrastructure investment increases the ability to absorb higher levels of debt.

Finally, the international banks can catalyze a dollar of infrastructure investment at a cost of much less than a dollar by providing a tranche of equity financing, a tax subsidy or a loan guarantee. When it takes these factors into account, the IMF finds that every dollar of public infrastructure investment increases GDP output by nearly three dollars. The budgetary mathematics associated with infrastructure investment is especially attractive at a time when there are unused human resources. Thus, greater infrastructure investment need not come at the expense of other spending. If we are entering a period of secular stagnation, unemployed human resources could be available for quite some time.

To prove that there were no white elephant projects, the tiger team had a rigorous evaluation system. There were macroeconomic indicators, such as job creation, per capita income and government revenue. The cost benefit analyses only included infrastructure projects in which there was a strong benefit to cost ratio. All others were rejected.

The Task Force's predictions of successful infrastructure projects also had demanding risk assessments. Oxford Analytica was rejected because their work only included economic risk. Instead, the task force opted for interdisciplinary company, which included political, military and economic algorithms. Soft infrastructure projects were also evaluated, including (a) legal, policy and regulatory reforms, (b) cross-border economic zones and (c) harmonizing regional customs.

The task force also developed plans to give the Afghan private sector persuasive reasons to stay in Afghanistan and enticing reasons for the Afghan diaspora to return.[19] Afghan rural communities lacked soft infrastructure to facilitate education and job creation. They lacked affordable electrical

Afghanistan 31

and internet services, resources and access to digital education libraries and entrepreneurship/mentorship programs.

The task force's strategic enablers involved building soft infrastructure in rural communities to create sustainable resources to support education and foster entrepreneurship. The plans for the small business center included a solar-powered convenience store and a micro-grid enhanced with a conferencing E-station. This would enable video teleconferencing and access to educational E-library centers and training videos to foster entrepreneurship.

Step by step, the CENTCOM task force was successful in getting 35 US government agencies onboard. While the policy planning council at the US State Department continued to oppose the New Silk Road Initiative we were building at CENTCOM, we were successful at getting Marc Grossman, the new and more powerful Special Representative for Afghanistan and Pakistan (or SRAP), onboard. The CENTCOM task force enjoyed a declaratory policy victory when US Secretary of State Hillary Clinton embraced its New Silk Road initiative in a speech she gave in Chennai, India on 20 July 2011.[20] With all of its persuasive feasibility plans done, the task force was ready to pursue an implementation plan. General Petraeus was the ideal choice to help get Wall Street onboard with the task force's finance plans and the media on board to mobilize public opinion. Petraeus holds a PhD in International Relations from Princeton University, and he taught economics at West Point.

But the task force suffered a fatal defeat when President Obama, who never understood the strategic value of its New Silk Road initiative, rushed to judgment and sent General Petraeus to "save the day" in Afghanistan.[21] Ill-advised decision meant that Petraeus would get bogged down with tactical military matters and have little time for the long view and the strategic New Silk Road Initiative. I personally believe that no Hollywood producer would ever miscast his military commanders the way Obama did. Like George Patton, General Mattis was a "legendary warrior" who should have gone to Afghanistan. "Mad-man" Mattis would have excelled as a battlefield commander in Afghanistan. Instead, Obama had Mattis replace Petraeus at CENTCOM.

Why did this change of command matter? While General Petraeus was a grand strategist and passionate supporter of the New Silk Road at CENTCOM, General Mattis did not understand either the economic or strategic importance of the CENTCOM New Silk Road. Therefore, he had no problem and throwing away all the work the New Silk Road task force had done at CENTCOM. He bottomed out the funding for the New Silk Road at CENTCOM and tried to eliminate the Chief Economist position that Admiral William "Fox" Fallon had insightfully created to link economics and security. General Lloyd Austen ignored General Mattis's advice and maintained the Chief Economist position after Mattis retired. But the self-inflicted damage to America's version of the New Silk Road at CENTCOM was fatal. Instead of either competing with China or collaborating with it

32 *Afghanistan*

in the region, the fall of CENTCOM's New Silk Road Initiative meant that the US retreated economically from the region. I respectfully believe that this was a huge strategic mistake and a lost opportunity for US economic diplomacy.

Why not just let the US State Department run the New Silk Road Initiative? As we've seen, the Policy Planning Council at STATE never wanted the New Silk Road. Secretary of State Colin Powell created the Coordinator for Reconstruction and Stabilization (C/RS) position in 2004 to address these matters in theory,[22] but it never had enough resources to go from policy to implementation. The Bureau of Conflict and Stabilization (CSO) replaced C/RS in 2011,[23] but it had similar resource shortfalls. Instead of beefing up its budget, it appears that President Trump now intends to take CSO to the chopping block. The Task Force for Business & Stability Operations (TF/BSO) in OSD was created in 2006 to develop pilot projects.[24] But TF/BSO and USAID had turf battles, and TF/BSO was bottomed out in November of 2014.

With no plans to fill the gap between (a) combat power and (b) stabilization and reconstruction, a muscle-bound America continues to win operational military victories, lose the peace and surrender US Silk Road Strategy to China. The New Silk Road task force members at CENTCOM may have felt partially vindicated when Beijing announced in 2013 that it would initiate its own scaled up version of the New Silk Road, which they called the One Belt One Road Initiative (or BRI). The BRI is China's massive new trade corridor project. The good news is that China is serious.

The bad news is that much of China's New Silk Road goes around Afghanistan. CENTCOM's idea was to build infrastructure through Afghanistan, which, in turn, would strengthen the Afghan economy and foster transcontinental shared security. In any event, when America ill-advisedly abandoned its New Silk Road, China happily initiated its own $8 trillion version of the New Silk Road.

The Challenge of Reconciliation

Now let's move forward to September 2019. President Donald Trump says 18 years of fighting in Afghanistan is long enough. He says he wants to declare victory and cut and run from Afghanistan. That means that all US soldiers will hopefully be home well before what Trump plans to be his re-election in 2020.

Trump picked Dr. Zalmay Khalilzad, an excellent former US Ambassador to Afghanistan, as his US Special Representative for Afghan Reconciliation to help make this happen. The problem is that the Taliban sees President Ashraf Ghani's Afghan government as illegitimate and therefore refuses to meet with it. So, Khalilzad must fill the gap and meet with the Taliban himself.

Khalilzad's talks with the Taliban have been relatively successful. In the most recent round of negotiations, the two sides say they are close to agreement on two issues: A timetable for US troops to leave the country and what the Taliban needs to do to prevent international terrorists (like ISIS) from operating on Afghan soil.

However, Khalilzad says that two other issues are important to the US. First, there must be a ceasefire, and second, there must be an intra-Afghan political settlement. Unfortunately, there has not been much progress towards reaching agreement on these two issues.

Khalilzad also insists that "nothing is agreed until everything is agreed." However, the Taliban continues to refuse to meet with the Ashraf Ghani government. So, an intra-Afghan political settlement is a non-starter with the Taliban. Thus, the US and the Taliban are at an impasse.

How should the US break the impasse? It might be useful to ask why it is so difficult to negotiate peace. In fact, the World Bank has done some useful research over the years on this very question (See The World Bank, Breaking the Conflict Trap: Civil War and Development Policy).

The World Bank notes that negotiating peace is difficult because the US, the Ashraf Ghani government in Kabul and the Taliban lack the means to lock into an agreement. For starters, the Taliban cannot guarantee that if it accepts a ceasefire, its more extreme members will not form a splinter group and keep fighting. Conversely, the Ashraf Ghani government cannot make binding commitments that the Taliban can trust once they disarm. That's not surprising. Results from other similar civil wars show that many of the agreements that end civil wars are unstable and collapse into renewed fighting.

The World Bank also notes that the difficulty of negotiating a lasting peace is due to the inability of a third party to credibly commit to the peace. Credible guarantees offered by a third party committed to enforcing the terms of an Afghan peace treaty are painfully lacking.

Could the US provide a credible US guarantee for a settlement? Does it have a credible and well-established self-interest in preserving the peace with enough US military resources? Is Khalilzad in a position to provide costly signals of US commitment by deploying US troops to provide credible guarantees?

A credible US commitment is problematic for two reasons. First, Trump reneged on the nuclear agreement with Iran. Why should the Taliban trust him for a credible commitment in Afghanistan? Second, given his interest in permanently cutting and running from Afghanistan, it seems unlikely that he would want to deploy US troops for peacekeeping after they leave Afghanistan. That being the case, without such a credible US commitment and without an Afghan government seen as legitimate by the Taliban, there is no apparent incentive for the Taliban to disarm. And since disarmament is typically a precondition for the implementation of peace, these glaring

34 *Afghanistan*

omissions at least appear to create a significant obstacle to Khalilzad's successful negotiation with the Taliban.

If an external US military solution appears unlikely while Trump is president, is there another way to make the peace self-enforcing? Some analysts say that integrating part of the Taliban into the national army might be such a solution. The problem is that the Taliban would lose its bargaining power in relation to the Afghan government once its fighters demobilize. If the Afghan government retained its military, it could easily renege on its promise after the Taliban disarmed. It would have both the power and the incentive to either re-negotiate the agreement or defect from it unilaterally.

Reducing Post-Conflict Risk

In peacetime, US politicians are fond of using the bumper sticker "peace through strength" when they speak to their base. "Peace through strength" is also music to the ears of the military industrial complex that President Eisenhower used to warn us about.

But what happens in the immediate post-conflict world? How does the government reduce the risk of fighting again? For starters, the pressure from the military industrial complex for high military spending is certainly present here as well. However, research findings from the World Bank indicate that high levels of military spending in the post-conflict world significantly increase the risk of reversion to war.

For starters, an important post-conflict problem is that neither side trusts the other. Thus, the more the government spends on the military, the more the rebel organization feels it must prepare for the renewal of conflict. Such mutual military escalation can easily trigger incidents that re-ignite the conflict.

Research indicates that high military spending may well increase the risk of reversion to conflict by inadvertently sending signals to the rebels that the government lacks confidence in the persistence of peace. Therefore, more Afghan government military spending is destabilizing. In addition to the problems resulting from higher military spending, the government could forego the opportunity to realize a peace dividend from reduced spending. Thus, getting to peace is difficult.

But even if peace is initially re-established with peacekeepers like the United Nations, research shows that it is often fragile. World Bank research indicates that countries like Afghanistan face two major risks:

First, when peace is re-established, it is often fragile. The 18-year Afghan civil war has developed a momentum of its own. Powerful forces tend to lock it into a syndrome of further conflict. Paul Collier calls these perpetuating factors the conflict trap. In other words, it does not take much to upset the apple cart. In fact, the best predictor of whether Afghanistan will be in a civil war next year is whether it is now in civil war.

Second, the likelihood of fighting happening again turns on whether or not the country inherits a severe economic and social decline from the period of conflict. Empirical research by the World Bank shows a striking pattern: Civil war is heavily concentrated in poor countries, like Afghanistan. In other words, poverty increases the likelihood of civil war. Thus, the World Bank's central argument is the failure of economic development is a root cause of conflict.

The Failure of Economic Development

18 years after the Afghan conflict began, the failure of economic development continues to keep the conflict going and make reconciliation difficult. "You learn what you're made of not when life is good, but when the ground beneath your feet gives way, and you are left afraid and uncertain what to do." Those words of Mel Allen, a writer from New England, could easily be describing Afghanistan, a country with a worsening civil war, which has now triggered a financial crisis.[25]

The Afghan foreign exchange rate against the US dollar fell during the first 9 months of 2018 and hit a record low in September. Foreign reserves were also falling.[26]

Not surprisingly, Afghan GDP growth was only growing at about 2%, not nearly fast enough to absorb 400,000 new labor market entrants every year.

Kabul also faces a humanitarian crisis. The most direct human effects of 18 years of civil war are fatalities and population displacements. For starters, the dynamics of conflict from 2001 to 2016 can be divided into four main periods. From 2001 to 2005, conflict deaths in Afghanistan were in the thousands, with some 4,500 deaths nationwide. From 2006 to 2010, as fighting intensified, deaths increased above 30,000, over half of these in the southern region. From 2011 to 2014, conflict deaths declined as foreign troop numbers peaked. Between 2015 and 2016, troops left, conflict intensified and deaths increased once again. If we include "mini surge of additional US and allied troops in 2018," the human death toll includes 38,480 Afghan civilians, 58,596 Afghan military and police, 42,100 Taliban fighters, 2,401 US military, 3,937 US contractors and 1,141 allied troops.[27]

Forced migration in Afghanistan broadly consists of two groups: Internally displaced persons (IDPs) and refugees, who migrate into neighboring countries for safety. Afghanistan has one of the largest percentage of IDPs in the world. The Watson Brown Foundation estimates that there were 3.7 million Afghan IDPs in 2018. That figure is over 10% of the Afghan population. The UN Refugee Agency reports that there are also 1.38 million registered Afghan refugees in Pakistan. Another one million Afghan refugees are believed to be living there, unregistered.

The violence from the war also creates fear. Businesses close, and people stop shopping. They flee from their homes, and many become IDPs inside Afghanistan. Along the way, most of the Afghans on the move lose the

36　*Afghanistan*

few assets they possess. Those who have financial assets move their wealth abroad. This capital flight doubles Afghanistan's private capital stock overseas.

There is also brain drain as many of the intellectual assets move to safer places. The disruption of civil war also shortens time horizons. Many Afghans retreat into subsistence and invest less. The war also severs family and community links.

As the constraints on criminal activity weaken, crime increases. The illicit opiate economy in Afghanistan was estimated at US$2.8 billion in 2014 – equivalent to 13 percent of its GDP (UNODC, 2016). In 2017, opium cultivation and refining in Afghanistan reached a record high. Meanwhile, US eradication operations in Afghanistan predictably backfired, pushing much of the Afghan workforce closer to the Taliban. News flash to Donald Trump: Supply reduction is a costly failure. Solutions to the global problem of drug addiction lie within consumer countries themselves. Try education, prevention and treatment to reduce the demand for drugs.

Fiscal Revenue Costs

Now, imagine you have the challenge of running Afghan fiscal policy during this debacle. What kind of challenges do you face? For starters, there are the devastating economic costs of the violence. The war diverts resources from productive activities to destruction. This cause a double loss for the Afghan economy. First, the country suffers from the loss of productive resources before the conflict began. Second, the country suffers from current wartime destruction.

In addition, increased Afghan military spending is an opportunity cost, crowding out what your fiscal policy could otherwise spend on basic public services (such as health care, education and better infrastructure for your citizens and businesses). Since lower fiscal revenues hamper the ability of the Afghan government to provide these basic public services to its citizens, its revenue losses contribute to the humanitarian costs of conflict. In Afghanistan, this loss appears very substantial.[28]

IMF estimates that conflict-related violence reduced annual national revenues in Afghanistan in 2016 by around 50%. This lost national revenue is about $1 billion.[29]

Looking ahead, the loss of these fiscal results implies a sizable potential fiscal "peace dividend" for Afghanistan, should political reconciliation lead to peace. In Afghanistan, almost all security spending is funded by foreign grants, which will most likely be scaled back gradually in the event of peace. Hence, any fiscal peace dividend is likely to come principally from increased revenues as reduced security spending will mostly be offset by reduced grants. In other words, the $1 billion fiscal revenue costs of the Afghan War imply a sizable potential fiscal dividend for Afghanistan, should political reconciliation produce a durable peace.

Root Cause of the Afghan Conflict

Now that we've understood how costly the Afghan civil war has been, several other questions come to mind. First, why was Afghanistan so prone to violence 18 years ago? And second, why has the war lasted so long? If US strategists knew the answers to these two questions, it stands to reason that they might have a better chance of achieving political reconciliation and durable peace in Afghanistan.

Some scholars look at each civil war as totally unique and distinctive, with its own personalities and events. Most of us would agree that any all-embracing, general theory of civil war would therefore be patently ridiculous. That said, when we look beyond the personalities and events, important patterns emerge. In fact, some of these patterns are surprisingly strong, which suggests that some characteristics tend to make a country prone to civil war. If so, what made a country prone to civil war?

Many people think they already know the initial circumstances or root causes of civil war. Those on the political right tend to assume that it is due to longstanding ethnic and religious hatreds. Those in the political center tend to assume that it is due to a lack of democracy and that violence occurs where opportunities for the peaceful resolution of political disputes are lacking. Some scholars on the political left point to a deep-rooted legacy of colonialism.

While each political group speculates, none of these narratives sits comfortably with the statistical evidence. Empirically, the World Bank's most striking pattern is that civil war is heavily concentrated in the poorest countries. Admittedly, war causes poverty. But more importantly, poverty increases the likelihood of civil war.

The World Bank's central argument is that the root cause of the Afghan conflict and other such civil wars is the failure of economic development. Countries with low, stagnant and unequally distributed per capita incomes, and that have remained dependent on primary commodities for their exports face dangerously high risks of prolonged conflict. In the absence of economic development, neither good political institutions, nor ethnic and religious homogeneity nor high military spending provide significant defenses against large-scale violence.

Now, let's turn to our second question. If the average civil war lasts 7 years, why has the 18-year war in Afghanistan lasted so long? IMF found that a wide range of poverty related indicators worsened during the Afghan conflict. These show that per capita income fell, food production dropped, exports growth declined and their external debt increased as a percentage of GDP.[30]

These economic forces in Afghanistan contributed in large measure to what is known as the conflict trap: Once a country like Afghanistan has stumbled into conflict, powerful forces, perpetuating economic forces, act as a conflict trap and tend to lock it into a syndrome of further conflict.

38 *Afghanistan*

Notes

1 Shannon Tiezzi, "Who Is (and Who Isn't) Attending China's 2nd Belt and Road Forum?" *The Diplomat*, 27 April 2019. See HSBC. "Reshaping the Future World Economy", 11 May 2017, www.business.hsbc.com/belt-and-road/reshaping-the-future-world-economy.
2 See Hillary Clinton, *Remarks on India and the United States: A Vision for the 21st Century*, US State Department, Chennai, India, 20 July 2011.
3 See Leo Shane III, "Mattis Tapped to Replace Petraeus at the Helm of Central Command", *Stars and Stripes*, 8 July 2010.
4 Mahsa Rouhi, "Trump's Decertification Doesn't Mean the Death of the Iran Nuclear Deal", *Boston Globe*, 8 December 2017.
5 CNN, "Obama Announces Afghanistan Troop Withdrawal Plan", 23 June 2011.
6 Hans Binnendijk and Stuart Johnson, *Transforming for Stabilization and Reconstruction Operations* (Paperback), 23 July 2012.
7 See Leif Rosenberger, *Economic Transition in Afghanistan: How to Soften a Hard Landing*, The Strategic Studies Institute, US Army War College, 25 October 2011.
8 See *The New York Times*, "Peacekeepers Exit East Timor", 31 December 2012.
9 *NPR*, "Did Obama Withdraw from Iraq Too Soon, Allowing ISIS to Grow?", 19 December 2015.
10 See *NBC News*, "Rare Earth: Afghanistan Sits on $1 Trillion in Minerals", 5 September 2014.
11 See *The Economist*, "Obituary: Walt Rostow", 20 February 2003.
12 Patrick Gitton and Murtaza Muzaffari, "Afghanistan's Integration in Regional Trade: A Stocktaking", IMF, December 2017.
13 Ibid.
14 Ibid.
15 See Fred Starr, *The New Silk Roads: Transport and Trade in Greater Central Asia*, Central Asia Caucasus Institute Silk Road Studies Program, 2007.
16 At this time, Michael Gfoeller was the Political Advisor at CENTCOM, his Deputy was Lewis Elbinger and I was Chief Economist. The three of us attended that frustrating and unsuccessful meeting with the Deputy Director of the Policy Planning Council at the US State Department.
17 See Leif Rosenberger, *Economic Transition in Afghanistan: How to Soften a Hard Landing*, The Strategic Studies Institute, US Army War College, 25 October 2011.
18 Larry Summers, *Building the Case for Greater Infrastructure Investment*, 12 September 2016, larrysummers.com.
19 For a graphic of these rural small business centers, see http://thinkrenewables.com/sbiz-centre/.
20 See Former US Ambassador Marc Grossman's support for China's BRI in Interview: "Belt and Road Initiative to Boost Sustainable Economic Development – Former US Diplomat", *Xinhua*, 4 April 2007.
21 See Leo Shane III, "Mattis Tapped to Replace Petraeus at the Helm of Central Command", 8 July 2010.
22 For more on C/RS, see https://2001-2009.state.gov/s/crs/c12936.htm.
23 For more on CSO see https://www.state.gov/j/cso/.
24 See www.rand.org/content/dam/rand/pubs/research_reports/RR1200/RR1243/RAND_RR1243.pdf.
25 Mel Allen, "The Town that Refused to Die", *Yankee*, Nov/Dec 2018.
26 EIU, "Afghanistan: Country Report", September 2018.
27 Costs of the War, Watson Institute, Brown University, November 2018.

Afghanistan 39

28 Data on Conflict and Revenue in Afghanistan comes from the Uppsala Conflict Data Program (UCDP).
29 This IMF estimate of the impact of the conflict on national revenue matches well with the output loss estimates of Mueller & Tobias 2016.
30 Philip Barrett, "Measuring the Fiscal Revenue Cost of Conflict in Afghanistan", *Afghanistan Selected Issues*, IMF Country Report No. 17/378, December 2017.

Bibliography

Fiscal Revenue Cost of the Afghan Civil War

Abadie, Alberto, and Javier Gardeazabal. "The Economic Costs of Conflict: A Case Study of the Basque Country", *The American Economic Review*, vol. 93, no. 1, 2003, pp. 113–32.

Besley, Timothy, Thiemo Fetzer, and Hannes Mueller. "The Welfare Cost of Lawlessness: Evidence from Somali Piracy", *Journal of the European Economic Association*, vol. 13, no. 2, 2015, pp. 203–239.

Besley, Timothy, and Hannes Mueller. "Estimating the Peace Dividend: The Impact of Violence on House Prices in Northern Ireland," *The American Economic Review*, vol. 102, no. 2, 2012, pp. 810–833.

Collier, Paul. "On the Economic Consequences of Civil War", *Oxford Economic Papers*, vol. 51, no. 1, 1999, pp. 168–183.

Dube, Oeindrila, and Juan F. Vargas. "Commodity Price Shocks and Civil Conflict: Evidence from Colombia", *The Review of Economic Studies*, vol. 80, no. 4, 2013, pp. 1384–1421.

Gupta, Sanjeev, Benedict Clements, Rina Bhattacharya, and Shamit Chakravarti. "Fiscal Consequences of Armed Conflict and Terrorism in Low-and Middle-Income Countries", *European Journal of Political Economy*, vol. 20, no. 2, 2004, pp. 403–421.

International Monetary Fund (IMF). "Gaining Momentum?" *World Economic Outlook*, Chapter 1, Box 1.1, International Monetary Fund, Washington, DC, 2017.

Knight, Malcolm, Norman Loayza, and Delano Villanueva. "The Peace Dividend: Military Spending Cuts and Economic Growth", IMF Staff Papers, vol. 43, no. 1, 1996, pp. 1–37 (Washington: International Monetary Fund).

Mueller, Hannes, "Growth and Violence: Argument for a Per Capita Measure of Civil War", *Economica*, vol. 83, no. 331, 2016, pp. 473–497.

Mueller, Hannes and J. Tobias, *The Cost of Violence: Estimating the Economic Impact of Conflict*, IGC Growth Brief Series 007, International Growth Centre, London, 2016.

Regional Trade

Arvis, Jean-François, Gaël Raballand, and Jean-François Marteau. *The Cost of Being Landlocked; Logistics Costs and Supply Chain Reliability*, The World Bank, Washington, DC, 2010.

Arvis, Jean-François, Robin Carruthers, Graham Smith, and Christopher Willoughby. *Connecting Landlocked Developing Countries to Market—Trade Corridors in the 21st Century*, The World Bank, Washington, DC, 2011.

40 *Afghanistan*

Cali, Massimiliano. *Trading Away from Conflict: Using Trade to Increase Resilience in Fragile States*, The World Bank, Washington, DC, 2015.

International Monetary Fund, *Middle East and Central Asia Department, Regional Economic Outlook*, International Monetary Fund, Washington, DC, 2016.

Islamic Republic of Afghanistan, Ministry of Foreign Affairs, Regional Economic Cooperation Conference on Afghanistan (RECCA). *Towards Regional Economic Growth and Stability: The Silk Road through Afghanistan* (Kabul), 2015.

Islamic Republic of Afghanistan, Ministry of Foreign Affairs, Regional Economic Cooperation Conference on Afghanistan (RECCA), Annual Review. *From Negotiation to Investment, Construction, and Trade: A New Decade of Progress* (Kabul), 2016.

Rastogi, Cordula, and Jean-François Arvis. *The Eurasian Connection—Supply Chain Efficiency along the Modern Silk Route through Central Asia*, The World Bank, Washington, DC, 2014.

Rocha, Nadia. *Trade as a Vehicle for Growth in Afghanistan: Challenges and Opportunities*, The World Bank, Washington, DC, 2017.

United Nations Conference on Trade and Development. *The Way to The Ocean— Transit Corridors Servicing the Trade of Landlocked Developing Countries*, United Nations, New York and Geneva, 2013.

World Bank, *Afghanistan Diagnostics Trade Integration Study (DTIS)*, The World Bank, Washington, DC, 2012.

World Bank. *Afghanistan Development Update*, The World Bank, Washington, DC, 2017.

Financial Inclusion

Atkinson, A. and Flore-Anne Messy. "Promoting Financial Inclusion through Financial Education: OECD/INFE Evidence, Policies and Practice," OECD Working Papers on Finance, Insurance and Private Pensions, No. 34, OECD Publishing, Paris, 2013.

Central Bank of Turkey, Prime Ministry Circular No. 2014/10 on Financial Access, Financial Education and Financial Consumer Protection Strategy and Action Plans published in the Official Gazette No. 29021, Ankara, 5 June 2014.

Dabla-Norris, E., Y. Ji, R.M. Townsend, and D. Filiz Unsal. "Distinguishing Constraints of Financial Inclusion and Their Impact on GDP and Inequality." NBER Working Paper 20821, National Bureau of Economic Research, Cambridge, MA, 2015.

Demirguc-Kunt, A., Leora Klapper, and Dorothe Singer. "Financial Inclusion and Legal Discrimination against Women: Evidence from Developing Countries." Policy Research Working Paper No. 6416, World Bank, Washington, DC, 2013.

Demirguc-Kunt, A., Leora Klapper, and Dorothe Singer. "Financial Inclusion and Inclusive Growth: A Review of Recent Empirical Evidence." Policy Research Working Paper No. 8040, World Bank, Washington, DC, 2017.

Demirguc-Kunt, A. and Leora Klapper. "Measuring Financial Inclusion: The Global Findex Database." Policy Research Working Paper No. 6025, World Bank, Washington, DC, 2012. https://openknowledge.worldbank.org/handle/10986/6042 Enterprise Surveys (www.enterprisesurveys.org), The World Bank. 2008–2015. Financial Services Authority of the Republic of Indonesia, 2013, "Indonesian National Strategy for Financial Literacy."

Afghanistan 41

Kyobe, Yen Nian Mooi, and Seyed Reza Yousef. "Financial Inclusion: Can It Meet Multiple Macroeconomic Goals?" IMF Staff Discussion Note 15/17, International Monetary Fund, Washington, DC, September 2015.

Sahay, R., Martin Čihák, Papa N'Diaye, Adolfo Barajas, Ran Bi, Diana Ayala, Yuan Gao, Annette Kyobe, Lam Nguyen, Christian Saborowski, Katsiaryna Svirydzenka, and Seyed Reza Yousefi. "Rethinking Financial Deepening: Stability and Growth in Emerging Markets." IMF Staff Discussion Note 15/08, International Monetary Fund, Washington, DC, 2015.

Other Works

Bizhan, Nematullah. *Aid Paradoxes in Afghanistan: Building and Undermining the State* (Routledge Studies in Middle East Development), Routledge, New York, NY August 14, 2017.

Chayes, Sarah. *The Punishment of Virtue: Inside Afghanistan after the Taliban*, Penguin, New York, NY, 2007.

Dorronsoro, Gilles. *Afghanistan: Revolution Unending, 1979–2002*, C. Hurst, London, 2004.

Felbab-Brown, Vanda. *Aspiration and Ambivalence: Strategies and Realities of Counterinsurgency and State-Building in Afghanistan*, Brookings Institution Press, Washington, DC, 2012.

Gregg, Heather Selma. *Building the Nation: Missed Opportunities in Iraq and Afghanistan*, NE Potomac Books, Lincoln, December 1, 2018.

Hogg, Richard and Nassif, Claudia. *Afghanistan in Transition: Looking beyond 2014* (Directions in Development), The World Bank, Washington, DC, March 21, 2013.

Hussain, Rizwan. *Pakistan and the Emergence of Islamic Militancy in Afghanistan*, Ashgate Publishing, Aldershot, 2005.

Ira and Cia. *Understanding Afghanistan: History, Geography and Economy*, August 3, 2013.

Lansford, Tom. *A Bitter Harvest: US Foreign Policy and Afghanistan*, Ashgate Publishing, Aldershot, 2003.

Lowe, Peter. *The Causes and Consequences of War in Afghanistan: Taliban, Terrorism & the Unwinnable War in Afghanistan*, April 6, 2018.

Misdaq, Nabi. *Afghanistan: Political Frailty and External Interference*, Routledge, London, 2006.

Preston, Diana. *The Dark Defile: Britain's Catastrophic Invasion of Afghanistan, 1838–1842*, Bloomsbury Publishing, London, 2012.

Ritchie, Holly A. *Institutional Innovation and Change in Value Chain Development: Negotiating Tradition, Power and Fragility in Afghanistan* (Routledge Studies in Development Economics), March 2, 2016.

Starr, S. Frederick, Editor. *The New Silk Roads: Transport and Trade in Greater Central Asia*, Johns Hopkins University-SAIS, Washington, DC, 2007.

U.S. Department of Commerce. *Business Opportunities in Afghanistan Paperback*, September 11, 2014.

4   Yemen

During the Arab Spring, Yemen appeared to be a rare success story. In contrast to the conflicts in Syria, Libya and Egypt, Arab Spring inspired the people in Yemen to organize a national dialogue and win a Nobel Peace Prize.

Those days are long gone. A vicious civil war has been raging in Yemen since 2014 and has created the world's worst humanitarian crisis. One million people have been infected with cholera, the largest documented cholera epidemic in history, and another eight million people are on the brink of famine.

Instead of trying to broker peace talks and foster shared prosperity, a militarized American foreign policy under Obama and Trump is responsible for huge arms sales to Saudi Arabia, which, in turn, have intensified and prolonged the fighting in Yemen for the past four years.

Things have gotten so bad that US Senator Chris Murphy has accused America of complicity in war crimes in Yemen.[1] To make matters worse, Saudi Crown Prince Mohammed bin Salman may be complicit in killing Jamal Khashoggi, a Saudi journalist working for the *Washington Post*.[2]

What went wrong? A good place to start is with Ali Abdullah Saleh's presidency.[3] When Saleh assumed power in Yemen in 1978, Yemen's new president had a strategic choice. He could start the slow but steady process of responsible nation building, a task Washington wanted no part of, then or now, or he could form a network of cronies and plunder the oil wealth in the country.[4] With military support from America, Saleh spent over three decades using a patronage system to loot and squander his strategic opportunity.[5] The system was increasingly destabilized when Saleh started to shift the power balance towards his eldest son.

The second destabilizer was Yemen's domestic oil production, which peaked at about 457,000 barrels a day in 2002 and then fell all the way down to 264,000 barrels a day in 2010.[6] By 2015, oil production was at only about 10% of the peak oil output of 2002. This created political and economic winners and losers as less and less oil wealth was available to spread around.

This struggle among the power elites for dwindling oil money took place just before another struggle, which would soon emerge at a grassroots level. In fact, the fight among the power elites meant there were relatively few resources left for ordinary Yemenis to share among themselves. Before long,

Yemen 43

Yemen had its own version of the Arab Spring. Hundreds of thousands of Yemenis protested peacefully at symbolic "Change Square" sites across the country to demand Saleh's resignation.[7] Along the way, Tawakkol Karman – a female Yemeni champion of women rights – made it clear that these were social protests, not just political protests. She was a worthy co-recipient of the Nobel Peace Prize in 2011 for her impressive efforts.

Arab Spring protests in Yemen caught Washington off-guard.[8] Since 9/11, America's foreign policy in Yemen had been like a one-trick pony. Washington was content with using Saleh as a willing conduit to let the US military use drones to attack al Qaeda targets in Yemen.[9] In return, Washington implicitly turned a blind eye to Saleh's autocratic ways.

That one-trick pony may have played well in the Obama White House, but it was ill-advised and shortsighted American foreign policy. Not only did America have no moral high ground in Yemen, but this quid pro quo, "drones for autocracy" deal was soon overtaken by events.[10] Arab Spring and Change Square were grassroots protests US backed autocratic strongmen across the Middle East.[11]

But the mindset at the White House was better late than never. US diplomats went to work at the 11th hour to quickly "rebrand" Saleh and try to salvage their man. They put pressure on him to make "bold" concessions in a disingenuous attempt to placate long-suffering protesters at Change Square sites all around Yemen. In February 2011, Saleh, the ruthless dictator, obediently took his cue from Washington and suddenly played the role of sensitive economic and political reformer who now said he wanted "reconciliation."[12]

Not surprisingly, the protesters didn't buy this hypocrisy. They had long lost faith with Saleh. They simply did not trust him to follow through and implement any of the "shake and bake" political and economic reforms he had never supported in the past. In addition, the political wind in Yemen was blowing in a radically new direction. Saleh was losing support on multiple fronts.

President Obama – who had been woefully behind the economic and political power curve in Yemen – finally got the picture. It was now too late for Saleh to reform, so it was time for a policy turnaround and to press the "change the regime button."[13] In Washington, the narrative quickly changed as Saleh had become more of a liability than an asset. He had no indigenous legitimacy, and his presidency was untenable. America supported a Gulf Cooperation Council (GCC) proposal for him to relinquish power. Saleh signed this agreement and left Yemen in June 2011.[14]

Protesters were happy see him go off to Saudi Arabia but not so happy that the GCC gave him domestic immunity, thus protecting him from prosecution in the future. Protesters had good reason to fear that domestic immunity as it left the door open for him to start meddling in Yemeni politics again. In fact, a vindictive Saleh could potentially return and harness his deadly patronage network for a return to power.[15]

44 *Yemen*

The departure of Saleh raised the question of who would assume power in Yemen. That turned out to be Vice President Abdu Rabbu Mansour Hadi. The constitution enabled him to serve on an emergency basis for 60 days; in February 2012, he was elected as Interim President for a two-year transition period. Initially, Change Square protesters and opposition groups to Saleh's regime were cautiously optimistic and had high hopes for Hadi personally and for his two-year transition. For a while, Yemen was even a role model for Arab Spring. Hadi had the United Nations (UN), US and the European Union (EU) diplomats and consultants help the cause. In accordance with the GCC initiative, Yemen launched a National Dialogue Conference (NDC) in March 2013 to discuss key constitutional, political and social issues. The national dialogue was supposed to provide an opportunity for all groups that had felt politically and economically marginalized under the old order to press for renegotiation. The rhetoric sounded wonderful. If successfully carried out, this democratic power shift would be the first and most diverse one in Yemen's history – even youth and women would be included. But there were two glaring omissions: Hadi marginalized the Houthis, who lived in the northern mountains and represented 40% of the population, and he marginalized the southerners, who wanted autonomy.

Hope soon turned to chaos. By the end of 2013, there was still no consensus on the future structure of the state among national dialogue delegates.[16] Hadi concluded the NDC in January 2014. To his credit, he said he wanted to implement subsequent steps in the transition process, including constitutional drafting, a constitutional referendum and national elections. But there was no sense of when, if ever, this would happen.

Hadi kept saying that the country needed more time for the principles of national reconciliation to be sorted out. But even if that were true, it was not a sure thing that this new political or economic system could be implemented anytime soon. That's because Yemen's collapsing economy did not allow for a gradual approach. The economy was rapidly running out of oil. Food prices were up for those lucky enough to have a job. But for the others, unemployment and poverty were an imminent threat. What was needed was economic crisis management, not marginal incrementalism. Unfortunately, Hadi relied on Prime Minister Mohammed Salim Basindwa to run the economy, and Basindwa was weak and indecisive. [17]

Hadi struggled to adjust to his new role as a caretaker president. At best, he was an indecisive politician heavily dependent on foreign consultants to prop him up. For their part, the UN and EU officials assigned to Yemen were equally ineffective. One problem was that they turned Yemen into a de-facto international protectorate and themselves into Hadi's salesmen for this new political entity.

A second problem, in 2014, was that the international community (from the UN and EU) was still riding the success of negotiating the transition agreement. Their approach was ill-advised. The UN and EU showed up in Yemen with too many political philosophers and not enough realistic, no-nonsense power brokers. They rested on their laurels. They could still be seen celebrating and congratulating themselves in 2014 for a rare success story in Yemen which "gave everyone a voice." The problem was that their pride in "giving everyone a voice" turned into almost 1,400 recommendations for change. Their chaotic process was "all over the place."

Thus, the big buildup for a national dialogue turned into a big letdown for lots of frustrated groups in Yemen. Take the original Change Square protesters: Due to the lack of a true social revolution, they felt betrayed. They felt that the revolution had been corrupted and hijacked by the regime's internal power struggle. While Saleh was gone, many of the old regime players were still in place. The protesters felt that Hadi was no different from Saleh in the sense that the system was corrupt and still rigged against them. The same eight to ten families dominated the economy and the political system. At best, one faction of the old elite power center had replaced another faction.[18]

Of course, the existing power centers had an understandably different take on the process. In their world, what had kept up political and economic stability under Saleh was an internal balance of power in a carefully calculated patronage system. That system had been destabilized by nepotism and falling oil production, but after Saleh left, instability turned into chaos. None of the key players were certain about their economic or political weight. They were the existing centers of power, and they resented emerging centers of power challenging their vested interests. Even after two years of transition, they saw a significant gap between formal power structures and informal networks of patronage.

This gap turned into rage for the Houthis. The Houthis felt that Hadi had failed to deliver on a number of substantive promises to address their grievances during the national dialogue, and they feared they would continue to be marginalized. To strengthen themselves militarily, they joined with Saleh's forces and expanded their influence in northwestern Yemen. This culminated in a major military offensive against Hadi's weak military units, and the Houthis seized the capital of Sanaa in September 2014.

In January 2015, the Houthis surrounded the presidential palace, Hadi's residence and key government facilities, prompting him and the cabinet to submit their resignations. In February 2015, Hadi fled to Aden, where he rescinded his resignation. He subsequently escaped to Oman and then moved to Saudi Arabia, asking the GCC to intervene militarily in Yemen to protect the "legitimate" government from the Houthis.

In March 2015, Saudi Arabia assembled a coalition of Arab militaries and began airstrikes against the Houthis and Houthi-affiliated forces. Ground fighting between Houthi-aligned forces and resistance groups backed by the Saudi-led coalition continued through 2016. In 2016, the UN brokered a months-long cessation of hostilities that reduced airstrikes and fighting, and initiated peace talks in Kuwait. However, the talks ended without agreement. Fighting resumed, with neither side making decisive military gains.

46 *Yemen*

Factionalism eventually developed in the Saleh-Houthis alliance. Saleh started to call for political reconciliation with Hadi's forces. Hardcore Houthis felt that he was betraying their cause and killed him in early December 2017. The civil war has continued unabated into the present.

Instead of acting as an honest broker to facilitate peace talks and foster shared prosperity, the militarized American foreign policy under Obama and Trump made the country complicit in the Saudi-led air campaign for Hadi against the Houthis.[19] Since the Saudi coalition started its air campaign in Yemen in March 2015, the US Air Force has provided operational support to Riyadh and its Arab allies, identifying Houthi targets, and American diplomats at the UN protect Riyadh from censure, water down resolutions and prevent war crime inquiries.[20] In addition, Saudi and the UAE jets have used US mid-air refueling capabilities to maintain their battle rhythm without having to return to a base. According to the Pentagon, the US Air Force has refueled Saudi aircraft more than 9,000 times.[21]

Bruce Riedel at Brookings notes that no president since Franklin Roosevelt has courted Saudi Arabia as zealously as Obama.[22] Nicolas Niarchos notes that Obama agreed in November 2015 to a giant weapons sale totaling $1.29 billion and signed off on the Saudis buying 7,020 Paveway-II bombs. By the end of President Obama's second term in office, the US had offered more than 115 billion dollars' worth of arms to Saudi Arabia, the largest amount offered under any US President in history.[23]

Obama's courtship with Saudi Arabia resulted in a US military assistance program which enabled the Saudi-led coalition to intensify and prolong the civil war. Unfortunately, America's strategy under Obama and Trump is not only failing but backfiring. Writing after his fourth visit to Yemen since the civil war began, *Washington Post* journalist Kareem Fahim underscores how embittered Yemen civilians have become as a result of the violence.[24] Dafna H. Rand, a Middle East expert who covered Yemen under Obama, says that the longer the war goes on, the higher the risk that deep resentment against the US will radicalize and lead to a rise in violent extremism.[25] In fact, US Senator Chris Murphy says that his first job is to protect US citizenry, and he feels that these arms sales put US lives in jeopardy.[26] Rising anti-Americanism plays right into the hands of al Qaeda propaganda, leading to the recruitment of more and more anti-US terrorists.

Since Obama's arms sales to Saudi Arabia are arguably counterproductive, why did he pursue such an ill-advised policy in the first place? And why does President Trump keep doing the same thing? The only plausible explanation is that Obama genuinely believed what Riyadh told him: that Saudi Arabia needs military assistance to counter Iranian support to the Houthis. But nothing could be further from the truth. The nature and extent of the US military assistance to Saudi Arabia for its air campaign in Yemen is far beyond what Iran is doing on the ground for the Houthis. Mareike Transfeld, a scholar at the Carnegie Endowment for International Peace, notes that Iran has a small hand to play in Yemen. As Transfeld puts it,

Iranian support for the Houthis has been marginal, and indigenous factors in Yemen are far more important. He argues that Saudi claims about Iran's influence over the Houthis are overblown. While he concedes that the Houthis do receive some support from Iran, he says that this is mostly political, with minimal financial and military assistance.[27]

The Saudi narrative that Iran has a close sectarian relationship with the Houthis is also fiction. The Houthis are a homegrown force, not a puppet of Iran. Transfeld notes that

> Until Arab Spring came along, the term 'Shia' was not used in the Yemen. That's because the Houthis do not follow the Twelver Shia tradition predominant in Iran, but adhere to the Zaidiya, which in practice is closer to Sunni Islam, and had expressed no solidarity with other Shia communities.[28]

Unfortunately, the US arms sales to Saudi Arabia and the Saudi-led campaign against the Houthis has finally turned into a self-fulfilling prophecy by pushing the Houthis closer to Iran.

Now that we've looked at America's militarized foreign policy toward Yemen and how Obama and Trump justify intensifying and prolonging the civil war, it's important to understand how a militarized American foreign policy toward Yemen creates a humanitarian crisis. As cited earlier, eight million people in Yemen are on the brink of famine. In addition, Yemen has endured the worst cholera epidemic in history, with more than one million people infected. US Senator Chris Murphy has even accused the US of complicity in war crimes from the floor of the Senate.[29]

For starters, US support for Saudi Arabia's de-facto air and naval blockade impedes both commercial and humanitarian food supplies, creating a reoccurring pattern. A ship carrying commercial supplies for southern parts of the country will sit off the port of Aden, awaiting permission to come in. On the humanitarian front, the various agencies have neither the access nor the funds to supply food or medicine. A ship carrying World Food Program (WFP) aid in the port of Hodeida will not get clearance to unload and transport food to areas where it is needed.[30] Even when food somehow gets into the country, fighting around ports makes food delivery difficult and dangerous. Thus, local markets do not have enough food to meet the needs of the population.[31] Yemen's escaping a full-blown famine in the past two years has been something of a miracle. Only heroic efforts by aid groups have kept trucks teetering up dangerous roads from Hodeida to regions where food and medicine are desperately needed.[32]

That said, there are good people with warm hearts lower down in the pecking order in the US government, and they genuinely wanted to mitigate the chances of famine in Yemen. Toward that end, the US Agency for International Development (USAID) responded to the humanitarian crisis by spending four million dollars on cranes to help take food and medicine off

48 *Yemen*

the ships at the port of Hodeida.[33] But Saudi Arabia felt that these cranes weakened the Saudi-led economic coercion of the Houthis. Not surprisingly, the US Department of Defense (DOD) outgunned USAID in a turf battle. And so, the American cranes were removed, making it increasingly difficult to expedite the movement of food and medicine to the port itself.

The removal of the cranes shows how economic coercion turns into a complicit American military action to intensify and prolong the civil war. Once the cranes were gone, and Hodeida was more vulnerable, in mid-June 2018, the Saudis and the United Arab Emirates (UAE) launched a reckless and potentially catastrophic attack. Because 70% of Yemen's food and aid shipments come through the port, the UN and every other major humanitarian agency have warned of dire consequences for the 22 million Yemenis who already depend on outside assistance, including millions on the brink of famine. They pleaded with the Saudis and Emiratis to hold off and allow more time for a diplomatic solution.[34] David Miliband, the former British foreign secretary, was also a critic of the attack on Hodeida. He said, "The attack on the port is an assault on the chances of a political settlement in addition to a danger to civilian life.[35]

The sad thing is that the Saudi-led attack was totally preventable, but US Secretary of State Mike Pompeo dithered, allowing it to move forward. In other words, the Saudi-led attack went ahead after receiving what amounted to passive assent from Trump. This means that Trump and his national security team will be complicit if their actions result is what aid officials say they could: starvation, epidemics and human suffering in Yemen surpassing anything the world has seen in decades.[36]

In what other ways do the Saudi-led coalition justify its attack on Hodeida? The UAE's minister of state for foreign affairs says that the Houthis are not willing to negotiate, and the seizure of Hodeida is necessary to bring them to the table, but that fiction is contradicted by Martin Griffiths, the relatively new UN envoy for Yemen, who is seeking to broker peace talks and tried to stop the attack. Griffiths has talked face to face with Houthi leaders, who have assured him that they are ready for political talks.[37]

Despite the UN failure to stop the Saudi-led attack on Hodeida, there is finally reason for cautious optimism that something can be done to end this humanitarian nightmare. In April 2018, Martin Griffiths stood up at the UN Security Council and provided a glimmer of hope. Since being appointed to this important position in early 2018, Griffiths has met most of the key players in the conflict and is preparing a plan for a new round of peace talks.

One key player Griffiths did not meet was Ali Abdullah Saleh, Yemen's former dictator, who was killed on 4 December 2017. Saleh was the most powerful stakeholder in Yemen, and responsible advocates of peace talks in the international community had hoped to use him to broker an end to the war. There are those who argue that Saleh's death leaves a power vacuum and will make it even more difficult for Griffiths to try to end the war. They may be right.[38]

But Griffiths is a qualified British diplomat who knows how to turn this power vacuum into a diplomatic opportunity. How? Saleh did more than anyone else to plunder billions of dollars from the Arab world's poorest state. He also drove the country into civil war and arguably would have continued increasing the demand for violence if he remained in power. Now that he is gone, it will arguably be easier to heal the country's wounds without him promoting violent solutions or his enemies harboring a burning rage for violent revenge.

If anyone can reset relationships and restart the long-stalled peace process, it is Martin Griffiths. He is an experienced mediator, with experience in Syria, Libya and Afghanistan. Most importantly, he is no stranger to Yemen. Since 2015, he has been meeting with the various warring groups on behalf of the UN. As a result, he was able to hit the ground running when he was promoted to the UN peace envoy.

In the month after he took the job on 19 March, Griffiths met Yemen's former President Hadi, along with the former Yemeni prime minister, Ahmed bin Daghir, and foreign minister Abdul Malik al-Mikhlafi. Griffiths also met with Saudi officials supporting Hadi. Shortly thereafter, he travelled to Sanaa, the Houthi-controlled Yemeni capital, to meet Houthi leaders, who greeted him warmly and were confident that he would be an honest broker. That's in sharp contrast with the way the Houthis treated his predecessor, Ismail Ould Cheikh Ahmed, whom they did not permit to visit the city for nearly a year. In fact, Ahmed somehow managed to antagonize both the Houthi rebels and the internationally recognized government.

While Martin Griffiths arguably provides a glimmer of hope, his biggest challenge may well be getting America to support his call for peace talks. As this study has explained, Washington turned a blind eye on Saleh's corrupt and autocratic ways as long as he let it use drones to kill al Qaeda terrorists in the country – until Arab Spring caught America by surprise. Obama tried to rebrand Saleh as a sensitive economic and political reformer. That disingenuous tactic didn't fly, so, America did a policy turnaround and started to say that Saleh had lost his "legitimacy." It did its part to throw Saleh out of the country, then Saleh allied with the marginalized Houthis.

This left Vice President Hadi, who was part of the same corrupt patronage system, waiting in the wings. US diplomats went to work trying to sell Hadi as a "Jeffersonian democrat." US diplomats said that he would be the new acting President for two years, while the country had a national dialogue. There would be democracy for all – all except the 40% of the population who were Houthis living in the northern mountains. In addition, southerners who wanted autonomy would be marginalized. Despite this democratic hypocrisy, Hadi asked the autocratic Saudis for help with "reviving democracy" and bringing the "legitimate" government back to power. The Saudis agreed and have been bombing the marginalized Houthis almost continuously for the past four years. As a result, America finds itself wallowing in the moral low ground in Yemen.

50 *Yemen*

What are the lessons learned in terms of American foreign policy? Don't pursue a militarized foreign policy which opts for narrow counterterrorism tactics and turns a blind eye to negative economic and political conditions in a country like Yemen. Hoping for the best is not a strategy. Don't think you can "rebrand" someone like Saleh with a laundry list of economic and political reforms at the 11th hour. It's hypocrisy. Don't force regime change when shake and bake reforms for Saleh don't click. Remember what Roland Paris, author of *At War's End*, says: Political and economic shock therapy simply intensifies competition, which quickly turns into conflict and civil war. Instead, America needs to take the long view and work hard to facilitate political and economic liberalization in Yemen over decades rather than media cycles. Finally, stop saying that America does not foster nation building. Rebalance American foreign policy in Yemen with diplomatic and economic actions rather than utilizing the one-trick pony approach of massive arms sales to an autocratic Saudi Arabia and expecting democracy to break out. Narrow US counterterrorism tactics against al Qaeda targets in Yemen are no substitute for fostering responsible nation building.

The longer the war goes on, the higher the risk that deep resentment against the US will radicalize and lead to a rise in violent extremism. The massive US arms sales to Saudi Arabia have put US lives in jeopardy. Rising anti-Americanism plays right into the hands of al Qaeda propaganda, leading to the recruitment of more and more anti-US terrorists.

What America needs to do is stop all military assistance to the Saudi-led coalition that is fighting the Houthis, let UN humanitarian assistance flow freely and bend over backwards to help Martin Griffiths and UN efforts to facilitate peace talks.

Notes

1 Alex Emmons, "Chris Murphy Accuses U.S. of Complicity in War Crimes from the Floor of the Senate", *Intercept*, 15 November 2017.
2 Kevin Sullivan Loveday Morris and Tamar El-Ghobashy. "Saudi Arabia Fires 5 Top Officials, Arrests 18 Saudis", saying "Khashoggi Was Killed in Fight at Consulate", *Washington Post*, 19 October 2018.
3 See Paul Dresch, *A History of Modern Yemen*, Cambridge University Press, Cambridge, 2000.
4 See Gabriele vom Bruck, *Islam, Memory and Morality in Yemen: Ruling Families in Transition*, Palgrave MacMillan, New York, NY, 2005.
5 For a good discussion of the patronage system in Yemen, see Sarah Phillips, *Yemen's Democracy Experiment in Regional Perspective: Patronage and Pluralized Authoritarianism*, Palgrave MacMillan, New York, NY, 2008.
6 BP, *Statistical Review of World Energy*, June 2011.
7 For the early response inside "Yemen to Arab Spring, see Waves of Unrest Spread to Yemen", *New York Times*, 27 January 2011 and Letter from "Yemen after the Uprising", *The New Yorker*, 11 April 2011.
8 Yemen protests inside "Yemen to Arab Spring", see "Waves of Unrest Spread to Yemen", *The New York Times*, 27 January 2011 and Letter from "Yemen after the Uprising", *The New Yorker*, 11 April 2011.

Yemen 51

9 See, "The Dangerous US Game in Yemen", *The Nation*, 30 March 2011.
10 See Ginny Hill, *Yemen Endures: Civil War, Saudi Adventurism and the Future of Arabia*, Oxford University Press, Oxford, 2017, p. 138
11 See Isa Blumi, *Chaos in Yemen: Societal Collapse and the New Authoritarianism*, Routledge, New York, NY, 2011.
12 Hill, *Yemen Endures*, p. 207.
13 US Shifts to Seek Removal of Yemen's leader, an Ally, *New York Times*, 3 April 2011.
14 Hill, *Yemen Endures*, p. 207.
15 Ibid., p. 210.
16 Ginny Hill et al., *Yemen: Corruption, Capital Flight and Global Drivers of Conflict*, Chatham House Report, September 2013.
17 Hill, *Yemen Endures*, p. 248
18 Ibid., p. 212.
19 Ibid., p. 282
20 Daniel Depetris, "The U.S. Is Enabling Civil War and Humanitarian Crisis in Yemen", *Los Angeles Times*, 9 October 2017.
21 Ibid.
22 Bruce Riedel, *Kings and Presidents*, Brookings Institution Press, Washington, DC, 2017.
23 Nicolas Niarchos, "How the U.S. Is Making the War in Yemen Worse", *The New Yorker*, 15 January 2018.
24 Editorial, "Catastrophe Could Lie Ahead in Yemen", *The Washington Post*, 14 June 2018.
25 Niarchos, "How the U.S. Is Making the War in Yemen Worse".
26 Ibid.
27 Mareike Transfeld, "Iran's Small Hand in Yemen", *Carnegie Endowment for Peace*, 14 February 2017. Mareike Transfeld is a PhD candidate at the Berlin Graduate School of Muslim Cultures and Societies at the Freie Universität Berlin, Germany.
28 Ibid.
29 Alex Emmons, "Chris Murphy Accuses the US of Complicity in War Crimes from the Floor of the Senate", *Intercept*, 15 November 2017.
30 See Leif Rosenberger, "Reconciling the Global Supply and Demand for Food", *Economonitor, Roubini Global Economics*, 28 February 2018.
31 Ibid.
32 Editorial, "Catastrophe Could Lie Ahead in Yemen".
33 Niarchos, "How the U.S. Is Making the War in Yemen Worse".
34 Editorial, "Catastrophe Could Lie Ahead in Yemen".
35 Ibid.
36 Ibid.
37 See *Economist Intelligence Unit*, "UN Mediator Pushes for Deal to End Hodeida Fighting", 28 June 2018 and Yemen, "New UN Peace Envoy Prepares Negotiation Plans", 20 April 2018.
38 *The Economist*, "An Ex-Dictator Slaughtered", 7 December 2017.

Bibliography

Brandt, Marieke. *Tribes and Politics in Yemen: A History of the Houthi Conflict*. Hurst, London, 2017.
Farrukh, Maher. *Yemen Crisis Situation Report*. CriticalThreats.org, October 30, 2017. www.criticalthreats.org/briefs/yemen-situation-report/2017-yemen-crisis-situation-report-october-30.

52 *Yemen*

Heinze, Marie-Christine. *Yemen and the Search for Stability: Power, Politics and Society after the Arab Spring*, I.B. Tauris, London, 2018.

Hill, Ginny. *Yemen Endures: Civil War, Saudi Adventurism and the Future of Arabia*, Oxford University Press, Oxford, 2017.

Karasik, Theodore and Cafiero, Giorgio. *Yemen's Humanitarian Disaster: Halting the Famine Threat*, Middle East Institute, October 30, 2017. www.mei.edu/content/yemen-s-humanitarian-disaster-halting-famine-threat.

Kendall, Elisabeth. "Iran's Fingerprints in Yemen: Real or Imagined?" *Atlantic Council*, October 2017. www.atlanticcouncil.org/publications/issue-briefs/iran-s-fingerprints-in-yemen-real-or-imagined.

Lackner, Helen. *Yemen in Crisis: Autocracy, Neo-Liberalism and the Disintegration of a State*, Saqi Books, London, 2018.

Lackner, Helen and Varisco, Daniel Martin. *Yemen and the Gulf States: The Making of a Crisis*, Gerlach, Berlin, 2017.

Nasser, Afrah. "The Unfolding UN Failure in the Yemen War", *Atlantic Council*, MENA Source, September 21, 2017. www.atlanticcouncil.org/blogs/menasource/the-unfolding-un-failure-in-the-yemen-war.

Robinson, Eric, et al. *What Factors Cause Individuals to Reject Violent Extremism in Yemen?* Rand Corporation, Santa Monica, CA, 2017.

Salisbury, Peter. "Yemen's Ali Mohsen al-Ahmar: Last Sanhan Standing", December 15, 2017. www.agsiw.org/yemens-ali-mohsen-al-ahmar-last-sanhan-standing/.

5 Syria

Henry Kissinger once said, "Opportunities cannot be hoarded; once past they are usually irretrievable."[1] In Syria, a good opportunity for shared prosperity instead of war came in 2009. Before then, the international community had been reacting negatively to one wave of domestic repression after another in Syria. The first wave started in 2001, and the second started in 2006. After each wave of repression, the international community treated Syria like a pariah, and when Syria feels threatened by a hostile external environment, it almost always becomes intolerant of domestic dissent and cracks down with a vengeance.[2]

To appreciate just how unique this 2009 window of opportunity was for shared prosperity in Syria, it's important to understand just how deep-rooted Syrian socialism had become since starting in the 1960s. When the Syrian Ba'ath party came to power in 1963, nobody in the Syrian government was thinking about free market reforms. In fact, the wind was blowing in the opposite direction. The economy was essentially closed. One of the first things the Ba'ath party did when it seized power in Syria in 1963 was nationalize the majority of the economy. An inefficient state controlled all the banks and many of the major industries after nationalization.[3] At this point in time, Syria frankly wanted nothing to do with America, so, there was no realistic opportunity for shared prosperity.

If we fast-forward to the twenty-first century, it's clear that Syria's economic growth was relatively buoyant from 2004 until late 2008 because of high oil prices. But then things took a turn for the worse. While the production of oil still dominated the economy, Syria's oil output fell from 600,000 barrels a day (B/D) in the late 1990s to just 380,000 B/D in 2008. In fact, it was a net-oil importer in 2008 for the first time in decades. Syria's oil revenues fell in 2008, despite high oil prices in the first half of the year.

To make matters worse, climate change slammed Syria. From 2006 to 2010, it suffered from its worst drought in at least 500 years. This drought devastated the countryside, where close to 60% of Syrians lived. Seventy-five percent of Syrian farms failed, and 85% of Syrian livestock died.[4]

Facing adversity, the Syrian government belatedly grasped the reality that it needed to adapt to survive. And so, in 2005, the government opted

54 *Syria*

for a "social market economy." The new policy was a de-facto acknowledgement that the old economic model was stagnant, and it was time to shake up the economy. The International Monetary Fund (IMF) helped Damascus draw up a new economic blueprint, whose purpose was to shift Syria away from a command economy and closer to a free market economy.[5] 2008 saw the growth of economic diversification and stronger non-oil sectors. Non-oil exports rose 23% in 2008 alone. Projects were underway to double Syria's natural gas output over next three years.

Frankly, Syria's economic transformation was impossible to miss. In 2003, its statist economy was closed to markets. It only had six state banks and only serviced the public sector. The private sector had to leave Syria to do its banking. In addition, Syrians could only dream of borrowing to buy a house, and ATMs were an alien concept. But between 2004 and 2008, Syrians started to use credit cards and apply for loans, not just to buy homes but to also buy new cars and computers. Syria boasted nine private banks, including two Sharia-compliant entities. Restrictions on foreign currency transactions were relaxed. As new sectors opened, and the business climate improved, private-sector contribution to growth of non-oil GDP rose 80%.

That said, Syria's movement toward a free market still had a long way to go. To make matters worse, the global financial crisis hit Syria in October 2008. Luckily, its tight regulations and weak global links to international banking partially protected it. Although Gulf construction firms were still buying land in Syria, Damascus worried that the financial crisis might cause these countries to cut investments.

An additional concern in 2009 was a reduction in remittances from abroad if foreign firms were forced to cut staff. This was already a big threat in Central Asia, but most Syrians working abroad were working in skilled sectors, and so, such a shift could mark a reverse of the brain drain. The problem, of course, would still be the lack of opportunity which drove them out in the first place.

Still, the global financial crisis hurt Syria's overall economic picture by causing a fall in Syrian export markets and restricting government spending due to lower oil revenue. That translated into a slowdown in the Gross Domestic Product (GDP) growth, from 5% in 2008 to 3% in 2009. As export growth slowed, the current account deficit was on track to worsen from 1% of GDP in 2008 to 5% of GDP in 2009.

Syria's economic reformers argued that economic reform was the only way to attack the massive unemployment rate, rampant inflation and dwindling oil reserves. But those calling for free market reforms – convinced that this was the only path out of chronic economic malaise – faced an uphill struggle.

The global financial crisis and an economic slowdown also had an impact on support for Syrian economic reforms evolving from pessimism to ambivalence to optimism. How did this roll out? Immediately following the collapse of the big US banks, it seemed that Syria's nascent reform program was doomed to fail. Among Syrian economic reformers, there was concern that the return of government bailouts to save the Western banking system would play into the hands of those hard-liners in Syria arguing against free market reforms. President Bashar al-Assad personified those in Damascus who struggled to decide which way to go. At times, Assad seemed to back reform, but he also put obstacles in their way. These same conflicting signals hurt Syria on the international stage, provoking even more US economic sanctions and frustrating accord with EU countries.

But then Syrian economic reformers had a second chance. French President Sarkozy travelled to Damascus in September, opening the door to rehabilitation. In addition, the Syrian foreign minister visited London. Although there was a noticeable slowdown in the pace at which Syria was implementing economic reforms, there was reason to be optimistic about their continuing in 2009. Syria continued its gradual shift to diversification. Inherent in this approach were more free market reforms. A case in point was the creation of a Syrian stock exchange. Just a few months before, the stock market appeared to be shelved, but then economic reformers were winning out. The Syrian stock market opening was back on track and slated for 23 February 2009.

Re-establishment of a stock market in Syria was arguably a crucial step to take the economic reform process forward. The stock market was the next piece of the puzzle. There were between 26 and 45 companies ready to list. Companies would require a minimum market capitalization of $5 million and three years of audited financial statements. Most importantly, the stock market would also be open to foreign investors.

Opening the Syrian stock exchange also sent an important signal to the Syrian bureaucracy. Once a stock market was up and running, it would be a symbolic success for those promoting free market reforms in Syria – an issue that became more pressing as the country's limited oil reserves declined. Opening a stock market was a positive signal meant to attract foreign investors. It's having a stock market showed that Syria was on its way to becoming an emerging market economy and was obviously an important indication that it was open for American trade and investment.

Thus, the Syrian domestic situation had changed. President Bashar al-Assad was pursuing economic reforms at home and abroad, and Syrian free market reforms created a strategic opportunity for America to reward Damascus with economic interdependence and shared prosperity. If the Syrian people were happy with job creation and rising incomes as a result of Western trade and investment in Syria, hope and opportunity would replace the anger and fear of Arab Spring. Therefore, there would be no incentive for President Assad to crack down on muted political dissent at home. He would think twice before throwing away shared prosperity with America and the West.

US Secretary of Defense James Mattis recently said, "You don't want to miss an opportunity because you were not alert to the opportunity. So, you

56 *Syria*

need to have that door open."[6] Unfortunately, neither President Bush nor the Obama administration were alert to the opportunity or had a door open to support Syria's movement toward a free market economy. Why did they squander this strategic opportunity? President Bush militarized American foreign policy after 9/11. Syrian President Assad would not support President Bush's Iraq War (2003–2011), which was based on the fiction that there were weapons of mass destruction (WMD) in Iraq.

President Obama promised to stop militarizing American foreign policy, but as Dr. John R. Deni, an analyst at the Strategic Studies Institute at the Army War College points out, Obama failed to implement his rhetoric about rebalancing American foreign policy with a greater emphasis on diplomacy and development.[7] Syria was a case in point.

If the US and Syria found common ground in shared prosperity, it's possible that they could build on this progress to find common ground in shared security. Or America could follow the George Clemenceau legacy of economic coercion. After World War I, this economic coercion led to German resentment, the rise of Hitler and World War II. In the case of Syria, a US policy of economic coercion and no viable alternative option could well lead to Syrian resentment and another wave of Syrian repression like those in 2001 and 2006. And as cited earlier, when Syria felt threatened by a hostile external environment, it almost always became intolerant of domestic dissent and cracked down forcefully for regime survival. America chose the George Clemenceau approach of economic coercion and another cycle of forceful Syrian repression at home.

Earlier, we cited Henry Kissinger, who said, "opportunities cannot be hoarded; once past they are usually irretrievable." Not surprisingly, America's decision to squander that creative economic opportunity with Syria led directly to Syrian resentment and civil war. The point is that President Assad would have arguably been more relaxed toward dissent at home if a more peaceful version of Arab Spring happened in Syria and had America pursued serious economic interdependence and shared prosperity with Syria.

By March of 2011, the windows for economic and political reform was closed. If anything, American economic coercion stiffened Assad's resolve. As Nikolaos Van Dam points out, "Historically, sanctions have only rarely been effective. They, often, have caused a lot of damage without ever achieving the results for which they were intended."[8]

At first glance, there was hope of a national dialogue to avert a Syrian civil war. A Ministry of Reconciliation was even set up,[9] but this was more public relations than anything else. The only thing the Baath Party and the Assad regime had in common was mutual distrust. The real power was in Assad's war cabinet, which reflected Assad's intention of a crackdown with brute force.[10]

In the past, the Syrian regime had successfully used brute force to suppress periods of Sunni protests and demonstrations in Homs and Hama in 1964–1965 and Hama again in 1982. President Assad tried the same

Syria 57

approach with brute force in March 2011, but this time, the attempted crackdown did not work so well. For one thing, radical Sunni Islamists (ISIS) had hijacked the revolution. For another thing, Arab Spring inspired a higher level of violence from the opposition. Feelings of Sunni revanchism, which had been suppressed for almost 30 years, burst out into the open. To make matters worse, radical Islamists highjacked the Syrian revolution. They saw Arab Spring as an opportunity to spread the rule of Islam.

President Obama was politically correct at home. He gave moralistic speeches about how President Assad was illegitimate and had to relinquish power. He also gave the opposition to Assad every reason to believe that the US military would intervene in Syria with enough military force to shove him out of power. But in the eyes of this opposition, it was a big buildup for a big letdown.

Before long, the Syrian civil war morphed into a war by proxy. Assad was receiving overwhelming military support from Russia, Iran and Hezbollah. In contrast, the Syrian opposition was receiving much smaller amounts of military assistance from the US, Turkey, Saudi Arabia and other the Gulf Cooperation Council (GCC) states, Qatar, France and the UK. Obama only gave the opposition enough military assistance to intensify and prolong the fighting, never enough to help the opposition to win.

As Richard Haas puts it, the West had limited will and limited means, so, it had to set limited goals for limited amount of good.[11] The opposition was a victim of false expectations and ultimately felt betrayed by American's ambivalence and dithering. America was a paper tiger.

Obama was fixated on the idea that the conflict could only be resolved if Assad was removed from power. The problem was that Obama grossly underestimated the strength of the Assad regime. The only way Western intervention would work would be if it put lots of American boots on the ground. Obama was not going to do that. He knew what he did not want – Assad to remain in power – but he had no idea who or what he wanted instead of Assad. Obama wanted to see a moderate, democratic, secular, pluralistic government replace Assad. The only problem was that such a possibility was not a realistic prospect.[12]

In contrast, Russia, Iran and Hezbollah knew exactly what they wanted – Assad to remain in power. This was a core interest for them. In contrast, Syria was never a core interest for Obama. Therefore, there was never any US political will to arm the political opposition to such an extent that they would have a chance to win battles against the Assad regime. There was never any clear US strategy in Syria, except that of defeating ISIS. Obama had no geopolitical clue in Syria other than counterterrorism tactics against ISIS.

What's interesting is that Robert Ford, US Ambassador to Syria, was reportedly opposed to calling for Assad's departure[13]; Ford argued that America would not be able to bring this about. In contrast, President Obama delivered stirring rhetoric calling for Assad's departure, but his demand

58 *Syria*

carried no intent to enforce that wish. The US may have been a superpower within its own borders, but it was a paper tiger in Syria.

Worst of all, Obama created false hopes among the opposition to Assad that decisive Western support was forthcoming. In the end, US support was not nearly as powerful as Obama's rhetoric. His moral high ground prevailed over pragmatism. Sadly, it took the political opposition to Assad a long time to accept the fact that they had been victims of false expectations.[14]

This raises a series of strategic questions for American foreign policy in the Middle East. Why was America such a paper tiger in Syria? The US military had sent large numbers of ground troops to Iraq, so, why didn't Obama do the same in Syria? Why was the US military involvement in Syria so much less than it had been in Iraq, despite Obama's soaring rhetoric that Assad had to relinquish power? Was he afraid of getting involved in a protracted ground campaign against Russia in Syria? If so, that raises the $64,000 question. Were his concerns about a US proxy war with Russia understandable? Could the Russian economy have afforded a protracted ground campaign in Syria against US military forces in 2015? That depends on the strength of the Russian economy.

That brings us back to Kissinger's original warning: "Opportunities cannot be hoarded; once past they are usually irretrievable." A grand bargain using creative economic diplomacy could have been made on the eve of the Trump presidency, but it arguably would have been much more difficult in 2017 than it would have been in 2009. Back then, Aleppo was falling, and the five-year Syrian Civil War appeared to be almost over. By all accounts, this was a massive humanitarian disaster. There will no doubt be lots of post-mortems that ask: How could the US, the biggest superpower in the world, turn a blind eye to this scale of de-facto genocide in Syria?

For starters, the Obama administration came to power determined to get America out of the wars in Afghanistan and Iraq. US Congress decided to opt for sequestration and cut military spending because the threats had gone away, then suddenly, two civil wars occurred: One in Iraq against ISIS and another in Syria against the Assad regime. Obama decided we could not walk and chew gum at the same time. The US would help the Iraqi government against ISIS but put the civil war in Syria on the back burner. Under the able leadership of General Lloyd Austin at CENTCOM, the US-led coalition arguably made steady progress against ISIS in Iraq. The ISIS territorial threat in Iraq was almost gone.

But why did Obama do virtually nothing to prevent massive genocide in Syria? For starters, an economically weak Syrian economy could not sustain a war economy for five years by itself. Of course, Syria was not operating by itself. Damascus had two major donors: Iran and Russia. Iran supported the Shia militia on the ground inside Syria, and Russia supported the Syrian Air Force. If Iran and Russia had had booming economies over the past five years, it would have been extremely difficult for the US to convince either of them to curb their support for the Assad regime, but the Russian and

Iranian economies have been struggling. Iran was under severe economic sanctions, and economically vulnerable countries are always willing to consider ways in which to improve their economies. Therefore, the US and its allies could have at least tried to make a grand bargain, such as Iran curbing support to the Shia militia in exchange for the US and its allies giving a green light to Western companies to invest in Iran. This offer would have been even more compelling when the price of oil fell.

Similarly, the US could have offered to lift sanctions against Russia and facilitate an agreement for all major global oil producers to cut oil output worldwide if Russia stopped its air campaign with the Syrian air force. None of this would have been easy, but the sad thing is that the US didn't even try to use asymmetric economic diplomacy to stop genocide in Syria.

Russia was extremely vulnerable to low oil prices, which had fallen from over $100 a barrel in mid-2014 to below $40 a barrel. Not surprisingly, the Russian economy was collapsing. The misery of ordinary Russians was rising due to high inflation. Western sanctions over Ukraine dried up desperately needed Western capital inflow. Capital flight was rampant, and Moscow's hopes for alternative financing from China dried up with China's own economic woes.

Moscow's economic black hole could be seen throughout the Russian economy. State-run banks with a huge pile of bad loans turned a blind eye to regional governments and corporations which were hopelessly in debt. Despite these economic woes, Putin opted for an air campaign in Syria. This was affordable – only costing 2–4% of the military budget – because Russia was relying on old Soviet-era bombs.

However, the Russian air campaign was arguably not enough to be militarily decisive. Russian strategists argued that only a ground offensive would enable Russia to achieve a decisive win. However, a ground offensive was unlikely because it is unaffordable. Russia would have to consider diverting scarce resources from military modernization to current operations in Syria, but escalated ground operations in Syria would seriously degrade Russian military power in the future. A Russian ground campaign would also have made Russia extremely vulnerable to domestic unrest. But Moscow didn't have to provide all the costly land power. The Shia militia were only too happy to play this role if Iran paid for it.

So, the ball was in Iran's court. Would it support the Shia militia? That depended on the strategic context in Iran, and persuading Iran to curb support for the Shia militia in Syria would not have been easy. While there were lots of obstacles to creative economic diplomacy, there were also economic incentives to give it a try. After all, following a decade of economic isolation, Iran had agreed to a nuclear deal with six world powers. The deal unwound its nuclear program in return for lifting international economic sanctions.

Economic sanctions had had a devastating impact on Iran's economic performance since 2012. At first glance, the deal offered many opportunities to tap into an attractive economic market. Iran's potential emergence

60 *Syria*

from economic isolation could have been the most significant opening of an economy since the fall of the Soviet Union and the US rapprochement with China, but nuclear verification and untangling a maze of sanctions would not happen overnight.

A failing economic model and self-imposed sanctions also explained Iran's economic woes. Chinese companies partially filled the gap while the sanctions were in place, but Iran was unhappy with Chinese technology. Would the Western companies fill the gap? US companies were predictably cautious and for good reasons. In contrast, some of the European firms with historic ties were more willing to re-enter the market first. That said, even foreign oil companies were unhappy about Iran's old oil contracts.

But in a buyer's market, Tehran claimed that it would make new oil contracts more attractive. Could Iran's business climate change? Reforming it would be a slow process due to the role of the Iranian Revolutionary Guard (IRG) in key industries. If sanctions had been lifted in 2016, rising Iranian oil output would arguably have boosted Iran's economic performance.

Critics like Netanyahu argued that $100 billion in unfrozen assets would almost certainly embolden Iran to finance the Shia militia in Syria, but Iran's support for instability was not inevitable. If given the right economic incentives, Iran could choose re-entry into global economy.

Most importantly, the US was not a helpless bystander at that time. The US could have worked with the US private sector to shape Iran's decision to benefit from shared prosperity and develop into a responsible stakeholder in Syria. To sum up, if the US had made attractive enough economic offers to weak Iranian and Russian economies, it's possible that President Assad's behavior might have been different.

A Decade of Lost Chances

That said, Ken Pollack, a long time Middle Eastern political-military affairs expert and a resident scholar at the American Enterprise Institute (AEI), likes to say that "the conventional wisdom in the Middle East is almost always wrong." If this is true, there may not be a perfect time for the US to engage Syria. In fact, Carsten Wieland, a diplomat with the German Foreign Office, has written a book with the descriptive title *Syria: A Decade of Lost Chances.*[15] Wieland documents numerous opportunities for Western engagement with President Bashar Al Assad when he was President in the lost decade from 2000 to 2010. For one reason or another, these opportunities were squandered by the West or by Assad himself.

Syrian Mismanagement of Natural Resources

In thinking about the Syrian civil war and whether it could have been avoided, many scholars tend to look to ideological, religious or political factors as the major reasons for the war. However, what is often overlooked is the Syrian government's gross mismanagement of its natural resources as an underlying root cause of the uprising in March 2011.[16] First, Syrian agricultural planners grew wheat and cotton, which used way too much water. Second, instead of using sprinklers or drip irrigation, they used flood irrigation, which wasted water in a few areas while using way too little in other areas. Half of all Syrian irrigation came from groundwater systems that were over-pumped. That, in turn, led to groundwater levels dropping.[17] In fact, estimates said that 78% of all groundwater withdrawals in Syria were unsustainable.[18]

Water Depletion

Syria was thus rapidly depleting its non-renewable water resources. By 2007, it was withdrawing 19.2 billion cubic meters of water against renewable resources of 15.6 billion cubic meters of water. In two badly affected areas – Mhardeh in Hama governorate and Khan Shaykhun in Idleb governorate – the groundwater table fell by up to 100 meters from 1950 to 2000. In the aquifers around Damascus, the water table is plummeting at a rate of 6 meters a year or more – and springs have dried up in many areas. Since 1999, the Khabur River has had no perennial flow.[19]

One of the largest karst springs in the world, the Ras al Ain Springs on the Syrian-Turkish border, has disappeared completely since 2001, following extensive over-extraction in the spring catchment area over the last 50 years. The area north of Damascus, which used to be renowned for its vines and wheat fields, has turned to desert following extensive over-exploitation of groundwater.[20]

This mismanagement of Syrian water resources made it increasingly vulnerable to drought. The extreme drought came in 2006 and lasted until the Syrian uprising broke out in 2011. Scientists are divided as to whether this drought was the worst in 500 or 900 years.[21] Gary Nabhan, a respected agricultural ecologist, says this dry period was the "worst long-term drought and most severe set of crop failures since agricultural civilizations began in the Fertile Crescent many millennia ago."[22] The drought was especially intense and devastating to many people in Syria. The rainfall was 60% less than usual, and some regions received no rain at all. The consequences for Syrian agriculture were devastating. The wheat harvest came in at 2.1 million tons in contrast to an average of 4.7 million tons before the draught. This forced Syria to import wheat for the first time in 15 years.[23]

That said, it's important to understand that drought is not unusual in Syria. In fact, Syria has experienced a drought in half the time in the last 50 years. Neighboring countries, like Iraq, Jordan, Lebanon and Israel, have also experienced high levels of drought, starting in 2006. But these four countries had all built robust resiliency programs before the droughts to help them soften the impact and recover afterwards. Syria, however, never bothered to create a resiliency program. So, it was predictable that it was there that a grave humanitarian crisis occurred.

62 *Syria*

Instead, we see the negative dominoes falling. The longstanding deterioration of Syria's natural resources was especially severe in its impact on the country's northeast. This was a region that has historically been poor and neglected by the government. In the two decades leading up to the Syrian uprising in 2011, the people in the northeast were hopeful things would improve. Twice, there was a big build, and twice, there was a big let-down.

First was the government's discovery of oil. This brought considerable benefit to government revenues and to the economy, but it did little to relieve the poverty in the region. Second was the rapid development of the northeast water resources.[24]

The paradox for this natural resource disaster and its grave humanitarian and ultimately political and military disaster occurred in this same a region where the government invested heavily in water resources. Over 35 years (from 1985 to 2010), Syria doubled its irrigated area, from 651,000 hectares in 1985 to 1.35 million hectares in 2010.[25]

But the water was diverted once again for a privileged few. The UN estimated that between 2008 and 2011, 1.3 million people were affected by the drought, with 800,000 people severely affected.[26] During this period, yields of wheat and barley fell 47% and 67%, respectively, and livestock populations also plummeted.[27]

Food Insecurity

The Syrian people became less and less able to cope with the disaster. With no crops for two consecutive years, farmers no longer had seeds, while herders were forced to sell or slaughter their flocks. The incidence of nutrition-related diseases soared. By 2010, the UN estimated that 3.7 million people or 17% of the Syrian population were food insecure.[28] Stephen Starr, Founder and Editor in Chief of *Near East Quarterly*, says that the drought and the food shortages were the single most important factors setting off the revolt in 2011.

Migration

300,000 people migrated due to the drought, leaving more than two-thirds of the villages in two governorates (Hassakeh and Deir ez-Zor) deserted. 65,000 families migrated from the northeast to the tent camps that lie around Damascus and Aleppo. By 2012, the United Nations Food and Agriculture Organization 2012 assessment said that 3 million Syrians were in urgent need of food aid, and agricultural water use was unsustainable.[29]

The combination of severe drought, persistent multiyear crop failures and the related economic deterioration led to a very significant dislocation and migration of rural communities to cities. These factors further contributed to urban unemployment, economic dislocations and social unrest.[30]

Political Unrest

All these factors added to growing economic and political uncertainty. Early warnings were prescient: Some of the earliest political unrest began around the town of Daraa, the historic breadbasket of Syria, where a particularly large influx of farmers was displaced off their lands by crop failures. Political unrest was also visible at Deirez-Zour and Hama. Deirez-Zour, one of the most dangerously dry areas, was full of deep-seated dissent. Hama was a major destination for drought-displaced farmers, despite its own water scarcity problems.[31]

It was not the drought, the decline in food production or the rise in food insecurity that ultimately contributed to the disaffection of the Syrian people from the government. What fueled the Syrian uprising was the indifference of the country's government to the social, economic and humanitarian consequences of its policies on water and its failure to protect vulnerable populations from the effects of climactic disaster using adequate social safety nets.[32]

Suzanne Saleeby – writing in the February 2012 issue of *Jadaliyya*, a magazine from the Arab Studies Institute – provides an excellent analysis of the links between economic and environmental conditions, and the political unrest.[33] She says that the uprising was triggered by the lamentable failure of the Assad government to respond with adequate humanitarian assistance or help farmers to ride out the drought and restore their productive capability.

US Embassy and Syrian Government Warnings

P.H. Gleick notes that as early as 2008, the US embassy was warning the White House that the drought, food insecurity and social unrest could trigger an uprising. UN FAO Syrian Representative Abdullah bin Yehia warned that the impact of the drought, combined with other economic and social pressure, could undermine stability in Syria. In July 2008, the Syrian Minister of Agriculture said that the economic and social fallout from the drought was "beyond our capacity" to fix as a country.[34]

Despite the clear and present humanitarian crisis developing year after year, Francisco Femia notes that "the day before the revolt in Syria, many international security analysts were predicting that Syria was stable and immune to the Arab Spring. They concluded it was generally a stable country."[35] What these analysts missed was an obvious connection between economics and conflict.

The contrast between indications and warning of a direct military threat and economic warnings could not be more different. If a Syrian ballistic missile was launched somewhere in the Middle East, shared early warning systems would alert affected nations while the missile was airborne. But if a country like Syria grossly mismanages its natural resources and year after year makes itself increasingly vulnerable to a massive drought, migration

64 *Syria*

and social unrest, the White House, regardless of party, dismisses these social and economic strategic warnings as strategically unimportant.[36]

The sad thing is that none of this horrible humanitarian crisis in Syria would have been inevitable if the White House had had officials who could put aside their "realism" school of international relations and open their eyes to the connection between economics and conflict. Imagine what it would have been like if a more attentive, prescient and creative US government had pursued a depoliticized "preventive defense" with Syrian farmers as partners before the drought. Former Secretary of Defense William Perry used to call this preventive defense. Using this method, you anticipate a problem and take actions to avoid it rather than standing flat-footed, then reacting with far more costly and less effective military responses to an economic problem.

It would have been relatively easy for experts from the foreign office of the US Department of Agriculture, US military civil affairs units, the US Army Corps of Engineers and the FAO to work in a depoliticized way to build robust resiliency programs in this earlier part of the lost decade. In a sense, the White House asked the wrong questions. Instead of saying, "How do we contain Syria?" it should have imagined this negative scenario and asked, "How do we help Syrian farmers build resiliency programs to protect the Syrian people? How do we help the Syrian people keep such a nightmare from occurring in the first place?"

Start Recovery

As fate would have it, in 2005, all the member states of the UN attended a UN Summit and endorsed the Responsibility to Protect (R2P). The idea was to prevent genocide, war crimes, ethnic cleansing and crimes against humanity. While the Syrian Civil War showed that the US had once again missed an opportunity to engage President Assad, it can at least help the Syrian people in the post-conflict period. Better late than never!

The definitive scientific study by Dr. Colin P. Kelley et al. – "Climate change in the Fertile Crescent and implications of the recent Syrian drought," Proceedings of the National Academy of Sciences, 17 March 2015 – predicts an increasingly dry and hot future for Syria and the surrounding Fertile Crescent.[37] Therefore, outside intervention needs to happen as soon as possible to create resiliency programs and hereby avoid another humanitarian crisis and civil war that would devastate even more Syrians.

This intervention needs to start with the approach that should have been applied during the early part of the lost decade. The US government should partner with the Syrian government, the UN and other stakeholders, and start the recovery in the rural and agricultural sectors of Syria. This is because agriculture is key to stabilization and recovery. The key concept in rebuilding food security in the shattered rural economies of Syria is resilience. Resilience is the capacity of systems and people, in the face of shocks, to absorb, adapt and transform.

Syria 65

For military "war planners," resiliency is basically phase zero: How to shape the environment so conflict is less likely. In this regard, Christopher Ward and Sandra Ruckstuhl, two scholars of natural resource management, note that the resiliency concept should "shape" the three lenses through which the Syrian crisis and its aftermath can be viewed.[38] The first lens is the immediate situation. This requires rapid intervention to support populations that are vulnerable in terms of food security.

The second lens focuses on the task of rebuilding resilient systems and restoring livelihoods through investment in infrastructure. Those penny wise, dollar foolish skeptics just need to imagine what another Syrian civil war would cost, then understand what Harvard Professor Larry Summers and the IMF say: For everyone dollar spent investing in public infrastructure, the economy provides almost three dollars in output. Larry Summers calls this a free lunch.[39]

The third lens looks further ahead to the task of undoing the systemic distortions in agriculture, natural resources and the rural sector in Syria. These distortions fueled the crisis in the first place. Food security intervention needs to fit within Syrian national policies. Skeptics say that this is the showstopper, but this is arguably the best time to approach Assad. After all, he is asking for help himself at this moment.

It's also important to get a 360-degree buy-in and leadership from all the local stakeholders. There needs to be cross-sector collaboration, with multiple agencies working together. There must be a flexible learning community for everyone. The goal is social inclusion and shared prosperity to reduce the demand for violence.[40]

Intervention also needs to be tailored to each situation. In Syria, that means improving food security. The immediate aim is to reduce Syria's vulnerability to drought. Benchmark the resiliency programs of Syria's neighbors. Ask how much of that works for Syria.

In the longer term, develop efficient, equitable and sustainable food systems.[41]

Tailor the resiliency program to help the small farmer integrate himself into commercial value chains. Sustainable use of natural resources is also critical. To be more sustainable, there needs to be more sustainable and more equitable use of groundwater and modernization of irrigation. Instead of wasting water with old flood irrigation, Israeli-style, trickle-down irrigation technology needs to be used. In addition, Ugandan President Museveni is spot on when he uses migrants and refugees as assets rather than liabilities.[42] Finally, rhetoric is not enough. Create stronger capacity and institutions in order to lock in resiliency reforms.

Notes

1 Harvey Starr, *Henry Kissinger: Perceptions of International Politics*, The University Press of Kentucky, Lexington, KY, 2015, p. 63.

66 *Syria*

2 See Carsten Wieland's chapter 11 in Raymond Hinnebusch and Tina Zintl's, Editors. Series on *Syria from Reform to Revolt, Volume 1 – Political Economy and International Relations*, Syracuse University Press, Syracuse, NY, 2015.

3 Andrew England, "Andrew England, Syria's Next Step to Reform", *Financial Times*, London, 1 October 2008.

4 James L. Gelvin, *The New Middle East*, Oxford University Press, New York, NY, 2018, p. 56.

5 Ibid., p. 55.

6 Dan Lamothe, "Mattis Arrives in Afghanistan, Says Some in Taliban May Be Willing to Pursue Peace", *Washington Post*, 13 March 2018.

7 John R. Deni, "The Real Rebalancing: American Diplomacy and the Tragedy of President Obama's Foreign Policy", The Strategic Studies Institute, US Army War College, October 2015.

8 See Nikolaos Van Dam, *Destroying a Nation: The Civil War in Syria*, IB Taurus and Company, London, 2017, p. 78.

9 Ibid., p. 75.

10 Ibid., p. 76.

11 Richard Haas, *A World in Disarray*, Penguin Books, New York, NY, 2017, pp. 179–170.

12 Van Dam, *Destroying a Nation*, p. 127.

13 Ibid., p. 133.

14 Ibid., p. 137.

15 Carsten Wieland et al., *The Syrian Uprising: Dynamics of an Insurgency*, University of St. Andrews Centre for Syrian Studies, Fife, Scotland, 2013.

16 For instance, the Syrian construction of the Tishrin Dam on the Euphrates River. While the dam brought benefits to a privileged few, families living in the area were driven off their land. They were forced to migrate into tents outside Damascus.

17 Maher Salman and Wael Mualla, "The Utilization of Water Resources for Agriculture in Syria: Analysis of Current Situation and Future Challenges", *Proc. Int. Seminar on Water Issues of the World Federation of Scientists*, Erice, Sicily, Italy, IPTRID, 2003.

18 Yoshihide Wada, L.P.H. van Beek, and M.F.P. Bierkens, "Nonsustainable Groundwater Sustaining Irrigation: A Global Assessment", *Water Resources Research*, 48, W00L06, 2012, doi: 10.1029/2011WR010562.

19 Christopher Ward and Sandra Ruckstuhl, *Water Scarcity, Climate Change and Conflict in the Middle East: Securing Livelihoods, Building Peace*, IB Tauris, New York, NY, 2017, p. 82.

20 Francesca de Chatel, "The Role of Drought and Climate Change in the Syrian Uprising: Untangling the Triggers of the Revolution", *Middle Eastern Studies*, vol. 50, no. 4, 2014, pp. 521–535.

21 James L. Gelvin, *The New Middle East*.

22 Gary Nabhan, as cited by Francesco Femia and Caitlin Werrell, "Syria: Climate Change, Drought, and Social Unrest", *The Center for Climate and Security*, 2013.

23 Ward and Ruckstuhl, *Water Scarcity, Climate Change and Conflict in the Middle East: Securing Livelihoods, Building Peace*, p. 81.

24 Chatel, "The Role of Drought and Climate Change in the Syrian Uprising".

25 Ibid.

26 Mahmoud Solh, "Tackling the Drought in Syria", *Nature Middle East*, 2010, doi: 10.1038/nmiddleeast.2010.206.

27 ACSAD, "Drought Vulnerability in the Arab Region: Case Study; Drought in Syria—Ten Years of Scarce Water (2000–2010)", *ISDR and the Arab Center for the Studies of Arid Zones and Dry Lands*, 2011.

28 UN Food and Agriculture Organization (FAO), "Syrian Arab Republic Joint Rapid Food Security Needs Assessment (JRFSNA)", FAO Rep., 2012.

29 Ibid.

30 Francesca Femia and Caitlin Werrell, "Syria: Climate Change, Drought, and Social Unrest"; UN Food and Agriculture Organization (FAO), "Syrian Arab Republic Joint Rapid Food Security Needs Assessment (JRFSNA)"; and Megan Perry, "How Climate Change and Failed Policies have Contributed to Conflict in Syria", *Sustainable Food Trust*, 6 May 2016.

31 Suzanne Saleeby, "Sowing the Seeds of Dissent: Economic Grievances and the Syrian Social Contract's Unraveling", 2012, www.jadaliyya.com/pages/index/4383/sowing-the-seeds-of-dissent_economic-grievances-an.

32 Ward and Ruckstuhl, *Water Scarcity, Climate Change and Conflict in the Middle East: Securing Livelihoods, Building Peace*, p. 81.

33 Saleeby, "Sowing the Seeds of Dissent: Economic Grievances and the Syrian Social Contract's Unraveling".

34 Peter H. Gleick, *Water, Drought, Climate Change, and Conflict in Syria*, Pacific Institute, Oakland, CA, 1 July 2014.

35 Brad Plumer, "Drought Helped Cause Syria's War. Will Climate Change Bring More Like It?" *The Washington Post*, 10 September 2013.

36 Francesca Femia and Caitlin Werrell, co-founders of the Center for Climate and Security, argue that factors related to drought, including agricultural failure, water shortages and water mismanagement have played an important role in contributing to the deterioration of social structures and spurring violence. Francesca Femia and Caitlin Werrell, "Syria: Climate Change, Drought, and Social Unrest".

37 Colin P. Kelley et al., "Climate Change in the Fertile Crescent and Implications of the Recent Syrian Drought", *Proceedings of the National Academy of Sciences*, 17 March 2015.

38 Ward and Ruckstuhl, *Water Scarcity, Climate Change and Conflict in the Middle East: Securing Livelihoods, Building Peace*, pp. 176–182.

39 Larry Summers, "Building the Case for Greater Infrastructure Investment", 12 September 2016, http://larrysummers.com/2016/09/12/building-the-case-for-greater-infrastructure-investment/

40 When we created the New Silk Road Initiative at the US Central Command (CENTCOM), we got 35 different US government agencies onboard. Yes, the process was time consuming and frustrating at times, but better to take the time to get everybody onboard in the planning phase than to have an angry and forgotten stakeholder throw a monkey wrench in the implementation phase. When the money was zeroed out at CENTCOM to pay for implementation, I was told, "The prophet is never honored in his own country!"

41 See Leif Rosenberger, "Reconciling the Global Supply and Demand for Food in Roubini Global Economics", 28 February 2018.

42 See Leif Rosenberger, "Can Uganda Step Up to New Economic Challenges?" EconoMonitor, Roubini Global Economics, 25 June 2017, www.economonitor.com/blog/2017/07/can-uganda-step-up-to-new-economic-challenges/.

6 Gaza

On Friday 30 March 2018, thousands of long-suffering Palestinians were peacefully protesting in Gaza. Israeli soldiers over-reacted to the peaceful protests with deadly violence. At least 41 Palestinians were killed, and more than 1,700 were injured.[1] When the UN Security Council tried to criticize this horrifying over-reaction to the protests, the US government blocked it.

Think about how much American foreign policy has deteriorated. Not long ago, retired US General John Allen was working as President Obama's envoy and bending over backwards to be an honest broker for peace between Israel and the Palestinians. Now, we have US Ambassador to the UN Nikki Haley turning a blind eye to a violent Israeli military over-reaction to peaceful Palestinian protesters. Are Americans really expected to believe the Israeli government version of this slaughter, described as Hamas using innocent babies as suicide bombers? It would be advisable for Donald Trump to stop condoning bad behavior. The Palestinians have a right to peaceful protest in Gaza.[2]

Not surprisingly, the failing Israeli government showed no remorse for its military's slaughtering peaceful Palestinian protesters. This is because Mr. Netanyahu has persuaded too many Israelis to believe that brute force and economic coercion are the only ways with which to deal with Palestinians. But as the recent attack on peaceful Palestinian protesters has shown, Israel keeps winning battles but ending up with strategic failure. Instead, the Israeli government should use this strategic moment to rethink its economic coercion in Gaza. Regardless of whether Israel ends up with a one-state or a two-state solution, its strategists will never achieve sustainable strategic success in their own country until they understand the strategic importance of social inclusion and shared prosperity with the Palestinians.

It's important to understand what Gaza is like. As *the Economist* puts it:

> Gaza is a prison, not a state ... it is one of the most crowded and miserable places on Earth. It is short of medicine, power and other essentials. The tap water is undrinkable; untreated sewage is pumped into the sea. Gaza already has one of the world's highest jobless rates, at 44%.[3]

Gaza 69

There is nothing new about Israeli economic coercion against the Palestinians. In fact, since the turn of the century, Israel has progressively clamped down on Gaza's economy, allowing fewer and fewer goods, people and money to enter and leave.

Gaza has been the scene of three wars between Hamas and Israel since 2007; it is always on the point of eruption. After Hamas won the election in June 2007, Israel did everything it could to weaken this new democracy. It tightened its restrictions in Gaza and moved to halt the flow of all but the most basic humanitarian supplies. Businesses in what was a commercial and industrial hub folded at an alarming rate. Ninety-eight percent of Gaza's industry was shut down, and 40,000 farmers and 70,000 workers lost jobs due to Israeli economic squeeze. Israel's long-running closure of Gaza starved companies of raw materials. Israel robbed businesses of a chance to ship goods abroad. Even small bakeries closed because of a lack of electricity.[4]

This economic coercion set the stage for the 3-Week Gaza War (27 December 2008–17 January 2009). In this war, 1,440 Palestinians were killed, while only 13 Israelis died. The war forced over 40,000 people to flee to UN shelters. The main university, mosques and most government buildings were attacked. Even the most basic infrastructure required for private sector activity lay in ruins. The results were nothing short of catastrophic.[5]

There was particular worry about long-term damage to infrastructure. Power, water and sewage networks were all hit in the bombing raids. Five out of ten electricity lines from Israel were damaged. Gaza's only power station was closed due to lack of fuel. Damage to the water and sewage systems triggered another crisis. Lack of drinking water was pervasive, and raw sewage spilled into neighborhoods and fields.

With Israel barring the flow of all but basic humanitarian supplies, all promises of aid from Arab and Western governments, and private donations were impossible to translate into reconstruction on the ground. In addition, rebuilding homes and fixing Gaza's broken infrastructure depended on Israel's willingness to let in cement, bricks and machinery. Israel was adamant that it would not allow such supplies in. It feared that a speedy reconstruction of the war-ravaged strip would benefit Hamas and enhance its legitimacy.

In addition, Israel blocked money coming into Gaza for two months. Workers faced insurmountable obstacles in receiving their salaries. Long lines formed at banks and at cash machines, and people began hoarding what cash they could get hold of as the liquidity crisis grew. In early December 2008, things went from bad to worse. Banks inside the Gaza Strip were forced to shut down because of a shortage of cash.

In a November 2008 letter, the Palestinian Monetary Authority warned the Israeli central bank that Gaza-based banks were facing "severe liquidity problems" and at the time had seen their cash reserves dwindle to a total of 47 million shekels ($12 million). The letter warned of a "huge contagious effect to the whole banking system in Palestine" if the request for the transfer of 185 million shekels was not met.

70 *Gaza*

The financial situation kept deteriorating. In early December 2008, customers reportedly stormed a bank branch in a town in southern Gaza after the bank ran out of cash. Fearing similar outbreaks of violence elsewhere and in light of the pervasive lack of notes and coins, almost all banks and cash machines in Gaza closed.

International organizations pleaded with Israeli authorities to prioritize allowing the transfer of cash into Gaza. The cash crisis prevented the payment of December salaries to tens of thousands of Palestinians in Gaza employed by the Palestinian Authority. To make matters worse, the lack of cash affected the work of international organizations. The United Nations Relief and Works Agency, which supplies aid to one in two Palestinians in Gaza, was forced to suspend cash distribution to 94,000 Palestinians.

This Israeli financial squeeze antagonized many Palestinians who had once given Israel the benefit of the doubt. The financial squeeze therefore played right into the hands of hardline Hamas recruiters and propagandists – who used the squeeze to "justify" their missile strikes.

The 50 Day Gaza War (8 July 2014–26 August 2014) was even more destructive than the 3 Week War in late December 2008/January 2009. In the 50 Day War, 2,205 Palestinians died, and it appears that over half the Palestinian deaths were civilians. Israel lost 71 young soldiers, but for what gain? By any yardstick, the kill ratio was disproportionate.[6]

Clausewitz reminds us that "the first, the supreme, the most far-reaching act of judgment that a statesman and commander have to make is to establish ... the kind of war on which they are embarking; neither mistaking it for, nor trying to turn it into, something that is alien to its nature." He also stresses the relationship between political objectives and military objectives in war.[7]

So, what kind of war was Israel fighting? The Israeli government viewed these wars against Hamas as narrow military campaigns against a conventional military enemy, so, Israel aimed to destroy as many Hamas targets as possible and reduce its military capability to launch more rocket attacks in the future. In this way, Israeli leaders argued that they were protecting the Israeli people from Hamas terrorism. However, in essence, Israel was only addressing the supply side of war. It focused on destroying weapons. Hamas rocket attacks on Israelis show that old rockets can be replaced with new ones almost overnight. At best, such a narrow operational approach to war as Israel's can only bring temporary gains.

In addition, the Israelis targeted Hamas "terrorists" wherever they could find them. Inevitably, this meant killing a handful of Hamas terrorists living amongst a multitude of Palestinian civilians. This explains why over half the deaths in the 50 Day War were Palestinian civilians. Heavy civilian casualties like this tends to turn their family members and friends into anti-Israeli Hamas "terrorists." Instead of changing tactics, the Israelis doubled down and became determined to bomb all these "new terrorists." This vicious circle of new terrorists produced an almost permanent state of conflict against

Gaza 71

the Palestinian people instead of Hamas. After a while, the Israelis desensitized themselves and wrongly dismissed the deaths as "collateral damage." Their thinking was short-sighted, ill-advised and conceptually flawed.

Why is the Israeli economic and military coercion a counter-productive strategy toward Hamas? While it's always dangerous to overgeneralize, Hamas certainly has its share of "true believers." These true believers feel that they do not fit into their societies. They quickly become frustrated and feel they deserve far better. Israeli coercion often fails because it feeds this Hamas frustration and confirms their very sense that they deserve better.

At best, Israeli-launched wars can sometimes control Hamas, but violence will never eliminate it. If the extremist ideas of Hamas are to wane, they will do so only at the hands of more attractive ideas, which the current Israeli leadership seems temperamentally incapable of creating.[8] Thus, it appears that Israel doesn't focus enough on shaping a web of economic integration and shared prosperity into durable peace and security for all concerned. It logically follows that Israeli leaders have a one-dimensional view of economics. Israel fears that Hamas's economic power will invariably generate military power to reach military goals. In a similar way, the Israeli government sees Hamas as a terrorist group that will never change its tactics. Therefore, the Israelis make no attempt to use serious diplomacy to address Hamas resentment or reduce its demand for counter-violence.

Finally, Israel dismissed the importance of the information war. No attempt was made to win hearts and minds. Not surprisingly, therefore, it lost this all-important information war. It is difficult to exaggerate the damage this loss has done to Israel's reputation. The international community increasingly sees its war as more a war on the Palestinians in Gaza than a campaign against Hamas.

The scale of the Israeli military assault was huge. After over 2,000 Israeli air strikes and daily pounding from land and sea, destruction in Gaza was significant. The losses to its farming sector alone totaled $450m, and 350 businesses in Gaza were destroyed or damaged. Its sole power plant was damaged three times in Israeli air strikes, as were water tanks and wells and other infrastructure. Seventeen thousand houses, mostly in the northern and eastern regions near Israel, have been destroyed, and half a million people have been displaced. Mosques; schools and police stations; the finance, education, interior, foreign, justice, public works, labor and culture ministries; the parliament; and every public building of significance have been damaged or destroyed.[9]

Understandably, the 50 Day Gaza War in July/August 2014 once more focused the world's attention on Gaza's shattered economy.[10] So, in October 2014, the international community met in Cairo for the third time in five years to fund the rebuilding of Gaza. In 2009, the cost of fixing the damage and rebuilding it was estimated at $1.3 billion. This time, the cost turned out to be over three times that amount.

72   *Gaza*

The Palestinians were initially seeking $4 billion from the Gulf States, Europe and other countries to clear away rubble, rebuild destroyed buildings and infrastructure, and provide short-term assistance to the 1.8 million people in Gaza affected by Israel's 50-day summer offensive.[11] But when all was said and done, the international donors pledged $5.4 billion to help rebuild Gaza. Qatar pledged $1 billion in aid to the Palestinians, and Kuwait, Turkey and the UAE each donated $200m. The US offered a further $212m.[12]

Unfortunately, pledges of support are not enough. The promised reconstruction aid needs to be delivered, and that has not consistently happened for a number of reasons. For starters, the Israelis show no sign of ending the economic embargo, and, even if that could happen, the Palestinians cannot speak or act with a single voice.

In June 2014, the Hamas-backed government in Gaza was dissolved, and a unified Palestinian Authority (PA) was created under the leadership of Palestinian President Mahmoud Abbas. The international community reached a consensus that Abbas was empowered to lead reconstruction in Gaza and make sure building materials were not diverted to make tunnels. Unfortunately, due to infighting between Hamas and Abbas's Fatah party, he has proven to be unwilling or unable to govern in Gaza. As a result, the money promised for reconstruction in Gaza has not been delivered.

But first things first. Donors are demanding that Israel (and Egypt) lift their blockade on trade and movement into and out of Gaza as a precondition for any future reconstruction plan. The Israeli blockade stunts Gaza's economy by severing its natural trade routes, leaving most of its 1.8 million population dependent on aid. Gaza's few exporters cannot sell goods such as furniture or flowers in Israel or the West Bank – their natural market – because Israeli authorities prohibit this for security reasons, so goods must be sent overseas by ship or air.[13]

Economic recovery in Gaza will simply not be possible without lifting restrictions on the movement of goods and people, reopening trade with the West Bank, Israel and beyond, and repairing and rehabilitating damaged social and economic infrastructure. Therefore, there can be no security for Israel without socio-economic development for Palestinians and respect for fundamental rights and freedoms.[14] Even the month before the 50 Day War started, Palestinian and foreign officials warned of a worsening humanitarian crisis in Gaza, with electricity and drinkable water in short supply. In a report published in 2012, the United Nations Relief and Works Agency for Palestinian Refugees (UNRWA) said that Gaza's population would grow by another half a million people by 2020, and its electricity, water and sanitation would struggle to keep pace. Its threadbare utility companies say that they have been unable to undertake large investments in new facilities because of the Israeli import restrictions.[15]

International aid to the power sector, for example, has focused on the shipment of emergency fuel rather than investment in new capacity. Efforts to rehabilitate Gaza's precarious water and waste system have also focused on emergency stopgap measures rather than investment in new plants because the approval process for construction materials takes so long.[16]

What has been the Israeli response? Have the Israelis relaxed their restrictions? To be fair, there have been glimmers of hope. The rebuilding of Gaza began. Israel lifted the ban on construction materials and allowed trucks carrying construction materials to enter the Gaza Strip for the first time in a year, marking the start of a massive rebuilding task following its war with Hamas in the summer of 2014.

While the Palestinians were happy to see Israel start to relax restrictions in order to rebuild Gaza, they were also frustrated with the slow pace of US-sponsored direct negotiations with Israel on both the political and the economic fronts.[17] Confident that support from the UN and the rest of the international community was on the rise, the Palestinians opted to join the International Criminal Court (ICC) in The Hague.[18] In retaliation for the Palestinians joining the ICC, Israel temporarily stopped paying the Palestinians the tax revenues it collects on their behalf (which covers most of the Palestinian Authority's wage bill).[19] For about two months, teachers, police officers and tens of thousands of other employees only received about 60% of their pay.[20]

Finally, on 27 March 2015, Israel's government said it would release tax revenues that it had been withholding since January to punish the Palestinians for their decision to join the ICC. The government of Benjamin Netanyahu said that it made the decision on the recommendation of military and security officials. In a prepared statement, Prime Minister Netanyahu said, "Given the deteriorating situation in the Middle East, one must act responsibly and with due consideration alongside a determined struggle against extremist elements." In short, there is another glimmer of hope that Netanyahu may be starting to see the connection between Palestinian frustration and Israeli security.

This chapter has asked the following questions: Does Israeli coercion work? Do Israeli operational military actions get Hamas to cave in and surrender? Do they make Hamas submissive? Do they win over the Palestinians in Gaza? The answer is no. Hamas will not become more submissive and less violent, and Israeli tactics will not win over the Palestinian people. The reason is simple. Hamas gets its political legitimacy from the Palestinians in Gaza by satisfying their socio-economic needs. While Israel has a legitimate right to curb the buildup of a Hamas weapons arsenal, destroying Gaza's economy has caused it to further lose the war for the hearts and minds of the Palestinians there and in many countries and populations around the world, and has strengthened the reputation of Hamas as the protector of Palestinian people in Gaza. That said, Hamas and Fatah must also reconcile their differences and allow the donors to deliver reconstruction funds.

Jared Kushner should focus more directly on Israeli economic coercion of the Palestinian people and less on Israeli operational victories over Hamas. He should use key leadership engagement opportunities to speak out

74   *Gaza*

against Israeli unwillingness to pursue social inclusion and shared prosperity between Israeli people and the Palestinians. The real friends of Israel need to argue that Israeli actions are not only morally wrong but are increasingly turning other nations and peoples against Israel. These coercive actions are therefore counter-productive and result in a permanent state of strategic failure for Israel.

One thing is certain: Both sides of the conflict – Israelis and Palestinians – must emerge with something that makes them willing to give peace a chance. The Israelis need reasons to believe that Gaza will no longer be used as a base for rocket or tunnel attacks on their country. The Palestinians need relief from the blockade that is imposed on Gaza by both Israel and Egypt. Any deal should be based around the idea of trading the demilitarization of Gaza for an easing of the blockade, combined with the rebuilding of vital infrastructure.

The Israeli-Palestinian issue directly impacts a critical strategic environment, so, it is important to discuss and debate it in President Trump's policy circles. The UN could play a larger role in postwar Gaza. The question of whether Israel, in particular, has committed war crimes over the years revolves around the issue of whether its military has taken all "feasible precautions to minimize harm to civilians" and whether the Israelis use "disproportionate" force in pursuing their military objectives.

Given the hatred and mistrust on both sides, Jared Kushner's efforts to negotiate an agreement between Israel and the Palestinians and then make it stick will be extremely difficult. How can mutual hatred and mistrust be reduced? Perhaps lessons from history can help. A good example of the strategic vision that is needed in Gaza appeared after World War II, when Jean Monnet called for a European Coal and Steel Community. At the time it was easy to dismiss Monnet for being hopelessly naïve and idealistic. Didn't Monnet know that France and Germany hated each other and had been fighting for centuries? But Monnet correctly argued that an alternative future was possible. If given a chance, French and German businessmen would bond. What was needed was a strategic vision and unwavering moral courage to execute a viable economic strategy and concrete economic plans for regional economic integration. Social inclusion and shared prosperity would outweigh security concerns. Before long, French and German businessmen reduced the demand for violence, and as the countries began to see mutual economic benefit, they turned from enemies into friends.

Like Jean Monnet, "Breaking the Impasse" is a group of Israeli and Palestinian business leaders who press their respective political leaders to use shared prosperity to foster peace in Gaza. This group was initially put on hold because of emotions inflamed by the 50 Day War. As a small first step, US strategic leaders should encourage Israeli and Palestinian businessmen to give "Breaking the Impasse" another chance to foster peace and stability.[21]

In conclusion, Israel's political right wing says that Donald Trump's surprising victory in the US Presidential election will allow Israel to "reset and rethink everything" in regard to its conflict against the Palestinians. If this is true, why don't they also rethink economic coercion in Gaza?

Economic recovery in Gaza will not be possible without lifting restrictions on the movement of goods and people; reopening trade with the West Bank, Israel and beyond; and repairing and rehabilitating damaged social and economic infrastructure. There can be no security for Israel without socio-economic development for Palestinians and respect for fundamental rights and freedoms.

As cited earlier, friends of Israel need to argue that Israeli actions are not only morally wrong but are increasingly turning other nations and peoples against Israel. These coercive actions are therefore counter-productive and result in a permanent state of strategic failure for Israel.

This Israeli coercive mindset against the Palestinians is self-defeating. The harsh socio-economic conditions which it has created in Gaza are now an incubator for violent extremism. Israeli coercion plays into the hands of Hamas. Palestinians needlessly see Hamas as freedom fighters and champions of their economic rights.

Instead of offering the Palestinians a worse alternative than Hamas, Israel needs to offer them a better economic alternative. It needs to learn that there can be no durable security for its people without social inclusion and shared prosperity between Israelis and Palestinians. Israel needs to lift the economic blockade to help reconstruction in Gaza. But even if it did, Palestinian infighting between Fatah and Hamas would prevent the subsequent delivery of reconstruction money to Gaza. Therefore, Gaza reconstruction cannot happen until there's Hamas-Fatah reconciliation as well.

Toward this end, friends of Israel need to persuade the Israelis and the Palestinians to support groups and initiatives such as "Break the Impasse," a group of Israeli and Palestinian businessmen who want to work together to turn enemies into friends. One thing is certain: Both sides of the conflict – Israelis and Palestinians – must emerge with something that makes them willing to give peace a chance.[22]

Notes

1 See David M. Halbfinger, "Hamas sees Gaza Protests as Peaceful – and as a Deadly Weapon", *The New York Times*, 15 April 2018.
2 See "EU: Israel Must Respect the Right to Peaceful Protest in Gaza", *EU Observer*, 15 May 2018.
3 "Gaza Erupts: How to End the Endless Conflict between Israel and the Palestinians", *The Economist*, 17 May 2018.
4 See BBC, "Gaza Economy Crushed by Embargo", 20 January 2008.
5 Ibid.
6 See William Booth, "In Blow to Gaza's Economy, Israeli Strikes Have Left Industries Hard-Hit", *The Washington Post*, 22 August 2014.
7 See Carl von Clausewitz, On War.

76 *Gaza*

8 See Martin Wolf, "How to Share the World with True Believers Behind Global Terror", *Financial Times*, 13 January 2015 and Eric Hoffer, *The True Believer: Thoughts on the Nature of Mass Movements*, Harper and Bros, New York, NY, 1951.
9 John Reed, "Donors Demand Israel Lifts Gaza Blockade to Help Reconstruction", *Financial Times*, 20 August 2014.
10 John Reed, "Gaza Conflict Sharpens the World's Focus on Gaza's Shattered Economy", *Financial Times*, 25 July 2014.
11 John Reed, "Palestinians Call for Help in $4bn Cost of Rebuilding Gaza", *Financial Times*, 9 October 2014.
12 Heba Saleh and John Reed, "International Donors Pledge $5.4bn to Help Rebuild Gaza", *Financial Times*, 12 October 2014.
13 John Reed, "Donors Demand Israel Lifts Gaza Blockade to Help Reconstruction".
14 Ibid.
15 Ibid.
16 Ibid.
17 For more details on political and security issues, see the CSAG Strategy Paper 2014–23 of 8 July 2014.
18 John Reed, "Palestinians to Turn to UN Amid Frustration with Peace Process", *Financial Times*, 1 September 2014 and John Reed, "Palestinians Join ICC in Politically Charged Move", *Financial Times*, 1 April 2015.
19 John Reed, "Israel withholds Palestinian Tax Revenue", *Financial Times*, 3 January 2015.
20 John Reed, "Palestinians Squeezed after Israel withholds Tax", *Financial Times*, 27 February 2015.
21 John Reed, "Israel Releases Tax Revenues to Palestinians", *Financial Times*, 27 March 2015.
22 See Jimmy Carter, "Rebuild Gaza and Avert Another War", *The Washington Post*, 27 March 2015 and *Financial Times Editorial*, "In Search of Lasting Peace in Gaza: Ease the Blockade in Return for Getting Rid of the Rockets", 5 August 2014.

Bibliography

Abunimah, Ali. "'Gaza Is a Graveyard,' Sing Joyful Israeli Youths", *Electronic Intifada*, July 28, 2014. https://electronicintifada.net/blogs/ali-abunimah/gaza-graveyard-sing-joyful-israeli-youths.

Blumenthal, Max. *Goliath: Life and Loathing in Greater Israel*. Nation Books, New York, NY, 2014.

Erakat, Noura. "Israel Will Invade Gaza Again—the Only Question Is How Soon", *The Nation*. July 8, 2015. www.thenation.com/article/israel-will-invade-gaza-again-the-only-question-is-how-soon.

Erakat, Noura. "Permission to Kill in Gaza", *Jadaliyya*, July 7, 2015. www.jadaliyya.com/pages/index/22093/permission-to-kill-in-gaza.

Esmeir, Samera. "Colonial Experiments in Gaza", *Jadaliyya*, July 14, 2014. www.jadaliyya.com/pages/index/8482/colonial-experiments-in-gaza.

Farsakh, Leila. *Palestinian Labour Migration to Israel: Labour, Land and Occupation* (Routledge Political Economy of the Middle East and North Africa). Routledge, New York, 2005.

Human Rights Watch. "Israel: In-Depth Look at Gaza School Attacks", September 11, 2014. www.hrw.org/news/2014/09/11/israel-depth-look-gaza-school-attacks.

Landler, Mark. "Gaza War Strains Relations between the U.S., Israel", *The New York Times*, August 4, 2014. www.nytimes.com/2014/08/05/world/middleeast/gaza-is-straining-us-ties-to-israel.html?_r=0.

Li, Darryl. "A Separate Piece?: Gaza and the 'No-State Solution'", *Jadaliyya*, December 4, 2012. www.jadaliyya.com/pages/index/8762/a-separate-piece_gaza-and-the-%E2%80%9Cno-state-solution %E2%80%9D.

Oswald, Nuriya. "Gaza Reconstruction Mechanism: Profiting Israel, Entrenching the Blockade", *Jadaliyya*, July 7, 2015. www.jadaliyya.com/pages/index/22089/gaza-reconstruction-mechanism_profiting-israelent.

Rabbani, Mouin. "Why the Gaza Truce Failed", *Jadaliyya*, August 24, 2014. www.jadaliyya.com/pages/index/18976/why-the-gaza-truce-failed.

Roy, Sara. "Gaza: New Dynamics of Civic Disintegration", *Journal of Palestine Studies*, vol. 22, no. 4, 1993, pp. 20–31.

Roy, Sara. "The Gaza Strip: A Case of Economic De-Development", *Journal of Palestine Studies*, vol. 17, no. 1, 1987, pp. 56–88.

Roy, Sara. *Hamas and Civil Society in Gaza*, Princeton University Press, Princeton, NJ, 2013.

Roy, Sara. "Rebuilding Gaza Needs Freedom and Normality – Not Just Aid", *Jadaliyya*, July 7, 2015. www.jadaliyya.com/pages/index/22098/rebuilding-gaza-needs-freedom-and-normality_-not-j.

Said, Edward. *Peace and Its Discontents: Essays on Palestine in the Middle East Peace Process*, Vintage, New York, NY, 1996.

7 Iran

At the start of *A Tale of Two Cities*, Charles Dickens tells us, "It was the best of times, it was the worst of times." On 14 July 2015, the Iranian people no doubt felt it would soon be the best of times when they poured out of their houses to celebrate in the streets. After a decade of economic isolation, Iran had reached a nuclear agreement with the US, the UK, France, Germany, Russia and China. Iran promised in the Joint Comprehensive Plan of Action (or JCPOA) that it would unwind its nuclear program in return for lifting international economic sanctions and reintegrating into the global economy.[1] In short, the agreement was meant to turn isolation and economic coercion into Jean Monnet's vision of a web of economic interdependence and shared prosperity.

The euphoria of the Iranian people reflected both the prospect of an end to the devastating impact of the sanctions on its economy and the economic promise of the lifting of the sanctions. The JCPOA allowed Iran to export crude oil and other energy products, source foreign direct investment (FDI) in most sectors and access about $100 billion in its foreign-exchange reserves in international banks.[2]

But not so fast. Donald Trump killed the joy and made it the worst of times for the Iranian people. On 12 October 2017, President Trump announced that he was de-certifying the nuclear agreement.[3] On 8 May 2018, he abandoned his belief in allies and withdrew from the agreement completely.[4] On 7 August 2018, he announced that "the highest level of economic sanctions" would "snap-back" again against Iran.[5] And on 12 September 2017, he slammed Iran for being "evil" in a speech he delivered at the United Nations.[6]

What does it mean for sanctions to snap back against Iran? When severe sanctions were in place against Iran, this economic coercion targeted everything from shipping and banking to foreign investment and exports. The sanctions limited Iranian revenues and stymied industry. They had a devastating impact on the economy. Over $100 billion in financial assets were blocked. The volume of oil exports fell over 50% (from 2.5 MBD to 1.4 MBD).[7] Car production fell by 40%. One out of every five Iranians was jobless. The economy was 15% to 20% smaller than it would have been without the sanctions – that's the equivalent of the Great Depression in the US in the 1930s.[8]

Foreign businessmen hoped the nuclear deal would pave the way for a flood of new business deals, opening up foreign investment and international trade in crucial sectors such as oil and gas, car production, aviation, tourism, technology, mining the stock market and banking.[9]

Iran's potential emergence from economic isolation could be the most significant opening of an economy since the fall of the Soviet Union and the US rapprochement with China. The potential of Iran is huge. As one of the last markets to be opened up to the world, its allure is unmistakable. Its nearly 80 million residents – 60% of whom are under 30 years old – already have an affinity for Western brands, especially American ones like Coca-Cola and Chevrolet. Some shops in affluent urban areas, particularly the nation's capital, are full of Western-made products, from sunglasses and designer jeans to laptops. In addition, the Iranian population is tech-savvy. Internet penetration is 53% across the population and 77% in Tehran. About 11 million Iranians have mobile Internet access. Many senior businesspeople were educated in the US and still prize American engineering. Iran's market for technology products and services is roughly $4 billion a year. If sanctions are lifted, the market rises to $16 billion annually, which makes it comparable to that of Saudi Arabia. Overall consumer expenditures are projected to be about $176.4 billion a year, with annual disposable income pegged at about $287 billion.[10]

While Iran enjoys huge oil and gas reserves, the economy is relatively diversified in a Middle Eastern context, with the oil and gas industry accounting for just 15% of the GDP.[11] In short, foreign businessmen have been eyeing a huge market in Iran for a long time.

Back in those heady days when the nuclear agreement was reached in 14 July 2015, the sanctions didn't disappear right away. The nuclear agreement wouldn't be adopted until 18 October 2015. Foreign companies could move in only after Iran implemented the nuclear part of the deal. The so-called P5 plus one countries – France, the European Union, Iran, the UK, the US and China and Russia plus Germany – had to ensure that Tehran was in compliance with its nuclear rollback commitments. Verification of its nuclear equipment and detailed inspections took place before the nuclear agreement was implemented in January 2016. Even then, the task of untangling a maze of economic sanctions that had been made against Iran since 2012 was not easy.[12]

But lifting sanctions was not enough for Iran to be competitive in the global economy. Iran also needed to end the crippling sanctions it had imposed on itself.[13] If it was to escape the trap of poor management and inefficiency, it still had to ensure that privatization created a real private sector rather than a semi-governmental sector. It took months to get a new company registered due to bureaucratic inefficiency and corruption. The Iranian economy suffered from price controls, import tariffs or other interventions. Efforts at corporate restructuring were frustrated by an archaic Napoleonic commercial code.

80 *Iran*

Finally, there was the banking sector, shut out for years from much of the international system by sanctions but also hobbled by problems of its own. Non-performing loans were alarmingly high, and liquidity was alarmingly low. In short, the nuclear deal was necessary but far from enough to reintegrate Tehran with the rest of the global economy.[14]

President Rouhani deserves kudos on the foreign policy front for working with the US and the other five world powers to negotiate the nuclear deal. But he has not yet implemented significant economic reforms. In many ways, the failing economic model has not fundamentally changed from that when his predecessor, President Ahmadinejad, was in power.

Now that we've looked at both the external sanctions and the self-imposed sanctions and failing economic model, we can note that, back in 2014, some of the world's largest companies – such as Chevron, Cisco and GE – were examining how the nuclear deal would affect their ability to do business in Iran even before Trump wrecked the nuclear agreement. In this sense, the hard work of weighing the pros and cons continues, albeit in an even more difficult way.

Of course, Trump's exit from the nuclear agreement makes everything even more difficult for international businesses previously trading with and/or investing in Iran. Trump was giving 3–6 months for corporations to wind down their operations with Iran.

Trump's new sanctions, which took effect on 7 August 2018, prohibit Iran from using US currency. The sanctions bar trading in cars and metals and minerals that include gold, steel, coal and aluminum. Iran is also barred from buying US and European aircraft. The sanctions bar imports of Iranian energy and prevent financial institutions from conducting transactions with Iran's central bank.[15]

So, imagine you are Patrick Pouyanne, CEO of the French oil company Total. You signed a multibillion dollar deal in July 2017 to develop the next stage of South Pars, the world's largest gas field, shared by Iran and Qatar, marking Tehran's first major contract with a Western company since the lifting of some international sanctions in 2016. Trump was telling you to wind down operations in Iran in three to six months, even though the International Atomic Energy Agency (IAEA) said that Iran was fully compliant with the nuclear agreement. Chances are you aren't going to send Donald Trump a Christmas card anytime soon.

How does this economic coercion work against America's former allies? Gideon Rachman notes:

> America's economic power goes well beyond market access. In extremis, European executives who continue to do business in Iran could become subject to arrest if they travel to the US. And European banks that do business with Iran could find themselves shut out of the US financial system, or subject to prosecution and massive fines in America.[16]

All of this reflected the role of the US dollar as the world's reserve currency. It was the dollar, as much as American military might, that allowed the US to coerce its allies – as well as its adversaries.[17]

Gideon Rachman, a writer for the Financial Times, predicted that 8 May 2018 – the day of the US exit from the nuclear agreement – would go down in history as the day Trump abandoned his belief in allies.[18] Gone are the days of George Marshall and US social inclusion and shared prosperity with its allies. Donald Trump was now using economic coercion against US allies as well as against Iran.

Europeans are angry and frustrated with Trump's America Alone approach, which arbitrarily bullies the Europeans with huge opportunity costs, taking billions of dollars out of their pockets. While Iran is relatively diversified, oil and gas would arguably have been its biggest attraction for Total and other European energy companies. Few of the oil and gas industry's big players could ignore the multibillion-dollar oil and gas "candy store" that is Iran. There are lots of reasons why Iran is a golden opportunity for oil and gas companies.[19]

So, what has been lost? Before Trump re-imposed new sanctions on 7 August 2018, Iran was preparing to open a multibillion-dollar shop window for 50 oil and gas projects that were up for grabs. Iran had the world's fourth-largest crude oil and second-largest natural gas reserves, which equates to more than 250 billion barrels of oil equivalent in reserves. Its energy resources have been mapped, and production costs are low. These costs are just $10 to $15 a barrel.[20]

If Trump had not wrecked the nuclear agreement, how much and how quickly could more Iranian oil have returned to the market? Presently, Iran has around 40 million barrels in storage on tankers which could be immediately released onto the market. However, a sustained pick-up in oil production and exports would take longer.[21]

While Iran is capable of accelerating production and exports by about 500,000 barrels a day (or b/d) to 800,000 b/d within 6 to 12 months of any sanctions being lifted, it is unlikely that it could have achieved pre-sanctions levels any time soon. That said, it claims that it has more ambitious goals and says it could ultimately increase its oil production capacity to 5m b/d by the end of the decade.[22]

This ambitious oil production goal would hinge on foreign direct investment (FDI) that would depend not only on sanctions relief but the terms under which western companies would be permitted to invest. What kinds of activities would be permitted in Iran, and with Iran, and by whom, are among questions being asked by the oil and gas industry before Trump wrecked the nuclear agreement.[23]

France's Total was not the only European oil company interested in Iran: Royal Dutch Shell and Eni of Italy had visited as well.[24] Total has a long history in Iran, and loyalty counts for a lot with the Iranians. If given a chance, these oil companies would likely return to the Iranian projects they were

82 *Iran*

interested in before the sanctions. ENI would go to Darquain, Shell would go to Yadavaran and Total would go to Azadegan and gas exports from the supergiant South Pars field. The Russian energy companies are politically important and would also play a significant role.[25]

Iran had experienced difficulties with Asia in recent years on both the trade front and the foreign direct investment (FDI) front. On the former, Iran faced a battle to win back its oil export market share in Asia. Before the US and European sanctions halved Iran's exports to 1 million of barrels per day (or MBD), four Asian countries – China, India, Japan and South Korea – accounted for 60% of Iran's exports. At that time, Iran was the second-largest exporter of crude oil to India. By 2014, however, Iran had fallen to the 7th spot. Despite this overall downturn, China increased its imports of Iranian oil by 30% over the last five years. It accounted for 40% of Iran oil exports in 2014.[26]

Until the sanctions were lifted, China would have a stranglehold on the Iranian economy. Therefore, Tehran wants to diversify. On the FDI front, Chinese oil companies continued to invest in Iranian oil fields at a low level during the sanctions period, but Chinese oil technology is unimpressive, and the Iranians are unhappy with China's performance.[27] The Iranians also say they want to do less business with China because the Chinese break their promises, and Chinese goods are shoddy.[28]

The Iranians wanted to be involved with US major oil companies (such as Exxon Mobil, Chevron, ConocoPhillips and Conoco) for political and technical reasons, but these US oil companies are well behind their European rivals because US sanctions and concurrent legal restrictions on trade with Iran are far more restrictive. US companies have been disconnected from Iran for longer, and the threat of legal action against any US oil company that tries to invest there before sanctions are lifted is far more severe, but at some point, they may be allowed to negotiate options to enter when it is possible.[29] However, the problem for US companies and the US economy is that the rest of the world, especially the European Union, will have a massive jump on the US. This is not helped by the outlook of many in Congress.

In the past three years, the cash-starved Iranians have lost $160 billion in oil sales. In addition, they have been laid low by mismanagement, corruption and under-investment. To reach its goal of increasing oil production by 1 MBD, Iran needs Western oil expertise to revive aging oil fields and creaking infrastructure. It is especially eager to attract Shell – which has pioneered gas to liquid technology – to help it catch up to Qatar's lead in liquid natural gas (LNG) output. But that dream is impossible if Donald Trump is the US president.

While the Iranian energy industry's enthusiasm for Western oil company expertise to boost oil production and exports would help its cause, this enthusiasm does not completely erase a long history of Iran frustrating Western oil companies. For instance, Eni has unresolved contractual issues that illustrate the hurdles oil companies may face when entering the country. Eni claims that Iran owes the company money for overruns at oil-and-gas

Iran 83

projects it was operating before sanctions were imposed. The disputed sum stemmed from old deals that, unlike most oil company contracts around the world, wouldn't pay for cost overruns. Eni Chief Executive Claudio Descalzi said that his company wouldn't return to Iran if contract terms remained largely the same. It wasn't even clear when oil companies like Chevron *could* return. In 1996, they were banned from investing in Iran's oil industry by a US law separate from the nuclear sanctions.[30]

With frustrating experiences like this, the Iranians would likely have found Western oil companies to be far from easy to deal with, even if there were no sanctions in place. The big question was whether the oil and gas contracts would be sufficiently attractive if sanctions were lifted again. Iranian law forbids foreign ownership of oil and gas reserves. In addition, Iran offered unpopular one-sided contracts in the late 1990s and early 2000s. These contracts put too much risk on the investor. In a buyer's market driven by low oil prices, this type of contract needs adapting. The new Iranian Petroleum Contract needs to be more attractive. Capital, investment, output and financing risk should be shared.[31]

The Iranian oil industry understands the business climate has not been good in the past. Would this situational awareness matter? Could the Iranian oil industry improve enough to offer more attractive production-sharing contracts? At a minimum, they would need to enhance the old contracts; otherwise, foreign oil companies would just say no. Iran is currently finalizing a new contract system to secure about $100 billion of new oil and gas deals with Western companies if or when sanctions are lifted. The new contracts would enable foreign companies to set up joint ventures with Iranian state-run oil companies. The new contracts would likely look more like production-sharing deals, with foreign companies winning the rights to output and reserves, and risk would be shared. Even when the terms and conditions are sorted out, actual implementation of the projects would take years, with investment needs easily rising to $200 billion.[32]

Could Iran change its business climate? Yes, but cultural change does not happen overnight. It would be a slow process to modernize its business environment. In recent years, hard-liners have come to play a key role in some of the country's biggest industries, such as energy and telecommunications. Its economic system has been hobbled by this cronyism, corruption and control by thuggish vested interests. The Iranian Revolutionary Guard Corps (IRGC), the arm of Iran's military charged with protecting its Islamic system, is heavily controlled in this and is likely to remain under sanctions for alleged terrorism and human rights violations. This could pose a risk for companies eager to enter businesses where local partners could trigger snap back to sanctions or fines from the US or European capitals.[33] This would moderate Iranian economic performance in much the same way it is held back in other countries in the Central Region, such as Egypt, Iraq and Pakistan.

Iranians rejoiced when the nuclear deal was signed. The international sanctions had taken their toll on the economy. At first glance, foreign

84 *Iran*

businessmen saw the Iranian economy as a large and attractive market, but it would likely have taken until 2016 for the country to achieve nuclear compliance and untangle its maze of international sanctions, even if Trump had not wrecked the nuclear agreement. That said, lifting international sanctions is not enough to make Iran competitive in the global economy. It also needs to end the crippling sanctions it imposed on itself in the form of a failing economic model. When self-imposed and international sanctions are lifted, its success in boosting oil output would turn on creating more attractive terms and conditions than in the past, especially in a buyer's market.

Chinese oil companies tried to fill the gap back when sanctions were in place. But Iran was unhappy with China's performance. US oil firms would be more cautious than the European oil companies because any US re-entry into Iran would most likely face tighter restrictions. European oil companies would re-enter the market sooner. But most foreign oil companies would not return to Iran until Iran changed its business climate.

Can Iran change? Yes, its Islamic forces would cause the process to be slow. In particular, the IRGC involvement in the economy poses risks for foreign oil companies. That said, had Hillary Clinton become president, the opportunities for shared prosperity for Iran and America would arguably have outweighed the risks.

But Donald Trump became president. That changed everything. Trump called the nuclear agreement with Iran a disaster. He claimed that Iran had been engaged in an "aggressive and expansionistic foreign policy" since its Islamic Revolution. So, when the nuclear agreement ultimately provided Iran with at least $100 billion in unfrozen assets, he argued that it would be "emboldened" to support even more instability across the region. Therefore, Trump believes it's a foregone conclusion that Iran will use this money to escalate its funding for Houthi rebels in Yemen, President Assad in Syria, Hezbollah in Lebanon and sectarian militia in Iraq.

However, President Trump was ill-advised. He forgets that the purpose of the sanctions is to coerce Iran to negotiate. This economic squeeze worked. Iran agreed to roll back its nuclear program. But then Trump killed the nuclear deal and "tightened the sanctions" in hopes of getting "a better deal."

That won't work. First, Trump threw away a ten-year agreement that froze the Iranian nuclear program and received no viable alternative agreement in return. He is left wishing and hoping that more sanctions and economic coercion will somehow force Iran to totally give up nuclear weapons. But guess again. Wishing and hoping is not a strategy. To make matters worse, Trump has undermined Rouhani, who trusted the United States to honor its side of the agreement.

Instead, Trump's withdrawal from JCPOA and his re-imposition of severe sanctions will almost certainly backfire by strengthening the hand of the hard-liners in Iran who argue that you can't trust America to honor an international commitment. America will just find another excuse to bully you with economic coercion. In short, America will betray you.

The IRGC hard-liners in Iran will likely gain the upper hand over Rouhani and the reformers. At home, the hard-liners will stifle political and economic reform. White House threats of regime change in Iran will raise concerns among the Iranian hard-liners of confrontation with the United States, Israel and Saudi Arabia. In response, the hard-liners in Tehran will shore up support for its regional proxy forces as a form of deterrence. This will increase tensions between Iran and Saudi Arabia and raise the risk of conflict between Iran and Israel in southern Syria.[34]

Much of the chapter reviewed how the previous round of economic coercion hurt the economy. Trump's "severe economic sanctions," which will begin in November 2018, will also hurt the Iranian economy, but they will also arguably backfire and hurt the global oil market and security in the Middle East.[35]

On the Iranian economic front, the US withdrawal from JCPOA and the re-imposition of sanctions will reduce oil export earnings. This kind of economic coercion will also deprive the economy of the Western capital, technology and managerial skills necessary to make the transition to a free market economic model easier. Instead, Trump's severe sanctions will force him to implement his "resistance economy." This will entrench an inward, nationalistic, socialistic economic model while protecting the militant IRGC and religious businesses in Iran at the expense of foreign (Western) investors.

Trump is also learning that sanctions are a double-edge sword and are already backfiring and hurting the US and global economy. Since Iran is a major global oil producer and exporter, Trump's plan to cut off its oil exports will likely cause global oil supplies to fall and oil prices to rise. The specter of high oil prices (and the trade war with China) has already been baked into the pie on Wall Street. As of late October 2018, The US stock market gains have been wiped out through October 2018.[36] Investors saw a sea of red on Wall Street on the eve of the November US Congressional elections in November 2018.

The only good news is that the other P5 plus 1 member want to continue the nuclear agreement with Iran. They are willing to develop their own financial agreement with Iran which does not require US banks or Trump's agreement. The bad news is that Trump's rejection of the nuclear agreement drives one more wedge between America and its post-World War II allies.

Trump looked at Iran with historic determinism. He argued that it was "inevitable" that Iran would use the "lion's share" of its $100 billion in unfrozen assets to fund instability. But the past does not have to be a precedent for the future. In fact, Iran has a choice[37]:

- Option 1: Use the money to finance more instability.
- Option 2: Use the money to rebuild its infrastructure and revive its economy.

86 *Iran*

Iran's support for instability is not inevitable. It can choose re-entry into the global economy. The United States is not a helpless bystander. If Trump loses in 2020, a new US president could work with the US private sector and shape Iran's decision to benefit from a web of economic interdependence as a responsible stakeholder. The United States and its allies could tilt the playing field and shape's Iran's decision to pursue option two, but instead of wishing for Iran to choose option 2, a new US president would need to work for it with the Iranians. Iran should consider using the $100 billion in unfrozen assets from the nuclear deal to recapitalize a restructured banking sector.

In a broader sense, a new US president in 2020 needs to work closely with the US oil companies, US carmakers, etc. to boost investment and trade with Iran. When this happens, a web of economic interdependence occurs. In this case, Iran develops a stake in shared prosperity. Once Iran becomes a responsible stakeholder, it will think twice before it does anything blatant to destabilize the region and throw it all away.

That does not mean that the US and Iran will always see the world in the same way. Their interests and policies may often diverge. But when US and Iranian interests largely converge, as they did in Iraq against ISIS, the US should not cave to political correctness. The US should cooperate with Iran to maximize our chances of success against terrorist groups like ISIS in Syria.

Notes

1 The nuclear deal is called the Joint Comprehensive Plan of Action (or JCPOA).
2 Economist Intelligence Unit, *Iran on a Knife's Edge: As Nuclear Deal Goes Up in Smoke*, The Economist Intelligence Unit Limited, London, 2018.
3 Katrina Manson, "Donald Trump Set to Repudiate Iran Nuclear Agreement", *Financial Times*, 13 October 2017.
4 Edward Luce, "Donald Trump Goes for Global Change", *Financial Times*, 8 May 2018.
5 Demetri Sevastopulo, Mehreen Khan and Najmeh Bozorgmehr, "US Reimposes Economic Sanctions on Iran", *Financial Times*, 6 August 2018.
6 See Jason Rezaian, "In UN Speech, Trump Fails (again) to Make His Iran Case", *The Washington Post*, 25 September 2018.
7 The fall of oil prices from over $100 a barrel to over half that made a bad situation worse.
8 Mark Glassman, "What Sanctions Have Done to Iran's Economy", *Bloomberg*, 2 March 2015.
9 See Najmeh Bozorgmehr and Monavar Khalaj, "Businessmen Eye Huge Opportunities in Iran", *Financial Times*, 14 July 2015.
10 Benoit Faucon, "In Iran, Business Deals are Rarely Smooth", *The Wall Street Journal*, 15 July 2015.
11 Steve Johnson, "Investors Eye Iranian Opening", *Financial Times*, 7 July 2015.
12 See Alex Barker, "Powers Face Daunting Task in Untangling Complex Web of Sanctions", *Financial Times*, 14 July 2015 and CSAG, "Some Consequences of Lifting International Sanctions Against Iran", *Snapshot Paper*, 2015–2019, 2 June 2015 and CSAG, "Sanctions and Iran – A Complex Web," *CSAG Strategy Paper*, 2015–2018, 14 April 2015.

Iran 87

13 Rouzbeh Pirouz, "Iran Imposed Crippling Sanctions on Itself", _Financial Times_, 20 July 2015.
14 Ibid.
15 Demetri Sevastopulo, Mehreen Khan and Najmeh Bozorgmehr, "US Reimposes Economic Sanctions on Iran", _Financial Times_, 6 August 2018.
16 Gideon Rachman, "The New World Order: Donald Trump Goes It Alone", _Financial Times_, 11 May 2018.
17 Ibid.
18 Ibid.
19 Chris Adams, Najmeh Bozorgmehr and Ed Crooks, "Iran: The Oil and Gas Multi-Billion Candy Store", _Financial Times_, 16 July 2015.
20 Ibid.
21 Anjli Raval, "Iran's Return to Oil Market to Weigh on Crude Prices", _Financial Times_, 14 July 2015.
22 Ibid.
23 Ibid.
24 Najmeh Bozorgmehr, Dave Sheppard and Neil Hume, "Glencore Executives Visit Tehran for Oil Talks", _Financial Times_, 2 July 2015.
25 Robin M. Mills, "Global Oil Companies will Welcome Iran Deal", _Financial Times_, 16 July 2015.
26 Eric Yep, "Iran Faces Battle to Win Back Asia Oil Market Share", _The Wall Street Journal_, 16 July 2015.
27 Ibid.
28 _The Economist_, "Iran's Economy: Fading Hope", 7 March 2015.
29 That said, European oil companies suspect that US oil companies have already secured oil deals with Iran, notwithstanding the sanctions. Time will tell. _The Economist_, "Iran's Economy: Fading Hope", 7 March 2015.
30 Benoit Faucon, "In Iran, Business Deals Rarely Smooth", _The Wall Street Journal_, 15 July 2015.
31 Adams et al., "Iran: The Oil and Gas Multi-Billion Candy Store".
32 Ibid.
33 Faucon, "In Iran, Business Deals Rarely Smooth".
34 Economist Intelligence Unit, "Iran on a Knife's Edge: As Nuclear Deal Goes Up in Smoke".
35 Ibid.
36 See Robin Wigglesworth, Steve Johnson and Katie Martin, "No Hiding Place for Investors in Markets Wobble", _Financial Times_, 26 October 2018 and Robin Wigglesworth, Adam Samson and Michael Hunter, "US Stocks Head for Worst Month since the Financial Crisis", _Financial Times_, 26 October 2018.
37 Anwar Gargash, "The Fate of a Febrile Middle East is in Iran's Hands", _Financial Times_, 16 July 2015.

Bibliography

Akbarzadeh, Shahram and Conduit, Dara. _Iran in the World: President Rouhani's Foreign Policy_, Palgrave MacMillan, London, January 20, 2016.
Albinson, Henry. _Iran History: Society, Economy, Government, Politics, the Iran-Iraq War, Relations with Regional Powers_, Smashwords, Los Gatos, CA, 2016.
Alizadeh, Parvin and Hakimian, Hassan. _Iran and the Global Economy: Petro Populism, Islam and Economic Sanctions_ (The Routledge Political Economy of the Middle East and North Africa Series), Routledge, New York, NY, June 30, 2016.

88 *Iran*

Calabrese, John. *Revolutionary Horizons: Regional Foreign Policy in Post-Khomeini Iran* (International Political Economy Series), Palgrave MacMillan, London, January 14, 2014.

Economist Intelligence Unit. *Iran on a Knife's Edge: As Nuclear Deal Goes Up in Smoke*, The Economist Intelligence Unit Limited, London, 2018.

Erlich, Reese. *The Iran Agenda Today: The Real Story Inside Iran and What's Wrong with U.S. Policy*, Routledge, New York, NY, September 17, 2018.

Kamel, Amir M. *The Political Economy of EU Ties with Iraq and Iran: An Assessment of the Trade-Peace Relationship* (The Political Economy of the Middle East), Palgrave Macmillan, New York, NY, 2015.

Maloney, Suzanne. *Iran's Political Economy since the Revolution Paperback*, Cambridge University Press, Cambridge, August 13, 2015.

Marvin, Uzo. *Iran History: Society, Economy, Government, Politics, the Iran-Iraq War, Relations with Regional Powers*, Adlibris, Finland, March 7, 2016.

Mason, Robert. *Foreign Policy in Iran and Saudi Arabia: Economics and Diplomacy in the Middle East* (Library of Modern Middle East Studies), I.B. Tauris and Company, London, December 31, 2014.

Nephew, Richard. *The Art of Sanctions: A View from the Field* (Center on Global Energy Policy Series), Columbia University Press, New York, NY, December 12, 2017.

Pesaran, Evaleila. *Iran's Struggle for Economic Independence: Reform and Counter-Reform in the Post-Revolutionary Era*, Routledge Political Economy of the Middle East and North Africa, Cambridge, March 5, 2013.

Rosser, J. Barkley Jr. and Rosser, Marina. *Comparative Economics in a Transforming World Economy*, The MIT Press, Cambridge, MA, January 26, 2018.

Saikal, Amin. *Iran at the Crossroads*, Polity Press, Cambridge, 2016.

United States Congressional Research Service. "Iran: U.S. Economic Sanctions and the Authority to Lift Restrictions", January 22, 2016, R43311, Available at: www.refworld.org/docid/56bc468f4.html [accessed October 12, 2018].

U.S. Government and Library of Congress. *Iran: Federal Research Study and Country Profile with Comprehensive Information, History, and Analysis*, Washington, DC, May 20, 2017.

8 Qatar

During Arab Spring, thousands of Shia protesters gathered in Manama, Bahrain, with longstanding and legitimate social and economic grievances. Instead of fostering an initial national dialogue, the Obama administration did nothing to stop Sunni ally Saudi Arabia's invasion of Bahrain in March of 2011, at the request of the repressive Bahrain Sunni royal family, to quell Shiite protests. In November 2011, the Bahrain government conceded that it had used "excessive force" against the peaceful demonstration,[1] and the US Secretary of Defense conceded that Iran had nothing to do with the demonstration.[2]

More recently, a similar Saudi invasion was planned for Qatar. The plan was reportedly for the Saudi and the United Arab Emirates (UAE) military forces to invade Qatar and advance 70 miles to conquer Qatar militarily. The good news is that then US Secretary of State Rex Tillerson was able to intervene and stop another Saudi invasion.[3]

The bad news is that the quartet had a back-up plan. On 5 June 2017, America found itself in the middle of the worst diplomatic crisis among Persian Gulf nations since Iraqi dictator Saddam Hussein invaded Kuwait in 1990. Four Arab countries (Saudi Arabia, the UAE, Bahrain and Egypt) slammed Qatar for its alleged support for terrorism and cut diplomatic relations with Doha. The quartet also imposed a regional embargo on Qatar. They cut land, sea and air links to the country.

About three weeks later, the quartet issued 13 demands to Qatar. The list included closing Al Jazeera (Doha's flagship satellite television network), cutting ties to Islamists and paying reparations. The list also demanded that Qatar curb its relations with Iran, close a Turkish military base and halt all military co-operation with Ankara before the embargo would be lifted.[4]

Unfortunately, Rex Tillerson was unable to stop this back-up plan because his boss, US President Donald Trump, reportedly tilted toward the Saudis and then openly supported the quartet's economic coercion of Qatar.[5] Once again, Washington had a strategic choice. It could opt for the logic of Jean Monnet and George Marshall and embrace economic diplomacy and shared prosperity with the quartet and Qatar, or it could cave into the quartet's economic coercion of Qatar.

90   Qatar

It's important to understand the larger stakes for the region. The Saudis were frustrated that a small Sunni country like Qatar was too independent in its foreign policy. Qatar had refused to toe the Saudi party line. The boycott was all about putting pressure on the maverick country to get onboard with a Saudi war by proxy against Shia Iran.[6]

That raises the question: Why was Sunni Qatar so friendly toward Shia Iran? The answer is that Qatar's cordial ties with Iran have nothing to do with religion. What's important is the fact that Qatar and Iran share ownership of the South Pars/North Dome natural gas field, by far the largest natural gas field in the world.[7]

Thus, shared prosperity far outweighs religious differences between Sunni Qatar and Shia Iran. Just as Jean Monnet used a man-made European Coal and Steel Community to turn German and French enemies into friends, Qatar and Iran have been successfully using the natural gas field to turn potential enemies (Shia Iran and Sunni Qatar) into economic partners.

That raises another important question: Did America have the leverage to foster an economic grand bargain of shared prosperity between the Sunni quartet and this Iranian-Qatar economic partnership? The answer is yes. America had a window of opportunity to use military and political leverage to mediate the conflict, promote shared prosperity and thus mitigate the demand for economic coercion and violence. What was missing was political will and strategic creativity.

In this regard, America has cross-cutting loyalties. On the one hand, Al Udeid Air Base, near Doha in Qatar, is the largest US Air Force base in the Middle East. The forward headquarters of the US Central Command (or CENTCOM) is located on the base, along with 10,000 US troops. Qatar also buys fighter jets from America, the United Kingdom and the French. On the other hand, America also has strong political and military equities with the quartet. The Fifth Fleet is in Bahrain, and the US military has strong military assistance programs with all four countries in the quartet.[8]

With strong military ties with all participants in the conflict, America did not have to play either the role of helpless bystander or be complicit in the boycott against Qatar. America could have stood up to the Saudi bully and insisted on shared prosperity rather than economic coercion. Unfortunately, Trump refused to support his embattled US Secretary of State Rex Tillerson, who pushed hard for shared prosperity. Trump caved to Saudi-led economic coercion against Qatar.

That raises another question. Even if one buys the Saudi logic of economic coercion, did this coercion work? Initially, it did exactly what it was intended to do. The sanctions slashed Qatari trade, shattered business confidence in Qatar and shook up its financial system.[9] Its Gross Domestic Product (GDP) growth fell from 2.5% in 1Q 2017 to 0.6% in 2Q 2017. Imports fell 40% month on month in June and July of 2017.[10]

In addition, there was the risk that a prolonged reduction of construction for the World Cup could threaten the global football tournament itself. Not surprisingly, Fitch downgraded Qatar's credit rating and gave it a negative outlook.[11]

As cited earlier, the quartet imposed a regional embargo by cutting land, sea and air transport links to Qatar. This embargo hurt various sectors of the Qatari economy. The boycott's impact was most visible in some of the service sub-sectors. Transportation, storage, lodging and food service were all down year on year.[12]

Before the embargo, the construction sector was a key driver of the Qatari economy and was partially dependent on overland routes for supplies. Once the embargo was put into place, quartet officials curbed building materials, which had previously come by truck over the Salwa border with Saudi Arabia (Qatar's only land border).[13]

Before the embargo, a significant portion of Qatar's food supply had also come over land via Saudi Arabia. The embargo curbed food shipments, which initially caused food prices and overall inflation to rise.[14]

Embattled Qatar businesses were forced to switch to more costly air and sea routes, but that wasn't easy either because the country is largely surrounded by the airspace of its three Gulf neighbors (Saudi Arabia, Bahrain and the UAE). Qatar Airways flights were forced to take a narrow northern air corridor to go around Saudi Arabia before heading to destinations to the west and south. This circuitous route sharply reduced Qatar's accessibility by air and increased travel times.

The loss of air routes and the costly circuitous routes hurt the bottom line of Qatar Airways. There was a 32% decline in passenger air traffic into and out of Hamad International Airport between May 2017 and the end of June. There was an 18% fall on an annual level, and passenger arrival levels dropped by 34%, as compared to July 2016 levels. There was also a 59% drop in hotel occupancy rates in July.[15]

In addition, there were financial jitters. Technically, the boycott only applied to trade and movement, and did not restrict financial transfer or investment in Qatar. But financial fears were initially pervasive. Not surprisingly, the embargo triggered sharp capital outflows in the early months after its launch in June 2017. At first glance, most of the capital outflows appeared to be withdrawals by non-resident depositors based in the boycotting states, but there also appeared to be panic transfers by Qatari residents and foreign investors worried about possible devaluation or capital controls.[16]

While the initial blow to Qatar's economy was sharp, it was also short and did not cripple the economy. That's because its government was well prepared to weather the storm. For instance, the initial panic buying of food did not give a fair representation of food inventories, which were enough to cover a year of domestic consumption, according to government officials. And fortunately for Qatar, it had large inventories of many key imported items (such as construction materials at major project sites).

92 *Qatar*

Qatar's government also had a medium-term resiliency plan. It established new direct shipping lines in several ports, including China, India, Malaysia, Taiwan, Turkey, Greece, Oman and Kuwait. Thanks to new trade routes, Qatar softened the blow to imports.

Qatar has been overhauling its supply chain by establishing new shipping routes with countries such as India and Oman, and developing the infrastructure around Hamad Port, the first stage of which had opened only a few months before the crisis began.[17]

Most importantly, Qatar had robust financial buffers. Thanks to over $300 billion in its sovereign wealth fund and $40 billion in foreign reserves, the central bank had 6.7 months of import cover in its foreign reserves in September – far more than the three months that is normally adequate. Thus, Doha could sell foreign reserves to prop up the riyal when the peg to the dollar came under pressure.[18] In addition, Doha injected ample liquidity into banks. Qatar's allies (Iran and Turkey) also helped to plug financial gaps.[19]

Despite the boycott-induced rise in food prices, inflation stayed low and stable after a spike in June. Low inflation reflected increased government spending on subsidies to shield consumers from higher import costs. As a result, interest rates remained within the central bank's low 2% to 4% comfort zone.[20]

Meanwhile, the quartet learned that sanctions are a doubled-edged sword. If the goal of the boycott was to get Qatar to toe the line against Iran, the boycott backfired in this area as well. For the foreseeable future, Qatar will remain in Iran's camp. The sanctions also rewarded Iran. In the summer of 2017, its exports to Qatar grew by 60%. Qatar's imports from Iran increased fivefold between 2017 and 2018. Iran's new wealth from lucrative overflight rights also strengthened its military power.[21]

Finally, the boycott was a negative financial blow to the UAE.

Take the UAE, for example. Before the boycott, Jebel Ali, just south of Dubai, was the busiest port in the region. It handled over 33% of cargoes in the Gulf and 85% of shipborne cargo for Qatar. Not anymore. The boycott accelerated the rapid decline of Jebel Ali's previously large market share. In September 2017, Qatar opened Hamad, a new $7.4 billion port that allowed shippers to bypass the UAE altogether. The boycott accelerated this shift away from Dubai. Qatar Navigation moved its regional hub from the UAE to Oman. Oman's trade with Qatar grew 2,000% in the summer of 2017. Traffic at its port, Salalah, rose 29%.[22]

Imports rose in August, and by October, the worst of Qatar's import disruptions were over, with imports close to pre-boycott levels. In October, imports rose by 53% month on month and 11% year on year, the steepest increase in over two years. In absolute terms, imports reached QR12.3 billion (US$3.4 billion), a record high and 32% above the average monthly level in the year prior to the crisis.[23]

Qatar's macroeconomics also bounced back in Q3 2017. After weak growth in 2Q 2017, reflecting the initial shock in June, Qatar's GDP rose 1.9% year on year and 5.5% quarter on quarter in Q3 2017.[24]

Fortunately, the core hydrocarbons sector was not visibly affected by the boycott and in fact posted its strongest quarter on record. The non-oil sector also performed well, despite drags on some sectors from the boycott. In fact, this sector posted record output, up by 3.6% year on year and 4.5% quarter on quarter. Two non-oil drivers of growth came from construction (up 14.7%) and manufacturing (up 5.1%).[25] Thankfully, declines in tourism did not cripple the economy. On the financial front, there was also improvement. Monthly banking sector data for November showed a continued stabilization. The deposit flight of non-residents continued to slow in November.

In addition to its economic bounce back, Qatar was projecting confidence about its future. It announced two new initiatives for the gas sector. Qatar Petroleum (QP) announced plans to double the size of its planned expansion of its North Field – the country's main source of liquid natural gas (LNG) exports. It also signed a new partnership with the oil major Royal Dutch Shell.[26]

The quartet was obviously frustrated about the fact that its economic coercion against Qatar was a strategic failure. That raises the question: Why didn't the quartet try to disrupt shipments of Qatar's vital export, natural gas? Doing that would have required preventing the hulking tanker ships that carry a super-cooled form of the fuel from reaching markets in Asia and elsewhere. Such a move would likely have involved militarily blocking Qatar's ports or preventing its ships from entering the Strait of Hormuz, the key passageway at the mouth of the Persian Gulf. Those measures would have been tantamount to a declaration of war against Qatar.

In this regard, Qatar's political/military actions make it clear to the quartet that its air force is well prepared to fight a war against the quartet. For over two decades, the core of the Qatar Air Force has been 12 third-generation Mirage 2000 jets, produced by France's Dassault. The total price tag of all these jets, and associated service contracts, is huge for Qatar – around US$28 billion (17% of GDP). The number and range of models is highly unusual. Qatar also signed orders for 120 more fighter jets. These orders put it ahead of the UAE and close to Saudi Arabia in number of fighter jets in service.

The message to the quartet is clear. The jets are intended as both a direct deterrence and as a way of consolidating key diplomatic relationships. Qatar uses these weapons purchases as a means of maintaining and securing diplomatic ties with the United States, the United Kingdom and France.[27]

Notes

1 See Ethan Bronner and Michael Slackman, "Saudi Troops Enter Bahrain to Help Put Down Unrest", *The New York Times*, 14 March 2011.
2 Michael Hughes, "Saudi-Backed Crackdown in Bahrain Exposes US Hypocrisy", *The Sunday Times*, Sri Lanka, 20 March 2011.

94 Qatar

3 See Alex Emmons, "Saudi Arabia Planned to Invade Qatar Last Summer. Rex Tillerson's Efforts to Stop It May Have Cost Him His Job", *The Intercept*, 1 August 2018.

4 Simeon Kerr, "Qatar Casts Aside List of Demands by Arab States", *Financial Times*, 24 June 2017.

5 Katrina Manson, "Qatar and Arabs Rivals Play Different Sides of Team Trump", *Financial Times*, 4 July 2017.

6 See Roula Khalaf, "The Rise and Fall of Maverick Qatar", *Financial Times*, 7 June 2017; Simeon Kerr, "Saudi Arabia, UAE, Bahrain, and Egypt Cut Ties with Qatar", *Financial Times*, 5 June 2017 and Simeon Kerr, "Crisis in the Gulf: Qatar Faces a Stress Test", *Financial Times*, 9 June 2017.

7 See Robin Mills, "Qatar Warms Up to Iran on Natural Gas", *Bloomberg*, 19 July 2017. Largest gas field in the world.

8 See "US (Military) Strength in the Persian Gulf", *Washington Post*, 24 February 2018.

9 See Economist Intelligence Unit, "Gulf Crisis Brings Significant Economic Disruption to Qatar", 9 June 2017 and David Sheppard, "Qatar Faces Higher Gas Shipments Costs after UAE Imposes Port Ban", *Financial Times*, 6 June 2017.

10 Qatar's Ministry of Development Planning and Statistics, for October 2017, Doha, Qatar.

11 See Simeon Kerr, "Qatar Crisis Sends Tremors through Banking in the Gulf", *Financial Times*, 12 October 2017.

12 Qatar's Ministry of Development Planning and Statistics for October 2017, Doha, Qatar.

13 Ibid.

14 See Simeon Kerr, "Crisis in the Gulf: Qatar Faces a Stress Test", *Financial Times*, 9 June 2017.

15 Qatar's Ministry of Development Planning and Statistics for October 2017, Doha, Qatar.

16 Simeon Kerr, "Qatar Sends Tremors through Banking in the Gulf", *Financial Times*, 12 October 2017.

17 See Gordon Platt, "Qatar: Economy Resilient Despite Boycott", *Global Finance*, 7 December 2017 and Economist Intelligence Unit, "Oman Opens up Shipping Routes to Qatar", 16 June 2017.

18 See Nicholas Megaw and Roger Blitz, "Gulf Dispute Sparks Worries Over Qatar's Currency", *Financial Times*, 6 June 2017.

19 Andrew England, "Qatar's Wealth Fund Brings $20bn Home to Ease Impact of Embargo", *Financial Times*, 18 October 2017 and Economist Intelligence Unit, "Qatar: Country Risk Service", December 2017.

20 Economist Intelligence Unit, "Qatar: Country Risk Service".

21 See Simeon Kerr, "Qatar Restores Diplomatic Ties with Iran", *The Washington Post*, 24 August 2017: and Simeon Kerr, Qatar pins hopes on domestic renewal, Financial Times, 18 October 2019.

22 Economist, "The Boycott of Qatar Is Hurting Its Enforces", *The Economist*, 19 October 2017.

23 Economist Intelligence Unit, "Qatar: Imports Surge in October", 14 October 2017.

24 Qatar's Ministry of Development Planning and Statistics.

25 Ibid.

26 See Economist Intelligence Unit, "Qatar Steps Up Gas Sector Expansion Plans Despite Boycott", 10 July 2017 and Economist Intelligence Unit, "Qatar Bets on LNG Demand Growth", 31 October 2017.

27 See Economist Intelligence Unit, "Qatar: Country Report", October 2018.

Bibliography

Anscombe, Frederick F. *The Ottoman Gulf: The Creation of Kuwait, Saudi Arabia, and Qatar*, Columbia University Press, New York, NY, 1997.

Cordesman, Anthony H. Bahrain, *Oman, Qatar, and the UAE: Challenges of Security*, Westview Press, Boulder, CO, 1997.

Crystal, Jill. *Oil and Politics in the Gulf: Rulers and Merchants in Kuwait and Qatar*, Cambridge University Press, Cambridge, 1995.

Ferdinand, Klaus. *Bedouins of Qatar*, Rhodos International Science and Art Publishers, Copenhagen, 1993.

Mallakh, Ragaei El. *Qatar: Development of an Oil Economy*, Croom Helm, London, 1979.

Rahman, Habibur. *The Emergence of Qatar the Turbulent Years 1627–1916*, Kegan Paul, London and New York, 2005.

Reed, Stanley. "Liquefied Natural Gas Makes Qatar an Energy Giant", *The New York Times*, August 5, 2015.

Sadik, Muhammad T. and Snavely, William P. Bahrain, *Qatar, and the United Arab Emirates: Colonial Past, Present Problems, and Future Prospects*, Lexington Books, Lexington, 1972.

Saud, Abeer Abu. *Qatari Women: Past and Present*, Longman, London, 1984.

Smith, Simon C, *Britain's Revival and Fall in the Gulf: Kuwait, Bahrain, Qatar, and the Trucial States, 1950–1971*, Routledge, London, 2004.

Zahlan, Rosemarie Said. *The Creation of Qatar*, Routledge, London, 1989.

Zahlan, Rosemarie Said. *The Making of the Modern Gulf States: Kuwait, Bahrain, Qatar, the United Arab Emirates and Oman*, Routledge, London, 1989.

9 Lebanon

Not long ago, American foreign policymakers would celebrate democracies around the world having free elections. On 6 May 2018, Lebanon had its first parliamentary election in nine years, so, one might think that the Trump administration would have welcomed this democratic event. Lebanon also had its first budget in 12 years. Would Trump praise them and celebrate their good fortune? Guess again.

Forget the democratic process. Forget the will of the Lebanese people, who work hard to have a socially inclusive country. Forget the fact that Hezbollah is popular because it is also a social movement which supports health care and education for downtrodden Shia in the country and throughout the Middle East. Forget the fact that Hezbollah's militia fought against the ISIS terrorist group in Syria when America put it on the back burner. Forget the fact that Hezbollah has its own military, which stands up to the Israeli army and protects the country. The Trump presidency didn't like the results.

The parliamentary election saw Hezbollah gain ground. Hezbollah, a Shia group, and its allies (which included the predominantly Christian Free Patriotic Movement (FPM) of President Michel Aoun) had a slight majority in parliament, having secured at least 67 of the 128 seats. Prime Minister Saad Hariri, who leads the Future Movement, a Sunni party, emerged as the biggest loser from the election.[1]

Since Hezbollah is a Shia group with good relations with Shia Iran, Trump has come down hard against it. In July 2019, the US Treasury Department announced that it was levying economic sanctions against Lebanon's Jammal Trust Bank for having "illicit" financial activities with Hezbollah. The US demanded that the Lebanese government close the Jammal Trust Bank, freeze its deposits and prevent it from paying any debts. Riad Salameh, Lebanon's central bank governor, quickly moved to carry out the order. He announced a freeze on the bank's operations and handed over account management to the central bank until a solution could be found. Apparently, President Trump didn't care that the Jammal Trust Bank had drawn praise in 2018 for close cooperation with the US Agency for International Development (USAID) and for its "Save and Win" campaign to encourage Lebanese citizens to increase savings.[2]

The Trump administration also announced sanctions on seven Lebanese companies for providing material support to Hezbollah amid renewed US threats to target any government ministries that are allocated to the party.[3] Needless to say, the democratically elected Lebanese government does not appreciate this kind of economic coercion from Donald Trump. The Lebanese government is trying to influence Trump to limit the impact of these new sanctions that reportedly target the allies of Hezbollah.

In July 2017, President Trump appeared at a news conference in the Rose Garden of the White House with Lebanese Prime Minister Saad Hariri. Trump lumped the Lebanese militant group Hezbollah with the militants and terrorists he praised Lebanon's government for fighting. President Trump praised Lebanon for being "on the front lines" of a shared battle against violent extremism. The only problem? Hezbollah is a political partner of the man who was standing next to Trump, Saad Hariri.[4] Oops. Was it possible that President Trump was content free on the democratic process in Lebanon? Or was he just ill-advised?

In any event, President Trump probably knows even less about Lebanon's complex economy, which has been struggling to foster social inclusion and make things work for all Lebanese people. After 12 years without a budget, this government, led by new Prime Minister Saad Hariri, also put together a $15.8 billion budget. It is difficult enough to strike a delicate political balance and build a consensus now that Hezbollah has a narrow majority in parliament. The last thing the country currently needs is Donald Trump unleashing economic coercion against the democratically elected Hezbollah.

While Trump's economic coercion against Lebanon is clear, what is not so clear is whether the new government will at least try to create a new economic model. One thing is certain. Lebanon's old economic model has dangerously over-borrowed, domestically and externally. The government borrowed too much money for political patronage rather than for infrastructure. Prior to the Syrian Civil War, Lebanon's financial offsets enabled it to resist economic collapse. Strategic enablers included strong banks and capital inflow from a rich diaspora and GCC countries.

That said, the Syrian Civil War and the rise of ISIS have seriously damaged Lebanon's economy.[5] Shocks include falling exports and tourism, the Gulf Cooperation Council (GCC) capital outflow and over 1.4 million Syrian refugees – 20% of the size of Lebanon's population.[6] Thankfully, the International Monetary Fund (IMF) notes that Lebanon's central bank and commercial banks are still rock-solid and have kept the shaky economy afloat. However, the deterioration of an over-borrowed Lebanese economy can't go on indefinitely. There are finite limits, even for the financial power of Lebanon's commercial banks. A new economic model needs to be created based on shared prosperity rather than on patronage.

The biggest threat to Lebanon's economy is a prolonged period of military conflict and political instability that could undermine investor confidence. This scenario could trigger capital flight – money moving almost overnight

98   *Lebanon*

from Lebanon bank deposits to safe-havens overseas. That scenario could threaten Lebanon's local bank's ability to meet the huge borrowing needs of its government. It is also a service-oriented economy, which makes it especially vulnerable to capital flight whenever confidence dips.

Even before the Syrian Civil War, Lebanon faced some serious economic challenges. These included high unemployment, poverty and an over-borrowed public sector. But the Syrian conflict has made things much worse, resulting in a broad-based deterioration of the Lebanese economy. This chapter explains how the Syrian conflict has damaged Lebanon's economy and how it tests its financial stability.

As the Syrian civil war spilled over the Syrian Lebanese border, the war polarized Lebanon, a country with a long history of sectarian conflicts. Shiite supporters of Syrian President Assad fight against Sunni supporters of Assad's opposition. Sunni towns, like Arsal, and Shiite towns in the Bekaa Valley are battlegrounds in the proxy war.[7] In this Syrian civil war that has spilled over into Lebanon, there is once again an absence of the social inclusion and shared prosperity, as we've seen in civil wars elsewhere in the Middle East. President Trump's economic coercion against a democratically elected government makes matters worse. In such extended war zones, it's not surprising that tourism, investor confidence and trade have all taken a hit.

In this regard, tourism plays a central role in Lebanon's economy. In fact, when times are good, it accounts for 20% of Lebanon's Gross Domestic Product (GDP). Times were good in 2010, when tourist arrivals reached 2 million, the most in 15 years. Many of these tourists came from rich GCC countries. But tourism has been all downhill since then. As violence from Syria spilled into Lebanon, it lost its attractiveness as a safe tourist destination.[8] The UAE and Saudi Arabia issued travel warnings to their populations against Lebanon.

As a result, in late January 2017, the IMF noted that "Lebanon's traditional drivers of GDP growth" – such as tourism (along with real estate and construction) – "have received a significant blow and a strong rebound is unlikely based on current trends."[9] Similarly, the Syrian conflict has also hurt foreign direct investment (FDI) inflows into Lebanon. FDI into Lebanon fell 23% in 2014.[10] Lebanon's Consumer Confidence Index fell in both May and June 2014.[11] The World Bank notes that remittance inflow (from Lebanese living outside Lebanon) fell 8.4% in 2014 and 3.3% in 2015.

In addition, the economies of Syria and Lebanon are inextricably connected. Nowhere is this more visible than in Lebanon's trade. Previously, 40% of all Lebanon's exports travelled through Syria for destinations such as Jordan, Turkey and Iraq, but due to the Syrian conflict, Lebanese trucks have been blocked from passing through Syria, and the road between Damascus and Amman is inaccessible. As a result, Lebanon's exports fell 35% in the first quarter of 2014 compared to the same period in 2013.[12] Two-way trade over land routes fell 55% between 2010 and 2013.[13] So, transport must take more expensive circuitous routes in and out of Lebanon. Consequently, its exports were about 25–30% lower in 2015 and 2016 than they were in 2012–2013.[14]

Why doesn't Lebanon use a maritime alternative to ship its exports? Actually, it has opened a ferry route through Suez to Aqaba, but the maritime route is slower and rougher, and damages exports of fruit and other perishables. This route is also more expensive for exporters, thus sapping their competitiveness.[15]

In addition, the most dramatic economic and social effect that the Syrian Civil War has had on Lebanon may be the influx of over 1.4 million Syrian refugees. That's the highest concentration of refugees per capita in modern history. Despite attempts to block further refugees, before long, the number of refugees is expected to make up half the Lebanese population. Syrian refugees increase the demand for basic infrastructure. Refugees put extra economic strains on water, electricity, primary education and health care.[16] Syrian workers also take jobs away from mostly poor Lebanese and push down wages for others.[17]

The impact of the conflict on Lebanon's weak labor market may be the biggest economic vulnerability and the biggest threat to social stability. Syrian workers accept wages 25% to 50% lower than those accepted by Lebanese workers. To make matters worse, the international community provides Syrian refugees with money to cover their health care expenses, while poor, unemployed Lebanese receive no health care support. Discontent and resentment from poor, frustrated Lebanese who have lost their jobs to Syrian refugees are understandable and provide fertile ground for extremists inside and outside of Lebanon to exploit the situation politically and militarily in a country that already has a culture full of violent sectarian conflicts.

Poverty and high unemployment were problems in Lebanon, even before the Syrian crisis, but the Syrian conflict now makes them much worse. The IMF expects the unemployment rate to nearly double in Lebanon from 11% to 20%. The World Bank estimates that the Syrian crisis will soon add 170,000 people to the number already living below the poverty line.[18]

Before the Syrian conflict, Lebanon's economy had been growing on average 9% a year from 2007 until 2010. But the decline in investment, tourism, retail trade and exports discussed earlier has taken its toll on Lebanon's overall economic growth. Its GDP growth slowed to just 1% in 2016. This slowdown has made it even more difficult for the Lebanese government to reduce its huge government debt. The financial burden can be seen in terms of the debt to GDP ratio. As GDP slowed from 9% growth to 1% growth, the burden of debt increases, even if the nominal debt does not increase much. In other words, the nominal debt becomes less affordable, but in the case of Lebanon, the large yearly budget deficit keeps increasing the financial burden.

How over-borrowed is the Lebanon economy? One way in which to measure financial vulnerability is to use EU yardsticks. An EU Maastricht

100 *Lebanon*

criterion says that entry into the EU club requires states to limit budget deficits to 3% of GDP. Another Maastricht criterion says that entry into the EU club requires governments to limit government debt to 60% of GDP. The EU says that anything over these two limits means that economies are vulnerable to a financial crisis and therefore should stay out of the EU. Unfortunately, the Lebanese government is heavily over-borrowed according to these criteria. The IMF notes that Lebanon is running a normally unstable government debt of 138% of GDP. That's huge – well over twice the 60% Maastricht limit.

In addition, the Economist Intelligence Unit (EIU) notes that Lebanon's budget deficit was about 10% of GDP in 2017. That's over three times the 3% Maastricht limit. Lebanon's trade deficit also appears to be in big trouble. If we use the more inclusive current account yardstick (which measures trade in goods and services), EIU notes that Lebanon is running a current account deficit of 17% of GDP. That means that it is running a current account deficit as a percentage of GDP that is over twice as big as those of Mexico and Thailand, both of which ran a financially unstable current account deficit of 8% of GDP prior to their financial meltdowns.

But appearances can sometimes be deceiving. This is because there is nothing conventional about the Lebanese economic model. This unorthodox system operates like no other economic model. Despite the rising costs associated with the Syrian civil war and the rise of ISIS, this unconventional economy keeps "defying gravity." How is this possible? Fortunately, the old Lebanese economic model has enjoyed numerous financial offsets, which have given it resilience to resist economic collapse. The short answer is that rich commercial banks provide liquidity to the central bank, which, in turn, constantly bails out the over-borrowed government.

But there is more to this story: (a) Investors know that the government has never defaulted on its debt payments, (b) most of the debt is held locally rather than in unforgiving foreign banks and (c) Lebanese commercial banks have assets that dwarf the real economy. So, they roll over government debt, which is relatively small, as a percent of their overall assets. Although Lebanon has labored under a massive government debt, confidence in Lebanese markets has been high in recent years due to internal financing from the central bank. Lebanon has also benefitted from large incoming foreign investment and the willingness of banks to maintain large liquidity as a buffer to defaults.

In addition, the Lebanese diaspora population is four times the number of Lebanese living inside Lebanon. It turns out that Lebanon has one of the highest numbers of diaspora billionaires. While this diaspora makes money outside of Lebanon, their hearts and loved ones still live in the country. Not surprisingly, this wealthy Lebanese diaspora consistently provides the country with high remittances of hard currency.

The IMF notes that Lebanon's remittance inflows are sizable and have averaged almost $7 billion in the last ten years. It is among the top five emerging-market receivers of remittances as a share of GDP, at 20% of output. In per capita terms, Lebanon tops the list by a wide margin. Most importantly, remittances to Lebanon also comprise a key part of its de-facto safety net. In addition, Lebanese banks find themselves in the enviable position of having excess capital. Bank deposits have been high, and the loan/deposit ratio has been low. In addition, the liquidity of its banks has been extraordinarily high.

Finally, if all else fails, the Lebanese central bank has lots of financial ammunition. A common rule of thumb is that three months of import cover is adequate for a country's foreign reserves. In fact, most over-borrowed economies would be hard-pressed to maintain three months of import cover. In contrast, EIU notes that the Lebanese central bank has amassed a huge supply of foreign reserves (or financial buffers), which could cover 18–20 months of imports. More importantly, the Lebanese central bank has this stockpile of foreign reserves to defend the foreign exchange rate of the Lebanese pound against financial attacks. But the same thing was said in 1993, when Mexico had $25 billion in foreign reserves. Things can change quickly. In January 1994, Presidents Clinton and Zedillo were toasting at a meeting of the North American Free Trade Agreement (NAFTA). Eleven months later, there was a run of the peso and capital flight, and Mexican reserves disappeared virtually overnight.

In conclusion, Syria's civil war and ISIS are ultimate tests for a deteriorating Lebanon's economy, in particular, its financial stability. The Lebanese commercial banks have been up to the test and have proven to be a pillar of strength. The booming banking sector has prevented further deterioration of the economy. Rich commercial banks provide liquidity to the central bank, which, in turn, draws from its huge stockpile of foreign reserves to bail out the over-borrowed government. But Lebanon's commercial banks are the last line of defense. Had the banks not been strong and resilient, the IMF would have been the next stop before financial turmoil. The deterioration of the Lebanese economy also can't go on indefinitely. Ultimately, there are limits to the financial power of its commercial banks. So, there is no time for complacency. Finally, Donald Trump's bullying and economic coercion will make things even more difficult.

Notes

1 Economist Intelligence Unit, "Lebanon: Parliamentary Election Sees Hezbollah Gain Ground", 8 May 2018.
2 Zvi Bar'el, "Lebanon Pays the Price for a Burden Called Hezbollah", *Haaretz*, 9 July 2019.
3 See Economist Intelligence Unit, "Lebanon: Fresh US Sanctions Announced on Hezbollah-linked Firms", 9 October 2018.
4 Anne Gearson, Trump erroneously says Lebanon is "on the front lines" in fighting Hezbollah, a partner in the Lebanese government, *Washington Post*, 25 July 2017.

102 *Lebanon*

5 See Mona Yacoubian, "Renewed Conflict in Lebanon, Council on Foreign Relations", *Council on Foreign Relations*, June 2014, and Faysal Itani, "Syria's War Threatens Lebanon's Fragile Economy", *Atlantic Council*, 9 July 2013.
6 World Population Review says Lebanon's population is almost 7 million people.
7 Barry Jongkees, "Drawn into the Conflict: The War in Syria and the Consequences for the Lebanese Economy", *Open Democracy*, 8 August 2013.
8 See Thomas Schellen, "The Ghosts of Seasons Yet to Come", *Executive*, 6 May 2014.
9 IMF, "IMF Executive Board Concludes Article IV Consultation", 24 January 2017.
10 *The Daily Star*, 25 January 2013.
11 *The Daily Star*, 27August 2014.
12 Economist Intelligence Unit, "Lebanon: Exports Suffer as Security Costs Reduce Competitiveness", 4 September 2014.
13 See Daniel Dombey, Shawn Donnan and John Reed, "Isis Advance Reverses Decade of Growth in Middle East Trade", *Financial Times*, 2 July 2014.
14 Discussions with Blominvest Bank Officials in Beirut in 2016.
15 Jongkees, "Drawn into the Conflict".
16 IMF, "Lebanon: Selected Issues", July 2014.
17 Toiufic Kasbar, "Syria War, Refugees Add to Lebanon's Economic Crisis", *Al Monitor*, 18 May 2014.
18 World Bank, "Lebanon: Economic and Social Impact Assessment of the Syrian Conflict", 24 September 2013 and IMF, "Lebanon: Selected Issues".

Bibliography

Daher, Joseph. *Hezbollah: The Political Economy of Lebanon's Party of God*, Pluto Press, London, 2016.

The Economist, "When the Music Stops", August 30, 2018.

Gaspard, Toufic. *A Political Economy of Lebanon, 1948–2002: The Limits of Laissez-Faire* (Social and Political Studies of the Middle East), 1st Edition, Brill, The Netherlands, 1992.

Gates, Carolyn. *Merchant Republic of Lebanon: Rise of an Open Economy*, I.B. Tauris and Company, London, 1998.

Makdisi, Samir. *The Lessons of Lebanon: The Economics of War and Development* (Library of Modern Middle East Studies), I.B. Tauris and Company, London, 2004.

Marois, Thomas, *States, Banks and Crisis: Emerging Finance Capitalism in Mexico and Turkey*, Edward Elgar Publishing, Cheltenham, 2012.

Safieddine, Hicham. *Banking on the State: The Financial Foundations of Lebanon*, Stanford Studies in Middle Eastern and Islamic Societies and Cultures, Redwood City, CA, 2019.

U.S. Government and Library of Congress, "Lebanon: Federal Research Study with Comprehensive Information, History, and Analysis – Politics, Economy, Military", Washington, DC, 2011.

10 Turkey

Turkey's economy appeared to be on a roll. But in economics, things can and often do change quickly. The country then headed for recession. To make matters worse, US sanctions are about to slam Turkey's economy in November 2018 because Turkey buys oil from Iran, a country whose nuclear agreement with the international community Trump just wrecked.

Needless to say, the timing of this US economic coercion against Turkey was not helpful to a North Atlantic Treaty Organization (NATO) country struggling to keep its economy afloat. Thus, it was just a matter of time before the vulnerable Turkish economy was in financial turmoil. In particular, the Turkish lira was vulnerable to shifts in foreign investor confidence. August 2018 was the month of reckoning. The Turkish lira fell 20% against a US dollar, which was getting stronger because the Federal Research (Fed) – the US central bank – was tightening US monetary policy to offset super loose US fiscal policy due to a huge US tax cut, soaring budget deficits and a trillion dollars more to be added to the national debt. In Turkey, inflation rose following the currency slide. That forced Turkey's central bank to raise interest rates to 24% on 13 September 2018. Turkish President Erdogan was unhappy because high interest rates would send the economy into a recession.

As stated earlier, there were five economic reasons for the currency crisis. First, Turkey has a structurally low national savings rate and large external financing requirement. The current account deficit was 5.6% of the Gross Domestic Product (GDP) in 2017. That made the lira vulnerable to a tightening in global liquidity due to rising interest rates in the United States, as cited earlier.

Second, the Turkish corporations cited earlier were highly indebted in foreign currency. Many were unable to service these debts. This triggered investor panic, capital flight and downward pressure on the lira.

Third, President Erdogan was implementing his executive presidency. Investors feared that he would politicize the central bank and be less willing to tighten monetary policy to offset Turkey's loose fiscal policy.

Fourth, Turkish tensions with Donald Trump were rising. In August, the United States imposed sanctions on Turkish individuals, and Donald

104 *Turkey*

Trump announced that US tariffs on Turkish steel and aluminum exports would double: US tariffs on Turkish steel would be 50%, and US tariffs on Turkish aluminum would rise to 30%.

Finally, Donald Trump also re-imposed sanctions on Iran. He wanted to curb Iran oil exports to countries like Turkey, and he would enforce this embargo with severe fines on any Turkish bank or company which used US dollars to finance purchases of Iranian oil. These American threats to punish Turkish banks or corporations caused Iranian bankers to be cautious about buying oil from Iran.

But because of Turkey's severe economic problems, as cited above, Erdogan needed to find ways to circumvent US sanctions and import Iranian oil. Therefore, he considered at least four ways to get around US sanctions. First, he could use euros or other local currencies instead of the US dollars to finance purchases of Iranian oil. Second, Turkey could try to arrange some barter deals that would offer Turkish goods instead of dollars in return for Iranian oil. Third, Turkey could buy oil from the Turkish private sector on the Turkish stock exchange. Fourth, it could use "ghost tankers" in an attempt to avoid the US tracking system.

To the casual observer, Turkey's currency crisis was a surprise because the economy appeared to be doing reasonably well. But in economics, things can and often do change quickly. The country is now headed for recession. To make matters worse, US sanctions were about to slam Turkey's economy in November 2018 because Turkey buys oil from Iran, a country whose nuclear agreement with the international community Trump just wrecked.[1] Needless to say, the timing of this US economic coercion against Turkey is not helpful to a fellow NATO country struggling to keep its economy afloat.

To be fair, President Trump may have had a positive image of Turkey's economic strength when he dreamed up economic coercion against it. At first glance, Turkey's economic performance appeared impressive. Its strong macroeconomic policies have dramatically improved socio-economic outcomes since the 2001 financial crisis. The Organization for Economic Co-operation and Development (OECD) predicted in 2014 that Turkey would enjoy the fastest GDP growth (4.9%) among its 35 members during the 2015–2025 time period.

But in economics, appearances can be deceiving. There are good reasons for Turkey's economic catch-up with advanced economies to have slowed since 2008. The rise of ISIS and trouble with Russia have hurt tourism and weakened Turkey's economic performance. A failed coup attempt and President Recep Tayyip Erdogan's sweeping reprisals have scared off foreign investors. To offset weak capital inflow, Erdogan has flooded the Turkish economy with domestic credit, hoping to boost short-term economic growth prior to the next presidential election in November 2019. In the process, Erdogan has failed to implement the kind of structural reforms that Turkey desperately needs to generate a stronger medium-term economic performance. More importantly, his blind eye to domestic and foreign financial

Turkey 105

imbalances makes Turkey increasingly vulnerable to financial turbulence. Therefore, its economic recovery was not sustainable and led directly to the currency crisis in August 2018.

That said, not long ago, Turkey's economy appeared promising to lots of analysts. Its GDP grew at 9% a year in 2010 and 2011. Exports were a bright spot and accounted for all of its GDP growth in 2012. Turkey successfully diversified its exports from traditional the European Union (EU) markets towards the Mideast, the Caucasus and the North Africa region. In fact, Turkey's share of exports to this increasingly important trading region more than doubled from 16% in 2004 to 34% in 2012.[2] This export success also helped to reduce Turkey's financial vulnerabilities. Strong exports and weak imports brought the current account deficit down as a percentage of GDP from 9.7% in 2010–2011 to 6.1% by the end of 2012. Inflation also fell from 10.4% in 2011 to 6.2% by the end of 2012. The credit rating agencies upgraded Turkish government bonds to investment grade in 2012.[3]

Turkey attributed this economic success to a "zero problems with neighbors" policy. Cordial relations with Syria were a showpiece of this policy. Turkey also enjoyed soaring trade with Iraq. In fact, Iraq was Turkey's second-biggest export destination in 2012. But before long, "zero problems with neighbors" turned into a region in flames. Turkey's cordial relations with Syria gave way to the negative environment of a bitter Syrian civil war and the rise of the terrorist group the Islamic State of Iraq and Syria (or ISIS).

ISIS-controlled areas in Syria and Iraq shut off Turkey's traditional export routes and forced it into time-consuming and costly circuitous alternatives. These circuitous routes added over a thousand extra miles to the journey and cost an extra $2,000 per truck.[4] Turkey's exports to Iraq fell 45% in July 2014 compared to same period in July 2013.[5]

Turkey also paid a high price for opposing the Gulf-backed military coup in Egypt against the Moslem Brotherhood. Turkey's exports to Egypt, Saudi Arabia and the UAE fell 11.6%, 15.7% and 5.9%, respectively, during the first seven months of 2014 compared to the same period in 2013.[6] Turkey's exports to Western Europe also faltered. The EU recovery faded, and countries like Germany and Italy started to battle economic contraction.[7]

With exports in the Mideast falling alarmingly, Turkey turned to domestic demand to keep growth up. At first glance, this seemed like a good idea. Thanks to interest rate cuts and more public-sector infrastructure spending, economic activity rose in early 2013. GDP went up 3.7% in the first half of 2013.[8]

But appearances can be deceiving. Domestic-led growth caused the external financial requirement to soar once more. Inflation rose to an unacceptably high 9%, and a combination of weak exports and a 10% rise in imports caused the current account to rise to almost 8% of GDP.[9] An 8% current account deficit was an alarm bell. That's where Mexico and Thailand were on the eve of their balance of payment crises.

When a country like Turkey runs such a huge current account deficit, it must somehow attract an equally huge amount of net capital inflow in

106   *Turkey*

the capital account of its balance of payments. When the Fed had a loose monetary policy to help embattled countries boost demand after the global financial crisis, there was plenty of global credit available for Turkey to meet its large current account deficit as long as the Fed policy did not tighten. But if the Fed ever tightened its loose monetary policy, Turkey would be vulnerable because its high current account deficit was financed mostly by short-term, foreign "hot money," with very little contribution from safer, more durable foreign direct investment (FDI).[10]

This negative scenario started to happen in late May 2013. Fears that the Fed would taper its bond buying program caused a large swing in market sentiment in emerging markets. A lower global appetite for emerging market assets exposed Turkey's large external financing gap and short-term funding needs. Investors attacked the Turkish lira, which fell 10% against the euro-dollar basket. Turkish stock prices fell 20%. Political demonstrations added to the uncertainty. To keep attracting capital inflow to finance its external imbalance, Turkey's central bank more than doubled its core interest rates from 4.5% to 10% on 28 January 2014. Not surprisingly, Turkey's GDP growth rapidly de-accelerated from 9% in 2010–2011 to only 2.1% in second quarter of 2014. Unemployment rose from 9.1% at the end of 2013 to 9.9% in June 2014. Recurring bouts of lira weakness pushed inflation to 9.5% in August 2014.[11]

During 2015, there were lots of other headwinds facing the Turkish economy. Turkey's exports fell to Russia (which was struggling with low oil prices) and to a Mideast in flames. Like other emerging economies, Turkey faced capital outflow due to Fed tightening. On the domestic front, investors stayed on the sidelines due to the political uncertainty surrounding two elections in Turkey. To make matters worse, terrorist attacks were driving away tourism, a key driver of the economy.

Given all these headwinds, Turkey opted to let domestic demand drive economic growth in 2015. At first glance, this seemed like a good idea. Surging private consumption filled the gap in GDP. In fact, a resilient Turkish economy enjoyed 4% GDP growth in 2015.

Unfortunately, Turkey pursued unbalanced growth. The flip side of high private consumption at home is a low private savings rate. In fact, there was rising private-sector and external indebtedness. In other words, Turkey was living beyond its means, not unlike Trump's America.

The International Monetary Fund (IMF) notes that this excessive private consumption creates two problems. First, there is low investment money inside Turkey to support high job creating growth. Second, there is a subsequent need to tap foreign savings to fund whatever investment takes place in Turkey. This macroeconomic imbalance turns into a high current account deficit in the balance of payments that Turkey must finance. If we disregard the effect of falling oil prices, the high current account deficit is potentially just as dangerous as was cited earlier (especially when oil prices were rising by nearly $85 a barrel in 2018). As a result, a high external debt and its refinancing became serious financial vulnerabilities for Turkey. Foreign debt amounts to 52% of GDP, while gross financing needs are about 25% of GDP every year. This dismal situation made Turkey extremely vulnerable to external shocks and a potential balance of payments crisis.

Following a strong performance in GDP growth in 2015, Turkey's economy slowed in 2016. In addition to the geopolitical tensions and other external shocks cited above, a number of unexpected domestic shocks slammed Turkey's economy. The most dramatic was a failed coup d'état against Turkish President Erdogan in July 2016. In response, Erdogan imposed a state of emergency. Over 140,000 public employees were suspended or dismissed; 40,000 people were detained, and over 4,000 companies and institutions, with assets close to $4 billion, were shut down and taken over by the state. The political instability, social polarization and economic uncertainty resulting from the failed coup attempt disrupted economic activity. The economy suffered negative growth in 3Q2016 (the quarter after the coup attempt). The chaotic events caused unemployment to rise to over 13%, and business confidence and foreign investment dried up. Security concerns and Russian sanctions reduced the number of tourists from Europe by a quarter and from Russia by over two-thirds. A year after the coup attempt, the Turkish lira was the world's worst performing currency outside of frontier markets. The lira lost 20% of its value against the US dollar. Its fall triggered a high level of Turkish corporate debt in US dollars. The run on the lira also drove inflation to a nine-year high. In response, Moody's cut Turkey's sovereign debt rating.

President Erdogan's fiscal expansion and rising private consumption helped him in three ways. First, GDP bounced back from contraction in 3Q2016 to 5% GDP growth in 1Q2017. Second, this growth spurt helped Erdogan win a narrow victory in the April 2017 referendum that gave him sweeping new executive powers. Third, the rise in GDP boosted Turkey's stock market. It rose 33% in the first half of 2017 and has risen 45% since the coup attempt. The Istanbul stock market posted its best gains since 2009 for January–July 2017, amid a surge in state-backed lending and one of the five biggest gains globally in 2017.

That said, Turkey's economy desperately needs bullish foreign investors to keep it afloat. Given its impressive economic bounce back in 1Q2017, foreign investors asked two questions: How financially stable is the economy? and How sustainable is the 5% growth we've seen in 1Q2017? As a result of his new executive power, Asli Kandemir at Bloomberg noted that President Erdogan was risking Turkey's future financial stability by flooding its economy with credit. He expanded state guarantees to rush $50 billion in lira loans to almost 300,000 companies, with little or no transparency on how the money was to be spent. This swelled a budget deficit that was already projected to be the highest since 2010. It's also threatened to prolong double-digit inflation.

In the process, Erdogan was bypassing the structural supply-side constraints of low savings rates, poor education and skill shortages. He was also

108   *Turkey*

shielding inefficient industries with some of the most protectionist policies in emerging markets. This supply-side neglect, together with debt buildup, risked making Turkey even more vulnerable to external shocks and a balance of payments crisis. Most importantly, its high current account deficit made it financially vulnerable in the medium term. Its current account deficit as a percentage of GDP was set to be the highest of the 20 largest economies in the world in 2017. Given these shaky financials, Istanbul stocks were expected to plummet in value once it became clear that Erdogan had randomly selected 300,000 companies to receive loans with no clue about their competitiveness or their ability to repay the loans. The day of reckoning was fast approaching.

Thus, it was just a matter of time before the vulnerable Turkish economy was in financial turmoil. In particular, the Turkish lira was vulnerable to shifts in foreign investor confidence. August 2018 was the "month of reckoning." The Turkish lira fell 20% against a US dollar, which was getting stronger because the Fed was tightening US monetary policy to offset super loose US fiscal policy due to a huge US tax cut and soaring budget deficits, and a trillion dollars more to be added to the national debt. In Turkey, inflation rose following the currency slide. This forced its central bank to raise interest rates to 24% on 13 September 2018. Turkish President Erdogan was unhappy because high interest rates would send the economy into a recession.

To briefly recap, there were about 5 economic reasons for the Turkish currency crisis. First, due to a structurally low national savings rate, Turkey had a large external financing requirement. The current account deficit was 5.6% of GDP in 2017 and therefore a cause for concern. That made the lira vulnerable to a tightening in global liquidity due to rising interest rates in the US, as cited earlier.

Second, the Turkish corporations cited earlier were highly indebted in foreign currency. Many were unable to service these debts. This triggered investor panic, capital flight and downward pressure on the lira.

Third, President Erdogan was implementing his executive presidency. Investors feared that he would politicize the central bank and be less willing to tighten monetary policy to offset Turkey's loose fiscal policy.

Fourth, Turkish tensions were rising with Donald Trump. In August, the US imposed sanctions on Turkish individuals, and Donald Trump announced that US tariffs on Turkish steel and aluminum exports would double: US tariffs on Turkish steel would be 50%, and US tariffs on Turkish aluminum would rise to 30%.[12]

Donald Trump was also re-imposing sanctions on Iran. He wanted to curb Iran oil exports to countries like Turkey, and he would enforce this embargo with severe fines on any Turkish bank or company which used US dollars to finance purchases of Iranian oil. These American threats to punish Turkish banks or corporations caused Iranian bankers to be cautious about buying oil from Iran.

But because of Turkey's severe economic problems, cited above, Erdogan needed to find creative ways to circumvent US sanctions and import Iranian oil. Therefore, he considered at least four ways to get around US sanctions. First, he could use euros or other local currencies instead of the US dollars to finance purchases of Iranian oil. Second, Turkey could try to arrange some barter deals that would offer Turkish goods instead of dollars in return for Iranian oil. Third, Turkey could buy oil from the Turkish private sector on the Turkish stock exchange. Fourth, it could use "ghost tankers" in an attempt to avoid the US tracking system.[13]

Conclusion

It's important to understand that Turkey's external financial vulnerabilities start at home. Its domestic savings rate has fallen dramatically over the last 15 years. Private savings, in particular, have fallen significantly. The IMF calculates that Turkey needs investment close to 21% of GDP in order for GDP to grow 4%.[14]

Since Turkey's domestic savings rate is only 14% of GDP, it has to fill this savings gap with an external financing requirement of 7% of GDP. Unfortunately, this capital is only available in the form of volatile, short-term "hot money," which is difficult to sustain over time. Turkey's gross external financing requirement is an alarmingly high 25% of GDP per year.[15]

Turkey also needs to implement key structural reforms in order to make its economy more competitive. These include boosting human capital, strengthening the business environment and making labor markets more flexible. Reducing Turkey's external deficit and making its economy more competitive are interconnected. Raising domestic savings, maintaining a strong monetary anchor and ensuring that structural reforms result in more foreign direct investment. That in turn are all critical components that will stabilize Turkey's economy.[16]

On the domestic front, President Erdogan's anti-democratic tendencies and a perceived weakening of central bank independence have damaged investor confidence since mid-December 2013.[17] As a result, Turkey is still vulnerable to capital flight. Therefore, the timing of President Trump's economic coercion against Turkey could not be worse.

Notes

1 See Holly Williams, "Turkey's Economy Suffers Amid U.S. Sanctions and Tariffs", *CBS News*, 15 August 2018.
2 Daniel Dombey, "Turkey: Business Shifts as Crises Rage from Syria to Iraq", *Financial Times*, 21 September 2014.
3 IMF, "Turkey: Staff Report for the 2013 Article IV Consultation", 1 November 2013.
4 See Elena Lanchovichina and Maros Ivanic, "Regional Economic Effects of the Syrian War and the Spread of the Islamic State", *World Bank*, 1 December 2014.

110 *Turkey*

5 Dombey, "Turkey: Business Shifts as Crises Rage from Syria to Iraq".
6 Ibid.
7 Chris Giles, "IMF Sees Risk of New Eurozone Recession, *Financial Times*, 7 October 2014.
8 IMF, "Turkey: Staff Report for the 2013 Article IV Consultation".
9 The current account deficit was 7.9% of GDP in 2013. Economist Intelligence Unit, "Turkey: Country Report", 26 September 2014, p. 8.
10 See Benn Steil, "Taper Trouble: The International Consequences of Fed Policy", *Foreign Affairs*, July/August 2014.
11 IMF, "Turkey: Staff Report for the 2013 Article IV Consultation".
12 Economist Intelligence Unit, "Turkey: Is Turkey Heading Towards a Financial Crisis?" 14 August 2018.
13 Economist Intelligence Unit, "Iran Energy: Outlook Worsens for Iran's Oil Exports", 28 September 2018.
14 IMF, "Turkey: Increasing Savings to Reduce Vulnerabilities", *IMF Survey Magazine*, 20 December 2013.
15 Ibid.
16 Ibid.
17 Economist Intelligence Unit, "Turkey: Country Report", September 2014, p. 5.

Bibliography

Faucompret, Eric and Konings, Jozef. *Turkish Accession to the EU: Satisfying the Copenhagen Criteria* (Routledge Studies in Middle Eastern Economies), Routledge, London, 2010.

Galip, Yalman and Marois, Thomas. *The Political Economy of Financial Transformation in Turkey* (Europa Perspectives: Emerging Economies), Routledge, London, 2018.

Kutlay, Mustafa. *The Political Economies of Turkey and Greece: Crisis and Change*, (International Political Economy Series), Palgrave MacMillan, New York, NY, 2018.

Onis, Ziya and Senses, Fikret. *Turkey and the Global Economy: Neo-Liberal Restructuring and Integration in the Post-Crisis Era* (Routledge Studies in Middle Eastern Economies), Routledge, London, 2013.

Togan, Sübidey. *Economic Liberalization and Turkey* (Routledge Political Economy of the Middle East and North Africa), Routledge, London, 2010.

Wigley, Arzu Akkoyunlu and Çağatay, Selim. *The Dynamics of Growth in Emerging Economies: The Case of Turkey* (Routledge Studies in the Modern World Economy), Routledge, London, 2019.

Zulkuf, Aydin. *The Political Economy of Turkey* (Third World in Global Politics), Pluto Press, London, 2005.

11 Trump and China

During his campaign for the US presidency, Donald Trump liked to wear a baseball cap that read, "Make America Great Again." He would tour the rust belt and promise who he called "the forgotten" blue-collar workers that he'd bring back their lost jobs.[1] These workers not only believed him – they helped to vote Donald Trump into office.

President Trump blames China for "stealing" American jobs. In an effort to bring these jobs back, in July 2018, he announced $50 billion of tariffs on products that America imports from China. His 25% tax on Chinese imports – including steel, aluminum, washing machines and solar panels – is the most extensive trade protectionism in nearly a century.

China predictably retaliated in force, with a 25% tax on imports of US automobiles, Boeing aircraft and soybeans, and many other agricultural products. This didn't faze Trump; he just raised the stakes. On 7 September 2018, he threatened new tariffs of an additional $267 billion on US imports from China.[2]

As expected, President Trump's high tariffs and China's retaliation have hurt US workers across America. For instance, US car exporters in Southern states like Tennessee were hit hard, as were Boeing workers in the Northwest.[3]

In addition, Trump's trade war with China has resulted in American farmers in the Midwest who produce soybeans' losing their export markets in China. China, the world's largest market for soybeans, is now looking to Brazil to replace America as a supplier.[4]

To be fair, President Trump has offered to compensate these Midwest soybean farmers. In fact, he has proposed a $15 billion farm bailout. But this subsidy is a misguided attempt to cushion the damage and is unlikely to address long-term risks. US soybean farmers fear that they may permanently lose their export market to China. Trump's subsidy could also trigger a challenge to the World Trade Organization.

US consumers are also being hurt. The high tariffs are a tax hike on embattled American consumers. In the past, American consumers were free to buy the lowest-priced, best-quality products, which often meant buying products with final assembly in China. The trade war means that Americans will be forced to buy inferior-quality, more expensive products from other

112   *Trump and China*

countries. That is tantamount to a large tax increase and a lower standard of living for struggling US consumers.

Trump's trade war with China plays well with his political base, who long for the days when those in the rust belt were doing better. To provide perspective, let's turn the clock back to the so-called "glory days" of US manufacturing. For instance, George Will says that President Trump would like to "make America 1953 again." Trump would say that America was "great" back then because it was "winning." America had a 30% share of global manufacturing. If this 30% market share of global manufacturing was all important to post-World War II US presidents, they could have tried to keep this manufacturing "success story" going into the future.[5]

But thankfully, back then, America had statesmen who had bigger things in mind – like internalizing the lessons learned from the punitive Treaty of Versailles, which ended World War I and led to the rise of a vindictive Adolf Hitler and World War II. Instead of repeating this strategic failure after World War II, US statesmen learned to be magnanimous.

One of the American heroes at this time was US Secretary of State George Marshall, who wisely created the Marshall Plan that helped Germany rebuild its manufacturing base. He had an implicit vision of "no (vindictive) victor" and no vanquished loser. Instead of pursing a fool's errand of trying to keep Germany forever defeated and in ashes, he fostered a web of economic interdependence and shared prosperity. He helped to turn a bitter enemy in World War II into a close friend and ally. The Marshall Plan enabled Germany to use its exports to earn hard currency to import American goods and services. The United States' shared prosperity, together with the North Atlantic Treaty Organization (NATO), helped to foster a responsible stakeholder in the heart of Europe for 70 years.

Just as George Marshall was an international hero, the scholars at the World Bank were equally impressive, connecting economics to global security. In their definitive 2003 study "Breaking the Conflict Trap: Civil War and Development Policy," the World Bank used statistical evidence to reveal a striking pattern: civil war does not occur randomly around the world. Instead, it is heavily concentrated in the poorest countries. The important reason for this concentration is that poverty increases the likelihood of civil war. Thus, the World Bank study concludes that the root cause of conflict is the failure of economic development.[6] More recently, scholars in the United Nations (UN) have highlighted the importance of free trade to counter this rising demand for violence. The UN finds that free trade across the world has cut the extreme global poverty rate in half since 1990.

In contrast, if Trump's protectionism and economic nationalism were to incite a global trend that rolled back this progress in free trade, he would also reverse this impressive decline in global poverty. This, in turn, would provide fertile ground for an even greater rise in demand for violent extremism, which would lead to the brave men and women of the US military being needlessly put in harm's way over and over again.

Trump and China 113

President Harry Truman once said, "the only thing new in the world is the history you don't know."[7] If we look at the past, we learn that protectionism was a bad idea then, and it was still a bad idea when President Trump opted for this kind of economic coercion against China in mid-2018.

Back in 1930, President Herbert Hoover's Smoot-Hawley Act's high tariffs achieved the glorious trade surplus that Donald Trump's economic nationalism calls "winning." But in economics, appearances can be deceiving, especially if you are obsessed with the wrong economic indicator. In 1930, shrinking the gains from trade by making the global economic pie smaller also produced a US unemployment rate of 25% – and the Great Depression.[8]

To be fair, Donald Trump and Herbert Hoover are not the only US president who have tried to "bring back American jobs." But President Trump has no problem listening to economists who dismiss lessons learned about protectionism from history and going instead with his uninformed "gut instincts."

Unfortunately, each time an American president makes this painful mistake, protectionism backfires and worsens the overall US economy. For instance, when President Carter tried to protect US manufacturers by restricting imports of Japanese televisions, imports from South Korea and Taiwan increased. When imports from South Korea and Taiwan were restricted, manufacturers in Mexico and Singapore benefited.[9] When this replacement happened, American consumers lost because they had to settle for higher prices and worse quality. Not exactly life, liberty and the pursuit of happiness!

The US middle class and other US businesses are also financially hurt by unhappy second- and third-order effects when the US government singles out one industry for special protection. In 2012, President Obama took credit for protecting over a thousand US jobs after there was a surge in Chinese tires. But this government interventionism cost $900,000 per job, paid for by American purchasers of now overpriced vehicles and tires. Meanwhile, imports of low-end tires from Thailand, Indonesia, Mexico and elsewhere largely replaced Chinese imports.[10]

To make matters worse, the Peterson Institute notes that this money's being needlessly taken out of the wallets of struggling US consumers had other negative consequences. It reduced their spending on other retail goods, which, in turn, brought the net job loss from the "job-saving" tire tariffs to about 2,500. To add insult to injury, China retaliated with duties on US chicken parts, costing this US industry (which had done nothing wrong) $1 billion in lost sales.[11]

Moreover, the number of Americans hurt far outnumbers the number of people who benefit from protectionism. For instance, Douglas Irwin from Dartmouth College asks: Is it fair to sharply increase the price of clothing for 45 million poor Americans just to save jobs in the US textile industry?[12] It also makes no sense for Trump to raise tariffs on imports and force

114 *Trump and China*

American businesses and consumers to pay more and have less freedom to choose. Foreign competition keeps prices affordable for consumers and increases the quality of US-made goods.

Instead of learning about the negative aspects of protectionism and the upside of free trade, President Trump is stuck on blaming China for US unemployment in the rust belt and says that his trade war with China is designed to "bring back American jobs." The problem is that there is nowhere to bring the manufacturing jobs back from because the lion's share of US manufacturing jobs were lost to technology, not trade.[13] A Ball State University study notes that out of the 5.6 million US manufacturing jobs lost between 2000 and 2010, productivity improvements accounted for over 85%.[14]

Take farming. Patricia Daly notes that half of all American jobs were in the agricultural sector in 1870. By 1980, only 4% of American workers were in agriculture. Thanks to stunning advances in agricultural technology, US agriculture is now a success story and certainly not what Trump would call a disaster. In many ways, America is now the bread basket of the world.[15]

A similar pattern of rising productivity happened in US manufacturing. Thanks to technological advances, US manufacturing output was at an all-time high in 2015. Over the past three and a half decades, US manufacturers have been able to produce more goods than ever with seven million less people. American factories are now producing twice as much as they were in 1984 with one-third fewer workers.[16]

Thanks to equally amazing advances in manufacturing technology, US manufacturing became just as much a success story as US agriculture. And for the past 40 years, the US market share of global manufacturing has held at around 20%. All the while, American manufacturing has moved up the value added ladder, thus fostering strategic stability and peace in the world by allowing developing countries to move into lower-end global manufacturing.

Somewhere along the way, President Trump missed this transformation in global manufacturing. Back in the old days that President Trump says were "great," manufacturing was one-dimensional. Victor Fung notes that it was done "in-house" ... in one factory, under one roof, and in one country ... before that product was exported and sold in another country."[17] But things changed, and products have become increasingly dispersed across different factories in different countries and thus globalized. Because of this dispersion of global production, countries previously omitted from manufacturing can now participate by performing just one or two pieces of the supply chain. Fung calls this the "democratization of the global production system." Dispersion also benefits American consumers because it reduces costs and makes products more affordable.

We now live in a world where global supply chains involve goods repeatedly crossing open borders, thus making traditional trade metrics relatively obsolete. In fact, two-thirds of international trade now takes place through these global value chains.[18] Therefore, when Trump criticizes China for its large trade surplus with the United States, there are simple reasons for this development. As it turns out, many Chinese exports are put together from parts produced elsewhere.[19]

With the dispersion of global production, China became a final assembly point for goods that the US previously imported from companies based in Japan, South Korea and Taiwan. As the final leg of the supply chain shifted to China, US imports from China rose as the United States imported less from the rest of Asia. In other words, there is nothing evil about China's last leg in this dispersion of global production.

It's important to understand that US and Chinese goods are often in different market segments – they therefore do not always compete head to head. So, when Trump's trade war increases the cost of US imports from China, the United States imports less from China and more from other, higher-priced Asian producers – not from producers in the United States. Not only is the result no net increase in US jobs, but it also means higher prices at Walmart for struggling US consumers.

Unfortunately, this inconvenient truth is not what President Trump tells his base in the rust belt. Instead, he also accuses China of stealing American jobs by manipulating its foreign exchange rate so that its export prices are lower than US export prices. Is this argument persuasive? Let's check China's foreign exchange rate against the US dollar in recent years.

If China wanted such a low foreign exchange rate to underprice US products, why did its foreign exchange rate rise so much against the US dollar? This rate rose from 8 renminbi (RMB) to $1 in the mid-2000s to 6.3 RMB to $1 in 2015.[20]

China's central bank depleted its foreign reserves numerous times in order to strengthen its foreign exchange rate. In fact, at the end of October 2016, its central bank's foreign reserves hit their lowest level since March 2011.

Since President Trump has come into office, the RMB has weakened. But that's because the Federal Reserve (or the Fed) had to raise interest rates to offset a super loose fiscal policy resulting from a huge tax cut. In other words, investors are chasing rising US interest rates, which strengthens the US dollar and weakens the RMB against the dollar.

Instead of blaming China, President Trump should blame himself for policies which end up strengthening the US dollar and therefore overpricing US exports. His huge $1.5 trillion tax cut increased public spending, a large percentage of which goes into imports. As imports grow faster than exports, the trade deficit rises. America must offset this deficit with a surplus in the capital account (financial flows) in the balance of payments. To attract capital inflow, the Fed must tighten monetary policy by increasing interest rates. Rising interest rates strengthen the demand for the US dollar, and a stronger US dollar overprices US exports, worsens US trade and current account deficits, and puts Americans out of work in export industries.[21]

116   *Trump and China*

In addition, President Trump likes to justify his trade war against China by pointing to what he calls "America's $500 billion trade deficit with China." For starters, the US trade deficit with China in 2017 was really only $375 billion.[22]

Second, the high US trade deficit with China also reflects national security realities regarding Taiwan and North Korea. US strategists must forego trade advantages with China when they have bigger fish to fry. To help protect Taiwan's security, America has placed an embargo on items which would give China's military advantages, even though this decision increases the US trade deficit with China. In addition, North Korean long-range missiles carrying nuclear weapons could blow up Seattle in about two years unless something is done to curb North Korea's military buildup. To avoid this existential threat to America, US strategists need China to use its economic relationship with North Korea to dissuade it from this unacceptable course of action. If the US launched a trade war against China with the hope of bringing back some US manufacturing jobs, China would see no incentive to put pressure on North Korea to curb its nuclear threat to Seattle.[23]

Third, President Trump fails to understand that this large trade deficit is what Nobel Laureate Paul Krugman calls a "statistical illusion." That's because over 50% of the value of these Chinese exports to America are parts and components produced in places like South Korea, Taiwan and Japan, even though China is the final assembler. As a result, over half the pain from Trump's tariffs will be felt by a wider group of countries, many of whom are close US allies and friends, and because of dispersion, Trump has much less trade leverage over China than he imagines.[24]

In addition, over 20% of the goods produced in China and then exported from China to the US are created by foreign companies working in China.[25] President Trump says that these American companies doing foreign investment in China should return to the United States. But US businesses have significantly benefitted from large US investments in China. Over the years, American and other foreign companies have dominated China's high-tech and industrial exports. Profits for these products are thus not China's alone. In the past, China has only retained $4 out of the $300 final price for the iPods that Apple produced in China. US corporations benefit by recycling their profits back into the United States and other foreign companies. US consumers benefit by getting lower prices, higher quality and greater variety.[26]

Instead of blaming China for America's high trade deficit with China, President Trump should blame himself. His huge $1.5 trillion tax cut has caused the budget deficit and national debt to soar. The federal budget deficit is headed back towards at least 7% of GDP over the next ten years.[27] That's over twice the 3% of GDP level which an EU Maastricht criterion says is financially unstable.

Similarly, the non-partisan US Congressional Budget Office (CBO) estimated that President Trump's public debt would hit 78% of GDP by the end of 2018, the highest level since 1950. The long-term projections are even worse. CBO says that the debt to GDP ratio is on track to hit 100% of GDP by 2030 and 152% by 2048.[28] That's a far cry from the 60% of GDP level which another EU Maastricht criterion says is financially unstable.

When President Trump says he wants to make America great again, he is half-right about one thing. In the 1950s, 1960s and 1970s, America's national savings rate was about 8% of GDP. By international standards, that was still low, but it's a lot higher than it is today. Unfortunately, the national savings rate fell sharply to just 2.4% of GDP in mid-2018. The problem is that President Trump is pursuing policies which are counterproductive. His 1.5% tax cut will send the already dangerously low national savings rate into negative territory.

The trade deficit that President Trump complains about exists because America is running a large deficit in national savings. The United States must import its savings from countries like China, Germany and Japan, which have large surpluses in savings, because America lives beyond its means by consuming way too much, thus leaving it with a large deficit in savings. As long as the United States maintains its large savings deficit, eliminating a trade deficit with China simply turns into a larger trade deficit with other US trading partners.[29]

In this regard, President Trump's own domestic economic policies are widening the US trade imbalance. He is running a loose fiscal policy that promises to generate rising budget deficits. The Fed has already said it will offset this loose fiscal policy with higher interest rates, which, in turn, is likely to strengthen the US dollar and increase the cost of US exports. More expensive exports will thus worsen the overall US trade deficit and lead to rising unemployment in US export industries.[30]

Trump officials are critical of Chinese economic initiatives in developing countries. They accuse China of "predatory" lending policies. They say its five year old "Belt and Road Initiative" (BRI) is dangerous because it gets developing countries hooked on excessive debt. That criticism is ill-advised for a number of reasons. First, no country in the world is as highly indebted to China as the United States. The American government owes China over a trillion dollars in debt. And America's debt is becoming far worse because the Trump administration's tax cut for millionaires and billionaires is increasing the national debt by over a trillion dollars. [31] Perhaps they should have hired former Admiral Michael Mullen, Chairman of the US Joint Chiefs of Staff, who said, "the most significant threat to our (America's) national security is our debt."

In the old days, America was a role model when it came to building modern infrastructure. Not anymore. The Trump administration has done virtually nothing to rebuild America's collapsing infrastructure. One of the biggest critics of China's BRI is Trump's Secretary of Defense James Mattis. And yet it was James Mattis who waved the economic white flag and zeroed out the funding for America's New Silk Road Initiative, which General Petraeus

118   *Trump and China*

had wisely started before him at the US Central Command (CENTCOM). Second, America is still offering developing countries virtually nothing in contrast to China's trillion-dollar initiative.

Notes

1 See Ben Bradlee, Jr. *The Forgotten: How the People of One Pennsylvania County Elected Donald Trump and Changed America*, Little, Brown and Co., New York, NY, 2018.
2 David Dollar, "Unpacked: The US-China Trade War", *Brookings*, 12 July 2018.
3 Ibid.
4 Ibid.
5 George F. Will, "A Plan to Make America 1953 Again", *The Washington Post*, 28 December 2016.
6 World Bank, *Breaking the Conflict Trap: Civil War and Development Policy*, Oxford University Press and the World Bank, Washington, DC, 2003.
7 Michael Beschloss, *Presidential Courage*, Simon and Schuster, New York, NY, p. 211.
8 See Robert Zoellick, "The Currency of Power: Want to Understand America's Place in the World? Write Economics Back into the Plan", *Foreign Policy*, 8 October 2012.
9 See Greg Ip, "When Presidents Defy Economic Gravity, Gravity Usually Wins", *The Wall Street Journal*, 7 December 2016.
10 Will, "A Plan to Make America 1953 Again".
11 Ibid.
12 Ibid.
13 See Knowledge at Wharton, "Can Trump – or Anyone Else – Bring Back American Manufacturing?", University of Pennsylvania, 30 November 2016; Claire Cain Miller, "The Long-term Jobs Killer Is Not China: It's Automation", *The New York Times*, 21 December 2016; Wolfgang Lehmacher, "Don't Blame China for Taking US Jobs", *Fortune*, 8 February 2017.
14 Will, "A Plan to Make America 1953 Again".
15 See Patricia A. Daly, "Agricultural Employment: Has the Decline Ended?" *Monthly Labor Review*, November 1981.
16 Drew Desilva, "Most Americans Unaware that as U.S. Manufacturing Jobs Have Disappeared, Output Has Grown", *Pew Research Center*, 25 July 2017.
17 Victor Fung, *William Fung, and Yoram Wind, Compering in Flat World*, Prentice Hall, New York, NY, 1979.
18 David Dollar and Zhi Wang, "Why a Trade War with China would Hurt the U.S. and Its Allies, Too, Order from Chaos", *Brookings*, 4 April 2018.
19 Paul Krugman, "Bumbling into a Trade War", *The New York Times*, 22 March 2018.
20 Kenneth Rapoza, "Is the Made in China Clothing Label a Thing of the Past?" *Forbes*, 11 October 2015.
21 See Barry Eichengreen, "Powerful Forces Will Lead to a Strong Dollar under Trump", *Financial Times*, 25 January 2017.
22 Krugman, "Bumbling into a Trade War".
23 Leif Rosenberger, *APEU 2007, Volume 1, US Pacific Command*, Camp Smith, Hawaii, 2007.
24 Krugman, "Bumbling into a Trade War".
25 Ibid.
26 Rosenberger, *APEU 2007*.
27 Stephen Roach is an economics professor at Yale University.

Trump and China 119

28 Economist Intelligence Unit, "Ballooning Deficits and Debt Cast a Long Shadow, United States", 5 July 2018
29 Stephen Roach, "US-China Trade Deficit Is Set to Keep Rising", *CNBC.com*, 26 March 2018; and Stephen Roach, "The Current Account Counts", *Project Syndicate*, 27 August 2018.
30 Eichengreen, "Powerful Forces Will Lead to a Strong Dollar under Trump".
31 William Baldwin, "Tax Breaks for Musk, Bezos and Various Other Billionaires", *Forbes*, 20 December 2018

Bibliography

Bradlee, Jr., Ben. *The Forgotten: How the People of One Pennsylvania County Elected Donald Trump and Changed America*, Little, Brown and Company, New York, NY, 2018.

Daly, Patricia A, "Agricultural Employment: Has the Decline Ended?" *Monthly Labor Review*, November 1981.

Desilva, Drew. "Most Americans Unaware that as U.S. Manufacturing Jobs Have Disappeared, Output Has Grown", *Pew Research Center*, July 25, 2017.

Dollar, David. "David Dollar, Unpacked: The US-China Trade War", *Brookings*, July 12, 2018.

Eichengreen, Barry. "Powerful Forces Will Lead to a Strong Dollar under Trump", *Financial Times*, January 25, 2017.

Fairbank, John King, Ernest R. May, and Alfred D. Chandler. *America's China Trade in Historical Perspective: The Chinese and American Performance. Harvard Studies in American- East Asian Relations, 11*. Committee on American-East Asian Relations of the Dept. of History, in collaboration with Council on East Asian Studies, Harvard University, Cambridge, MA, 1986.

Fung, Victor K. "Business Perceptions and Expectations Regarding the WTO Doha Negotiations, the UNESCAP Macao Dialogue Delivering on the WTO Round", *Luncheon Address*, October 4, 2005.

Hao, Yen-p'ing. *The Commercial Revolution in Nineteenth-Century China: The Rise of Sino-Western Mercantile Capitalism*, University of California Press, Berkeley, 1986.

Hao, Yen-p'ing. *The Comprador in Nineteenth Century China: Bridge between East and West*, Harvard East Asian Series, 45, Harvard University Press, Cambridge, MA, 1970.

Hufbauer, Gary Clyde, *The Free Trade Debate*, Priority Press, New York, NY, 1989.

Knowledge at Wharton, "Can Trump – or Anyone Else – Bring Back American Manufacturing?" University of Pennsylvania, November 30, 2016.

Lehmacher, Wolfgang, "Don't Blame China for Taking US Jobs", *Fortune*, February 8, 2017.

Miller, Claire Cain. "The Long-term Jobs Killer Is Not China: It's Automation", *The New York Times*, December 21, 2016.

Overholt, William H. *The Rise of China: How Economic Reform in Creating a New Superpower*, W.W. Norton and Company, New York, NY, 1993.

World Bank, *Breaking the Conflict Trap: Civil War and Development Policy*, Oxford University Press and the World Bank, Washington, DC, 2003.

Zoellick, Robert. "The Currency of Power: Want to Understand America's Place in the World? Write Economics Back into the Plan", *Foreign Policy Online*, October 8, 2012.

12 Taiwan

China's twentieth-century economic rise began with the implementation of Deng Xiaoping's 1979 economic reform plan. The rise has been nothing short of an economic miracle. For three decades, China's export-led economy has enjoyed a success story second to none. During the 1980s, it was the world's fastest-growing economy. The Gross Domestic Product (GDP) expanded on average over 9% from 1980 to 2002.

Poverty reduction was particularly impressive. In 1975, 570 million Chinese were living in poverty. By 1998, China had reduced this number to 200 million. The contrast to a protectionist India is striking. In 1975, 400 million Indians were living in poverty. By 1998, India still had 400 million people living in poverty.

China's astonishing trade performance was a key reason for its economic success story. Between 1980 and 2002, China's share in global exports and imports rose from 1.2% and 1.1% to 5.2% and 4.2%, respectively. From 1993 to 2002, the volume of its exports of goods rose at an annual rate of 17.3%.

Over the 12 months to May 2003, Chinese exports, at $366 billion, were the world's fourth largest, after those of the US, Germany and Japan. Its imports, at $323 billion, were the sixth largest but will soon be bigger than those of Japan, the UK and France. Chinese trade was truly global in nature. Particularly interesting is the fact that the US and Japan are far and away China's biggest trading partners.

In the early 1990s, China only received 18% of the foreign direct investment (FDI) coming to developing Asian economies. By 2001, it was receiving 61%. China's strong trade performance and huge capital inflows have generated a rising tide of foreign reserves. Its foreign reserves increased from about $50 billion in 1994 to almost $200 billion by 2001.[1]

But the story back then does not end with the rise of Mainland China alone. China, Hong Kong and Taiwan were in the process of creating "Greater China," an integrated economic powerhouse. This was emerging as one of the biggest economic mergers in history. The concept had been developing since the 1980s, with the mass influx of manufacturers from Hong Kong, and then Taiwan, to the Southern China coast soon after Beijing opened its doors.

Starting with China's entry into the World Trade Organization (WTO) in 2002, the industrial unification of the three economies accelerated and spread deep into the Mainland. Political barriers to investment in once-strategic industries – such as semiconductors, oil and banking – started to crumble. Infrastructure systems were fusing. Hong Kong and Chinese officials collaborated on economic affairs.

There are numerous manifestations of this accelerated convergence. The number of Taiwanese people officially living on the Mainland swelled from 300,000 to 500,000. Several thousand Taiwanese students pursued degrees in China rather than at US universities. China overtook the US as Taiwan's biggest export market in 2002. In addition, it passed Taiwan as the world's third-largest maker of information-technology products. But many of the benefits flowed to Taiwan companies, who controlled 70% of the output. China overtook Taiwan as a maker of desktop PCs, optical drives and liquid crystal displays. The share of Taiwan notebook PCs made in China leaped from 4% in early 2001 to 30% by 2006.

Hong Kong's role as an international capital window for China was also growing. Bank of China (Hong Kong) placed its initial stock offering in Hong Kong rather than New York. Dozens of other Chinese companies have been listed on Hong Kong's new second board aimed at startups. The impact of Greater China as an export powerhouse was felt around the world. Its share of total world exports went from 6.9% to 9.6% in just four years (1998 to 2001), surpassing Japan.[2] This concept of Greater China can be expanded even further if the huge populations of overseas Chinese who still consider the Mainland home and returned to start businesses there are considered.

In many ways, Greater China was becoming the commercial hub of Northeast Asia. What emerged was an integrated Chinese network in which dozens of growth zones essentially rented themselves out to foreign investors. The real architects of this growing economic colossus were the entrepreneurs of Greater China and the officialdom of cities such as Shanghai, Chongqing, Shenzhen, Dongguan and Hong Kong. They spent two decades creating networks of influence and putting down roots – advantages that would be extremely difficult for other foreigners to match. Equally important, these players provided China with the capital, technology and managerial expertise needed to compete in the world.

Several factors were driving the process. The biggest was China's economic reforms, now anchored by its entry into the WTO. Another was the ever-deeper integration of Hong Kong after the departure of the British in 1997. Calmer relations across the Taiwan Strait also helped.

Meanwhile, Mainland companies, such as Bank of China, which used to be shadowy presences in Hong Kong, started to use it as a base to learn international management standards. China's foreign trade ministry transported delegations of private Mainland entrepreneurs to Hong Kong to consider opening offices there. Mainland China was a magnet for Hong Kong

122   *Taiwan*

residents. After years of trying to keep its distance from the Mainland, Hong Kong began to see the Mainland as a savior. People on Hong Kong were willing to commute by hydrofoil or air-conditioned bus to factories in the Pearl River Delta. Previously, very few Hong Kong residents had wanted to live on the Mainland. That changed. Hong Kong residents started to fight for jobs there. Thousands flocked to Mainland job fairs.

Talent from Taiwan and Hong Kong was pivotal to China's ability to maintain annual growth rates of at least 7%. It played a key behind-the-scenes role at advanced plants and research labs provided by multinationals such as Cisco Systems, Ford Motor, Nokia, Sony and Motorola. All the Chinese plants were being built with managers from Taiwan.

Why were Taiwan businessmen investing on the Mainland? As Taiwan's GDP growth slowed from almost 7% in 1997 to less than 4% in 2001, its unemployment rate rose from less than 3% in 2000 to over 4% in 2001. Its corporations saw business opportunities drying up in Taiwan and starting to grow on Mainland China.

Taiwan's business community poured money into the Mainland to take advantage of the growing opportunities to make money there. Taiwan's pledged cumulative investment increased almost tenfold between 1991 and 2000. In addition to slow GDP growth and rising unemployment in Taiwan, the rise in its Foreign Direct Investment (FDI) on the Mainland reflected the magnetic effect of the Chinese Mainland market (which was characterized by the cheaper cost of land and labor). The Chinese government also provided numerous incentives to Taiwanese investors in China.

Social and economic interactions between Taiwan and Mainland China took off in the late 1980s. Before then, there were almost no direct contacts between citizens of the two countries. They would be allowed to visit relatives on the Mainland for humanitarian purposes. Once the door was opened, visitors poured across the strait, "like waters rushing through a breached dam."[3] By the end of 1989, nearly 1 million Taiwanese visited the Mainland.[4] By October 2002, over 27 million visits to the Mainland had been tallied.[5] In the year 2002 alone, the figure was more than 3 million.[6]

At the same time, by the 1980s, Taiwan's prosperity had driven up wages. Its wages were so high that it was losing competitiveness in its labor-intensive production sector. Many Taiwanese business people saw the Mainland as a prime location for new factory sites. In the eyes of Taiwanese business, the Chinese Mainland enjoyed almost unlimited low-cost labor. In addition, the language and cultural ties were very strong. Finally, pragmatic provincial leaders on the Mainland offered substantial incentives for Taiwan's investment in export industries.

In the meantime, in the late 1980s, China embarked on a "coastal development strategy" aimed at attracting the light and labor-intensive industries that were being priced out of Hong Kong and Taiwan. China also began to emulate the export-led industrialization of the East Asian capitalist nations.[7]

The result was a confluence of fundamental economic changes in Taiwan and the new Chinese economic strategy. This confluence produced tremendous growth in cross-strait economic interactions.[8] While the Taiwanese and the Chinese numbers differ, the trend lines show a similar upward trajectory. Taiwan's exports to China grew nearly six times between 1987 and 1991 (from $1.2 billion to $6.9 billion). Between 1992 and 1996, Taiwan's exports to China more than doubled again (to $19.1 billion).

Therefore, Taiwanese businessmen saw rising economic relations with the Mainland as an economic blessing rather than as a problem. This upward trend in cross-strait trade and investment was so strong and resilient that it shrugged off political turbulence, including the Tiananmen Square massacre of 1989 and the Taiwan Strait crisis of 1995–1996. Taiwan's exports to China remained steady at $21.2 billion from 1997 to 1999, despite the Asian financial crisis of 1997–1998 and Lee Teng-Hui's 1999 declaration of "two-state theory." Nor did the presidential election of Chen Shui-bian change this economic growth trend. In 2000, Taiwan's exports to China were estimated at $26.1 billion, while the bilateral trade volume jumped to $32.3 billion.

In 2002, Taiwan's exports to China increased to an estimated $33.05 billion, while the bilateral trade volume jumped to $41 billion. Statistics from China's Ministry of Commerce suggest that in the first quarter of 2003, cross-strait trade volume increased by 39% to reach $12.12 billion.[9]

According to Taiwan's Board of Trade (BOFT), from January to March 2003, the cross-strait trade volume was $10.06 billion, a 33.2% increase over the same period in 2002, which, in turn, was 16.4% of Taiwan's total trade volume. The value of Taiwan's exports to China in the same period was $7.8 billion, a 29.9% increase from 2002.[10]

The value of Taiwan's imports from China was valued at $2.26 billion, a 45.6% increase, for a total $5.53 billion trade surplus with China. Similarly, China became the single most important source for Taiwan's foreign trade surplus from 1995 to 2006. In 2002, its trade surplus with China was $25.3 billion, while its total trade surplus was $18.05 billion. If it were not for its large trade surplus with China, Taiwan's balance of trade would be in deep deficit.[11]

Therefore, Chinese and Taiwanese businessmen saw their economic interdependence as mutually beneficial. Taiwan's trade with the Mainland was for the most part investment driven. Its investors on the Mainland mainly depended on the island for their supplies of machinery equipment, spare parts and certain raw materials.

Prior to 1987, there was virtually no Taiwanese investment on the Mainland. Then things changed. The growth of investment from Taiwan to the Mainland is particularly impressive. Following its decades-long martial law, in July 1987, Taipei relaxed foreign exchange controls. Adventurous Taiwan businessmen then began to invest in the coastal cities on the Mainland, especially in the city of Xiamen, located directly across the Taiwan Strait.[12]

The initial level of Taiwan's investment on the Mainland was very moderate. Its investment sharply increased after 1990, when new capital poured into real estate in the coastal cities of Eastern China. Between 1991 and

124 *Taiwan*

1995, 11,254 investment applications to the Mainland, with a total value of $56.45 billion, were approved, while Beijing's statistics show 31,780 Taiwan investment applications for a total of $114.27 billion.[13]

In addition, the Mainland became the most important outlet for Taiwan's overseas investment.[14] It accounted for 44.53% of the island's total investment abroad from 1991 to January 2003. The Mainland far exceeded Taiwan's second country of investment, the US (11.25% from 1969 to January 2003).[15]

Taiwan's investments on the Mainland started to change in several ways: For instance, the nature of its foreign investment became more long term as well. Its investors moved from joint ventures to solely owned enterprises; they also began to build their own factories in China. The structure of Taiwan's business ventures on the Mainland was also upgraded – from simple assembly to upstream heavy and more capital-intensive or high-tech production. By the mid-to-late 1990s, the mix of Taiwan's investment on Mainland China began to shift from predominantly small business in labor-intensive exports to much larger businesses seeking to penetrate the Chinese market in heavy industry (e.g. Formosa Plastics) and consumer goods (e.g. President Enterprises). There was also a geographic spread of Taiwanese investment, from an initial concentration in Fujian and Guangdong provinces to Shanghai and, most recently, to almost all regions of China.[16]

By 2002, this economic integration began to generate another round of economic interactions between Taiwan and China. Cross-strait trade jumped. It rose 37% from about $30 billion in 2002 to about $41 billion in 2003. Taiwan's FDI on the Mainland also soared. Its investment surged even more dramatically, up to $20 billion, in 2000–2002, reaching an estimated cumulative level of $80 billion–$100 billion.[17]

These strong economic ties also augmented informal people-to-people diplomacy and created substantial Taiwanese communities in many Mainland cities. By 2006, there were an estimated 400,000 to 700,000 Taiwanese nationals living and working on the Mainland, concentrated in the high technology and high economic growth areas of Shanghai and Shenzhen. Some sources say that the number of Taiwanese living in Shanghai alone was about 300,000 in 2006.

The year 2000 was a benchmark year for Taiwanese investment in China, which moved from low- and medium-tech sectors into high-tech sectors. Furthermore, investment in services showed for the first time that Taiwanese businesses had finally begun to view Mainland China as a major export market. For the year 2000, Taiwan-owned production lines manufactured an astonishing 72.8% of the total $25.535 billion production value of China's information technology (IT) hardware sector.[18]

By the end of 2000, up to 48% of desktop computers exported by Taiwan were manufactured in Mainland plants. Plants in Taiwan turned out 18%. The remaining 34% were produced in other parts of the world.[19] In 2000, Taiwan-operated plants in Mainland China assembled 6.5% of Taiwan's notebook output, doubling the 1999 figure. About 56% of Taiwan's motherboard makers also had production lines on the Mainland, which, by the end of 2000, produced over 50% of its total motherboard shipments. Of Taiwan's computer monitor producers, 58% had major production lines in the Mainland. Seventy-four percent of its CD-ROM drive makers moved to Mainland China, and 88% of scanner manufacturers had moved to the Mainland by the end of 2000.[20]

Most importantly, cross-strait economic ties between China and Taiwan blossomed. By 1992, Taiwan's trade and investment with the Mainland were the most dynamic in the world. Cross-strait exceeded $7 billion in 1992. Taiwan businessmen took their capital, technology and managerial skill to the Mainland and created 7,500 projects totaling $8.4 billion. Taiwan tourists made over 3 million visits to the Mainland between 1987 and 1992.[21]

This trend has continued into more recent times. Bilateral trade between China (including Hong Kong and Macao) and Taiwan rose from $35 billion in 1999 to $181.76 billion by 2017. In 2017 alone, trade between China and Taiwan increased 14%. China is Taiwan's largest trading partner, with over 30% of the island's total trade. Since 1988, over 93,000 Taiwanese businesses have invested on the Mainland.[22]

The Kuomintang Party (or KMT) has been a champion of rising cross-strait economic ties. It also supports the 1992 Consensus which says there is only "one China." It implicitly says that Taiwan will not seek political independence. Ma Ying-jeou supported this KMT position when he was Taiwan's president from 2008 to 2016.

This raises an important question. How do the rising cross-sector economic ties we have been discussing correlate with national identity in Taiwan? Back in the heady days of the 1992 Consensus which underscored close cross-sector ties, he Election Study Center at the National Chenghi University did a survey which pleased Beijing. The survey said that only 17.6% of the Taiwanese population saw themselves as Taiwanese; 25% said they were Chinese and almost half – 46.4% – said they were both Chinese and Taiwanese.[23]

The problem is that not everyone on Taiwan sees rising cross-strait economic ties with the Mainland as such a good thing. The other major political party in Taiwan – the Democratic Progressive Party (or DPP) – says that Taiwan is becoming too dependent on the Mainland economy. And if we fast forward to the 2016 election in Taiwan, we find DPP's Tsai Ing-wen becoming the Taiwanese president. Tsai rode an apparent counter-trend of rising Taiwanese identity. A 2017 survey by the National Chengchi University angered Beijing and helps to explain why Tsai Ing-wen did so well in 2016. The survey says that 55% of the island's residents regard themselves as exclusively Taiwanese, 37% say they are both Taiwanese and Chinese, and only 4% consider themselves only Chinese.[24]

The DPP wants to reduce its reliance on Mainland China by diversifying its economic relations. Taiwan President Tsai Ing-wen is trying to strengthen its economic links with Southeast Asia and India with the implementation of the five-year "New Southbound Policy."[25]

126   *Taiwan*

On the political front, Tsai has antagonized China by refusing to support the 1992 Consensus (of one China), leaving the door open for political independence. Chinese President Xi Jinping has responded to Tsai's rejection of the 1992 Consensus by suspending a cross-strait communication mechanism with the main Taiwan liaison office in June 2016. Beijing has excluded the island from international entities addressing civil aviation and global health issues.[26]

Beijing also restricted Chinese tourism to Taiwan. Chiu Chui-cheng, Taiwan's Deputy Minister for the Mainland Affairs Council, stated in late June 2018 that Chinese tourists to Taiwan fell 15% in May and June 2018.[27] Chinese President Xi Jinping is therefore sending Tsai Ing-wen a signal. Be careful what you wish for. If you want Taiwan to be less reliant on the Mainland economy, we can make that happen. Fewer Chinese tourists will come to the island. Does this mean Taiwan is headed for political independence, which would almost certainly trigger a China-Taiwan war?

Not so fast. Chinese President Xi seems to be rushing to judgment that the trend towards Taiwanese identity is equivalent to support for political independence. This is not true. Although Taiwanese identity has obviously been rising since 1992, there has been no parallel change in attitudes towards unification and independence. The Election Study Center finds that over half the Taiwanese population still supports the status quo.

Another survey by Taiwan Brains Trust in 2016 found that almost 80% of respondents said they would like to see the status quo continue. Finally, a Shelley Rigger survey found that Taiwan's younger generation harbors no hostility towards China. They believe that increasing economic ties have benefits for Taiwan. In other words, Taiwan's younger generation has grown up in an era of normalized relations with China and frequent interaction. This has made them more open and rational towards China.[28]

If so, Washington should be pleased that political independence for Taiwan and a China-Taiwan war is not inevitable. The status quo can theoretically hold, but it arguably can't if Washington is a helpless bystander. The ongoing US-China trade war is not helpful if President Trump wants to avoid a China-Taiwan war.

Even in the best of circumstances, holding the status quo in the Taiwan Strait has not been easy for Washington. Mao Zedong came to power in China in 1949, but it took 30 years for the US to establish formal diplomatic relations with Beijing in 1979 under US President Jimmy Carter. A US-China Communique in 1979 states that "there is but one China and Taiwan is part of China." The US also terminated diplomatic relations with Taiwan at that time. That said, Washington has made it clear that it wants the integration of China and Taiwan to be peaceful.[29]

Toward that end, the US Congress passed the Taiwan Relations Act (TRA), which allows the US to send arms to Taiwan to deter or help it defend itself against a possible Chinese military attack. Washington implicitly hoped that closer cross-strait economic ties would make it less likely that

Taiwan would declare political independence and less likely China would attack Taiwan militarily. That won't happen if Washington puts cross-strait relations on autopilot. Nimble US diplomacy is required.

Take DPP accusations, for example, that Beijing is guilty of economic coercion of Taiwan. The logic behind the "economic coercion theory" comes from Tse-Kang Leng's book *The Taiwan-China Connection: Democracy and Development across the Taiwan Strait*.[30] In his book, Tse-Kang Leng points out that a state that is heavily involved in the international economy and cannot shift to relative autarky (or self-reliance) is vulnerable to political leverage exercised by its trading partners. Economic dependence not only limits Taiwan's capacity to intervene effectively in economic transactions but also gives China leverage to manipulate its domestic economy for political ends.

Is Beijing guilty of economic coercion against Taiwan? There are numerous problems inherent in the logic train of the coercion school of thought as well as its so-called evidence. At best, the so-called Chinese coercion strategy is an interesting hypothesis that is searching for more compelling evidence to support its judgments. The following is meant to be constructive criticism of Tse-Kang Leng's rush to judge China's alleged coercion strategy.

First, the definition of coercion is forcing someone to do something they would ordinarily not do. Is Beijing forcing Taiwan investors to invest on the Mainland? There is no evidence of this. Quite the contrary. Is Beijing forcing Taiwan importers and exporters to engage in international trade? Again, this is voluntary. There is no coercion.

Second, Tse-Kang Leng points out that a state that is heavily involved in the international economy and cannot shift to relative autarky (or self-reliance) is vulnerable to political leverage exercised by its trading partners. For a reality check, let's apply this statement to the US. The US is heavily involved in the international economy and cannot shift to relative autarky (or self-reliance) in energy production. Is it vulnerable to undue political leverage exercised by oil exporters? Why would it want to shift to relative autarky (or self-reliance) in energy production and pay huge costs for alternative energy just to be self-reliant in energy? Would Taiwan's economy be better off if it chose a path of economic self-reliance and no trade with or investment in China? Quite the contrary.

Third, the coercion school is critical of China for creating the economic ties that are binding Taiwan and allegedly coercing it into surrendering its sovereignty. But what if China suddenly cut off all economic relations with Taiwan? What if it suddenly refused to trade with Taiwan and said that all future Taiwan investment on the Mainland would be illegal? Wouldn't this PRC economic nationalism be a bigger threat to Taiwan? Wouldn't this be more provocative?

Fourth, the coercion school seems to think that China has all the economic cards and can use these to coerce Taiwan to surrender and accept unification on its terms. The coercion school has created the image of China as an omnipotent economic superpower capable of coercing Taiwan as a helpless victim. Is China's economy really this strong? Quite the contrary. Yes, China has impressive economic strengths, but it also has its own economic problems. China has been in a trade war with the US since 2018. Domestic economic demand is softening. Investors have been pricing in these economic headwinds, with a 20% fall in the stock market between January 2018 and July 2018. Added to these concerns has been the downward pressure on the renminbi. After strengthening against the US dollar in 2017, the currency lost momentum in early 2018, with the renminbi falling 3.2% against the US dollar in June 2018, its largest recorded monthly fall up to that point in 2018.[31]

These Chinese economic weaknesses are a potential vulnerability to the PRC. Therefore, if China was ill advised enough to attempt to use its economic relationship with Taiwan to "coerce" it, Taipei could use the same "coercive" tactics to exploit China's serious economic and financial vulnerabilities.

Fifth, the coercion school generally sees economics as a zero-sum game. Admittedly, economics can be a zero-sum game at the microeconomic level of head-to-head business competition. But that's the free market at work, not coercion. At the macroeconomic level, economics is also a positive sum game. Taiwan is not losing because of international trade with the PRC, and China is not winning at Taiwan's expense. The Taiwan-Chinese economic relationship is not a struggle over which side is more economically independent or dependent on the other side. It is a mutually beneficial relationship, and it reflects economic interdependence. Both sides gain from their trade and Taiwan's investment on the Mainland. Taiwan's Vice President Annette Lu is wrong. This economic relationship is not a "crisis." It is positive and fosters shared prosperity.

There's no question that cross-strait relations between China and Taiwan have worsened since Taiwan President Tsai Ing-wen came to power in 2016. Instead of moving closer to One China, her rejection of the 1992 Consensus means that she is moving closer to political independence, a red line which would trigger a Chinese attack on the island and a possible US-Chinese naval confrontation in the Taiwan Strait.

On the other hand, not everyone sees China's economic trajectory as such a bad thing. In fact, many people in Asia and around the world are benefiting from China's commercial success. They see it as a blessing rather than a threat, a partner rather than an enemy. As its economy grows, its appetite for imports also rises. Asian exporters benefit from the Chinese importing capital goods for their factories. As China's middle class grows, they travel more and spend tourism dollars around the world. US and Asian consumers benefit from high-quality, low-cost Chinese products. As a result, China and Taiwan enjoy mutual gains from free trade, economic interdependence and shared prosperity. Even those who don't currently benefit from China's success story stand to benefit in the future as new commercial opportunities develop.

Can China's economic interdependence with Taiwan reduce its incentives to use military force? There is obviously no easy answer to this question, but an increasing number of Chinese and Taiwanese businessmen on the Mainland are becoming vested in the cross-strait economic relationship. That, in turn, creates a growing force within China for moderating tensions with Taiwan. These economic benefits may become an increasingly important component of Beijing's political calculations, should the economic relationship continue to grow. In other words, China has a vested stake in economic interdependence and shared prosperity.

Put another way, if Beijing had no significant economic relationship with Taiwan, the chances of a PRC attack on Taiwan would be much higher since China would have nothing to lose. Perhaps Thomas Friedman puts it best when he says that strong economic ties between Mainland China and Taiwan greatly reduce the possibility of military conflict between the two sides since such a development would cause "mutual assured economic destruction."[32]

What if Taiwan decides to pursue economic nationalism and the kind of protectionism that effectively locks China out of the global economic system? The Chinese would arguably become more dangerous as they logically concluded that only military force would enable them to reach their economic objectives.

That said, in a crisis, the Chinese might still decide to use military force. Still, at least they would think twice before they threw away all they've gained from their amazing economic success story. This would also give the US and other Asian leaders more time to use diplomacy to explore a settlement.

To encourage either side to move back from the brink of war in the Taiwan Strait, Washington needs to make it clear that China and Taiwan have a strong strake in the shared prosperity and financial and economic interdependence. Don't throw away all this progress. The current political and military tensions in cross-strait relations are serious threats to peace and stability. Every effort must be made to de-escalate the military and political tension, and work toward even closer economic and financial integration of China and Taiwan.

As fate would have it, closer economic and financial integration of China and Taiwan appears to be happening, although the US appears to be the odd man out, economically. While Taiwan still enjoys strong security ties with the US, it has been moving economically away from the US and closer to China. Dr. Charles I-hsin Chen, Executive Director of the Institute for Taiwan-America Studies in Washington, D.C., notes that this is a long-standing trend for Taiwan. Its trade dependency on the US was largely replaced by dependency on China after 2001. The share of Taiwan's total trade involving the US has halved, falling from 23% to 12%, from 1998 to 2018, while China's share doubled from 15% to 31%. Taiwan's export reliance on China increased 2 percentage points to 41% in 2018, peaking historically at 45% in March 2018.[33]

130 *Taiwan*

Dr. Chen also notes that China's economic attraction for Taiwan is growing at the regional level. China's GDP per capita has increased 9 times on a purchasing-power-parity basis since 1990. It is now capable of offering lucrative incentives to convert the loyalty of Taiwan. For example, China's Belt and Road Initiative (BRI) includes the Chinese-led Asian Infrastructure Investment Bank (AIIB), which is far more accessible than the US-led World Bank in terms of granting large loans for Taiwan.[34]

Most importantly, Dr. Chen emphasizes that China's economic attraction for Taiwan is growing at the local level. China's economic influence on Taiwan has become more tangible and comprehensive. Since the late 1980s, Taiwanese investment had been lured by preferential policies from Chinese central and local governments. As of last year, the total amount of Taiwanese investment in China has accumulated to $180 billion – 10 times the Taiwanese investment in the US during the same period. As a result, over 400,000 Taiwanese quality managers and talents are currently working and living in Chinese cities with their family members. The total number may grow to surpass 2 million people, close to one-tenth of Taiwan's population.[35] In short, China's social inclusion and shared prosperity with Taiwan is more attractive to Taiwan than President Trump's US economic nationalism. This trend should also reduce the demand for violence.

Notes

1 The economic data comes for the rise of China from Joint BIS-IMF-OECD-World Bank Statistics.
2 Data from talks with World Bank officials.
3 Denny Roy, *Taiwan, a Political History*, Cornell University Press, Ithaca, NY, 2003, p. 150.
4 Ibid.
5 Taipei's Mainland Affairs Council (MAC).
6 Online at www.mac.tw/English/foreign/28.gif.
7 See Cal Clark, "Economic Development in Taiwan: A Model of a Political Economy", *Journal of Asian and African Studies*, vol. 22, 1987, pp. 1–16.
8 Ibid.
9 Online at www.chinadaily.com.cn/news/2003-05-29/116889.html.
10 Online at http://udn.com/NEWS/WORLD/WORS/1351386.shtml.
11 Chu-yuan Cheng, "Economic Relations across the Taiwan Straits: Mutual Dependence and Conflicts", in Winston L. Yang and Deborah A. Brown, ed., *Across the Taiwan Strait: Exchanges, Conflicts and Negotiations,* Center for Asian Studies, St. John's University, New York, 1999; and Board of Foreign Trade, Ministry of Economic Affairs.
12 See Lung-chu Chen, *The U.S.-Taiwan-China Relationship in International Law and Policy*, Oxford, New York, NY, 2016.
13 These are official Taiwan statistics. The discrepancies between Taiwan and Beijing's statistics result from the indirect trade and investment between Taiwan and the Mainland. Since most Taiwanese businessmen made their investment on the Mainland through Hong Kong and another third country, their records of investment are generally excluded from the official Taiwan statistics, while they are included in Beijing's statistics.

14 Department of Economic Affairs, Mainland Affairs Council, Executive Yuan, ROC, February 2003.
15 Taiwan's Mainland Affairs Council (MAC).
16 Chen, pp. 19–20.
17 The cumulative statistics on Taiwanese investment on the Mainland vary. For example, nongovernment sources estimate that Taiwan has actually invested well over $140 billion on the Mainland.
18 John Thacik, "Taiwan Dependence: The Strategic Dimension of Cross-Strait Trade and Investment", in Andrew Scobell, ed., *The Costs of Conflict: The Impact on China of a Future War*, Strategic Studies Institute, Carlisle, PA, October 2001, pp. 35–62.
19 Taiwan's Ministry of Economic Affairs.
20 Ibid.
21 William H. Overholt, *The Rise of China: How Economic Reform Is Creating a New Superpower*, W.W. Norton, New York, NY, 1993, pp. 327–328.
22 Eleanor Albert, *Backgrounder: China-Taiwan Relations*, Center for Foreign Relations, New York, NY, 15 June 2018.
23 Marie-Alice McLean-Dreyfus, *Taiwan: Is there a Political Generation Gap?* The Interpreter, Lowy Institute, Sydney, Australia, 9 June 2017.
24 Ibid.
25 Economist Intelligence Unit, *Taiwan Economy: Southbound, for the Fourth Time*, 30th September 2016.
26 Eleanor Albert, *Backgrounder: China-Taiwan Relations*, Center for Foreign Relations, New York, NY, 15 June 2018.
27 Economist Intelligence Unit, *Taiwan: Tourism Finding Its Feet Again*, 29 June 2018.
28 Marie-Alice McLean-Dreyfus, *Taiwan: Is There a Political Generation Gap?* The Interpreter, Lowy Institute, Sydney, Australia, 9 June 2017.
29 For earlier American perspectives of cross-strait relations, see Nancy B. Tucker, "If Taiwan Chooses Unification, Should the United States Care?", *The Washington Quarterly*, Summer 2002; Endnote – For earlier threat perceptions of a possible Mainland attack on Taiwan, see Economist Intelligence unit, *Leaping Dragon, Trailing Tigers?* Hong Kong and the Challenge of Mainland China, Taiwan, see Bill Heaney, "Fear not China, says EIU", *Taipei Times*, 30 June 2003, p. 10.
30 Tse-Kang Leng. *The Taiwan-China Connection: Democracy and Development across the Taiwan Strait*, Westview Press, Boulder, CO, 1996.
31 Economist Intelligence Unit, *Risk Returns to China's Economy*, 4 July 2018.
32 See Thomas Friedman, *The Lexus and the Olive Tree: Understanding Globalization*, Farrar, Straus and Girous, New York, NY, 1999.
33 Chen, *The U.S.-Taiwan-China Relationship in International Law and Policy*.
34 Ibid.
35 Ibid.

Bibliography

Betts, Richard K. and Christensen, Thomas J. "China: Getting the Questions Right", *The National Interest*, vol. 62, Winter, 2000/2001, pp. 17–30.

Bush, Richard C. *Untying the Knot: Making Peace in the Taiwan Strait*, Brookings Institution Press, Washington, DC, 2005.

Cheng, Chu-yuan. "Economic Relations across the Taiwan Straits: Mutual Dependence and Conflicts", in Winston L. Yang and Deborah A. Brown, ed., *Across the Taiwan Strait: Exchanges, Conflicts and Negotiations,* Center for Asian Studies,

132   *Taiwan*

St. John's University, New York, 1999; and Board of Foreign Trade, Ministry of Economic Affairs.

Chiu, Hungdah. *China and the Question of Taiwan; Documents and Analysis.* Praeger, New York, NY, 1973.

Clark, Cal. "Economic Development in Taiwan: A Model of a Political Economy", *Journal of Asian and African Studies*, vol. 22, 1987, pp. 1–16.

Clough, Ralph N. *Cooperation or Conflict in the Taiwan Strait?* Rowman & Littlefield, Lanham, MD, 1999.

Friedman, Thomas. *The Lexus and the Olive Tree: Understanding Globalization*, Farrar, Straus and Girous, New York, NY, 1999.

Klaus, Michael. "Red Chips: Implications of the Semiconductor Industry's Relocation to China", *Asian Affairs: An American View*, vol. 29, no. 4, 2003, pp. 237–253.

Leng, Tse-Kang. *The Taiwan-China Connection: Democracy and Development across the Taiwan Strait*, Westview Press, Boulder, CO, 1996.

Overholt, William H. *The Rise of China: How Economic Reform Is Creating a New Superpower*, W.W. Norton, New York, NY, 1993.

Republic of China, Mainland Affairs Council. *Relations across the Taiwan Straits*, Mainland Affairs Council, Taipei, 1994.

Rigger, Shelley. *Why Taiwan Matters: Small Island, Global Powerhouse*, Rowman & Littlefield, Lanham, MD, 2011.

Roy, Denny. *Taiwan: A Political History*, Cornell University Press, Ithaca, NY, 2003.

Rubinstein, Murray A., ed. *Taiwan: A New History*, Expanded ed., M. E. Sharpe, Armonk, NY, 2007.

Sicherman, Harvey. "A Conversation with Taiwan's Chen Shui-bian", *Orbis*, vol. 47, no. 2, Spring 2003, pp. 329–335.

Su, Chi. *Taiwan's Relations with Mainland China: A Tail Wagging Two Dogs*, Routledge, New York, NY, 2009.

Taiwan Affairs Office. *The One-China Principle and the Taiwan Issue*, Taiwan Affairs Office and the Information Office of the State Council, People's Republic of China, Beijing, 2000.

Thacik, John. "Taiwan Dependence: The Strategic Dimension of Cross-Strait Trade and Investment", in Andrew Scobell, ed., *The Costs of Conflict: The Impact on China of a Future War*, Strategic Studies Institute, Carlisle, PA, October 2001, pp. 35–62.

Tsai Ing-wen. "Current Cross-Strait Relationship, an Address Delivered to the Taiwanese Chamber of Commerce", *San Francisco Bay Area*, January 21, 2001.

Wu, Yu-Shan. "Mainland China's Economic Policy toward Taiwan: Economic Needs or Unification Scheme?" *Issues and Studies*, vol. 30, no. 9, September 1994, pp. 20–49.

Zhao, Suisheng. "Economic Interdependence and Political Divergence", in Zhao, Shuisheng, ed., *Across the Taiwan Strait: Mainland China, Taiwan and the 1995–1996 Crisis*, Psychology Press, London, 1999.

13 Bangladesh

In addition to his criticism of China's Belt and Road Initiative (BRI), Trump also accuses the Chinese of "unfair business practices." If there were truth in this accusation, one would expect to find the Chinese "cheating" (by using subsidies or currency manipulation to reduce China's export prices) to maintain market shares. To test out this hypothesis, let's turn the clock back to 2005 and look at over a decade (2005–2016) of Bangladeshi efforts to compete with China in the cut-throat global market industry.

The garment trade in Bangladesh was possible because of the 30-year-old Multi-Fiber Arrangement (MFA) which gave it and other poor countries preferential access to important markets in the European Union (EU) and America. So, when the MFA rules governing garment exports to rich countries were changed at the start of 2005, Bangladesh faced a time bomb. It feared huge jobs losses because of the potential collapse of its garment industry.[1]

Why so devastating? The garment industry anchors the economy and sustains millions of families. Bangladesh gets 75% of its hard-currency earnings from garment exports. Garment factories employ as many as two million workers or half the nation's industrial workforce. About 85% of these workers are women.

Bangladeshi garment makers were afraid they wouldn't be able to compete against China. Why? For a six-year period – 1998 to 2004 – China faced price deflation in textiles and other low-end manufacturing. The Chinese price seemed more and more unbeatable.

Some people said, "Don't worry, it will take China a long time to capture new market shares after MFA expires on 01 January 2005." Well, guess again. China enjoyed virtually overnight success. In the first quarter of 2005, its cotton shirt sales in the US market rose 1,250% from the same period in 2004. Its cotton trouser sales in the US market rose 1,500% from the same period in 2004.

Bangladesh appeared to be on the verge of losing a key industry. The garment industry in Bangladesh accounted for 80% of its exports and lifted 13% of the country's poor households out of poverty.

134 *Bangladesh*

World Bank estimated that China would corner the market by controlling 50% of global garment exports by 2010, up from about 20% today. Why? The Chinese garment makers enjoyed vast economies of scale; a deep pool of cheap labor easily bent to the political will; and fully integrated cotton, textile and garment industries.

China's growing market share in garments did not bode well for Bangladesh once the remaining quota barriers disappeared. The end of MFA would sharply diminish the demand for garments stitched in Bangladesh.

Unemployment in Bangladesh could soar. Most experts predicted that the country would lose one million garment jobs. Also at risk were the jobs of many of the 15 million people who worked in related industries, such as button-makers and truckers. For them, there was no state social security plan and no unemployment benefits.

To make matters worse, Bangladesh – a poor and overpopulated country with rising income disparity – was always fertile ground for extremism. Now, however, the extremists had an issue they could exploit. Violent extremists blamed the United States for globalization and the end of MFA, and they planned to exploit this ill-advised but pervasive perception of social and economic injustice. The concern was that these young men might not find jobs outside Bangladesh. But these angry young men might get politicized and fall for an extreme version of violent extremism. Over time, this could tip the scale of a relatively moderate Muslim country and turn it into a more extreme one.

This connection between the economy and violence contributed to a "great debate" in the country. Given the specter of rising unemployment, would terrorism break out in Bangladesh? One "supply" school of thought said that the Bangladeshi government had beefed up its "capacity" (or supply of intelligence and counter-violence) to combat terrorism. A competing "demand" school of thought said that capacity building – while necessary – was not sufficient. This demand school said that the socio-economic demand for violence was rising. Frustrated people were at risk of buying the propaganda lines of violent extremists.

Who was right? Was the terrorist threat up or down? In August 2005, the worst fears of the demand school played out. Five hundred bombings occurred in Bangladesh in just one month.

But at a time when things looked especially bleak, things were changing in the Chinese countryside that would reverberate in every nook and cranny in the international garment industry. These developments would also reduce the demand for violent extremism in Bangladesh.

Social unrest was rising in the Chinese countryside. In 2005, there were 87,000 public disturbances in China. That's a 13% rise from 2004. Frustrated Chinese farmers were pouring into Chinese coastal cities looking for work in the garment factories. An oversupply of Chinese workers in the cities pushed Chinese wages below those of Bangladesh. Most of these ex-farm workers stayed in the cities. If the great American singer Eddie Cantor were still alive and visited China at this time, he might have sung, "How you gonna keep 'em down on the farm after they've seen Shanghai?"

Then everything changed. In September 2005 – one month after 500 bombings in Bangladesh – Beijing announced that the agricultural tax – which dates back over 2,000 years – would be eliminated. What was the impact of abolishing the agricultural tax in China? At first glance, eliminating this seemed like a good idea to Beijing. It was more affordable for Chinese farmers to stay on the farm, now that their taxes were gone. This also reduced at least some of the social unrest in the countryside.

But be careful what you wish for. There were unintended consequences for Beijing. Improving life in the rural areas of China meant fewer migrant workers leaving the countryside, looking for work in urban garment factories along the PRC coast.

So, imagine you're running a garment factory in Shanghai. You now have a shortfall of workers knocking on your door. How are you going to attract more? You have to boost wages. And in 2005, there was a double-digit rise in Chinese wages. It didn't just happen in the textile industry. It happened across the board in Chinese low-end manufacturing. As a result, its manufacturing competitiveness fell in 2005. It was no longer the low-cost producer.

Who benefited from rising prices in China? It was a godsend for the garment factories in Bangladesh. Back then, garment workers in Dhaka earned 39 US cents an hour, while the hourly wage for sewing and stitching in coastal China rose to 88 cents. In Bangladesh, orders started to soar at its garment factories. Thanks to rising prices, Bangladeshi garment exports rose by $500 million in 2005 compared to those in 2004. The United Nations (UN) fears of a million Bangladeshi garment workers being laid off never happened.

Bangladesh nearly doubled its garment exports from 2004 to 2009.[2] China's garment workers made about $117 to $147 a month in 2010, while Bangladeshi workers made about half that. That spurred production in Bangladesh. The production of Walmart and Liz Claiborne products in Bangladesh rose 20% in 2010, while China's production for the same two companies fell 5%.[3]

If we fast forward to 2015, we discover that China's rising production costs (particularly, for labor and land) allowed Bangladesh and other rival producers to eat into China's market share. In fact, China's wages in the garment industry have doubled in recent years, while those in Bangladesh have remained relatively flat.[4] Over the first eight months of 2015, US garment imports from China fell by 7.7% year on year. Those who most clearly benefitted from China's decline were Bangladesh, Vietnam and India. EU imports from China fell by 9.7% year on year from January–July 2016, while those of Bangladesh and Vietnam surged by 6.3% and 8.8%, respectively.

News flash to Trump officials – that doesn't sound like China cheats. Far from it. In fact, it deserves three cheers for fostering shared prosperity with

136 *Bangladesh*

Bangladesh. In the past, it suffered from unreliable energy utilities and inadequate logistics infrastructure.[5] Beijing is committed to helping Bangladesh overcome these challenges. China's government will contribute to Bangladesh's ability to cope with the rapid growth in shipment volumes at its ports by providing Bangladesh the financing for port and power infrastructure upgrades (i.e. more port capacity) under its "One Belt, One Road" initiative (BRI).[6]

The point is that China believes in shared prosperity in the region, even when its own percentage of the garment pie declines. BRI is all about a rising tide lifting all ships of state. This Chinese positive sum game and support for shared prosperity stands in sharp contrast to Trump's zero sum game of "America First" economic nationalism.

Now, imagine you're a recruiter for a violent extremist group in Bangladesh. Bashing globalization has lost its punch. China's shared prosperity has reduced the demand for violence. Jobs and incomes at Bangladesh textile factories are rising. Globalization is wonderful. The free market has marginalized you. The demand for violent extremism has therefore fallen. Nobody believes your propaganda.

In conclusion, the logic of shared prosperity not only outweighs President Trump's ill-advised ideas of protectionism but also promotes shared security. In addition, there is almost nowhere overseas to bring manufacturing jobs back from. That's because the lion's share of manufacturing jobs was lost to technology, not trade.

In recent times, the dispersion of global manufacturing among many countries has promoted an inclusive economic democracy which, in turn, fosters even more peace and stability. In addition, the high US trade deficit is not because China is manipulating its exchange rate to get cheaper exports. The real reason America is running a large trade deficit is macroeconomic in nature. It's because it is consuming way too much. Therefore, eliminating 100% of China's trade surplus would simply turn into a larger trade deficit with other US trading partners.

US attempts at trade protectionism in the past have only made things worse. In contrast, free trade has dramatically reduced global poverty. If protectionism spreads, get ready for a rise in global poverty, which, in turn, is fertile ground for increasing the demand for violent extremism.

Notes

1 *The Economist*, "Garments in Bangladesh – Knitting Pretty: The Clothing Business Is Flourishing Despite Chinese Competition", 16 August 2007.
2 Vikas Bajaj, "Bangladesh", *The New York Times*, 16 July 2010.
3 Vikas Bajaj, "With Low Pay, Moves in on China", *The New York Times*, 16 July 2010.
4 Kenneth Rapoza, "Is the Made in China Clothing Label a Thing of the Past?", *Forbes*, 11 October 2015.
5 Ibid.
6 Economist Intelligence Unit, "Cutting into China's Apparel Market", 18 October 2016.

Bibliography

Absar, Syeda Sharmin. "Women Garment Workers in Bangladesh", *Economic and Political Weekly*, vol. 37, no. 29, 20 July 2002.

Agrawal, Gourav. "Impact of FDI on GDP: A Comparative Study of China and India", *International Journal of Business and Management*, vol. 6, no. 10, 2011, p. 71.

Begum, Flora. "Bangladesh Ready-made Garment Industry and Women Workers", Deutcthland, 2015.

Drennan, Kelly. "Picking Up the Threads: Fast Fashion Led to Rana Plaza Tragedy in Bangladesh", *Alternatives Journal*, vol. 41, no. 3, 2015, p. 21.

The Economist. "Garments in Bangladesh – Knitting Pretty: The Clothing Business Is Flourishing Despite Chinese Competition", 16 August 2007.

Economist Intelligence Unit. "Cutting into China's Apparel Market", 18 October 2016.

Human Rights Watch. "Whoever Raises Their Head Suffers the Most: Workers' Rights in Bangladesh Garment Factories", USA, 2015.

International Labour Office. "ABC of Women Workers' Rights and Gender Equality", Geneva, 2007.

International Labour Office. "Global Wage Report 2012/13: Wages and Equitable Growth", Geneva, 2013.

International Labour Office. "Fundamental Rights at Work and International Labour Standards", Geneva, 2003.

International Labour Office. "Wages and Working Hours in the Textiles, Clothing, Leather and Footwear Industries", Geneva, 2014.

International Labour Office. "Working Conditions Laws Report 2012", Geneva, 2012.

International Labour Office. "Workplace Safety and Labour Rights in the Bangladesh", Dhaka, 2016.

Khondker, Habibul Haque and Jahan, Mehraj. "The Social Context of Female Labour Force Participation in Bangladesh", *Southeast Asian Journal of Social Science*, vol. 17, no. 2, 1989, pp. 102–120.

Kurpad, M. R. "Made in Bangladesh: Challenges to the Ready-Made Garment Industry", *Journal of International Trade Law and Policy*, vol. 13, no. 1, 2014, pp. 80–96.

Rapoza, Kenneth. "Is the Made in China Clothing Label a Thing of the Past?", *Forbes*, 11 October 2015.

Rubya, Tamanna. "The Ready-Made Garment Industry : An Analysis of Bangladesh's Labor Law Provisions After the Savar Tragedy", *Brooklyn Journal of International Law*, vol. 40, no. 2, 2015, p. 685.

Sikdar, Md. Mehedi Hasan. "Socio-Economic Conditions of the Female Garment Workers in the Capital City of Bangladesh Department of Statistics", *International Journal of Humanities and Social Science*, Vol. 4, no. 3, 2014, pp. 173–179.

Spero, Juan E. and Jeffrey Hart. *The Politics of International Economic Relations*, Routledge, Boston, MA, 2003.

Vasja, Badalic. "Our Workers in Bangladesh: Toiling for $50 Per Month", *New Politics*, vol. 14, no. 3, 2013, p. 8.

Conclusion

This book began with a simple proposition. After World War I, the economic coercion pushed by George Clemenceau in the Treaty of Versailles led to German resentment, the rise of Hitler and World War II. After World War II, Jean Monnet had a better idea. It would be called shared prosperity rather than economic coercion. Despite centuries of war and hatred between the French and the Germans, Jean Monnet and his cohorts planned to create a European Coal and Steel Community (ECSC). The French and Germans would bond by working together on common tasks. The ECSC, along with the collective defense of the North Atlantic Treaty Organization (NATO), would turn French and German enemies into friends. The ECSC and NATO would reduce threat perceptions on each side. George Marshall would follow much the same vision of Jean Monnet with his Marshall Plan, which helped Germany rebuild its factories. Instead of punishing it once again with economic coercion, the idea was to create a web of economic interdependence and shared prosperity.

Over the years, the shared prosperity of Jean Monnet and George Marshall was largely forgotten. American foreign policy was militarized. The US military dominated what was called US national security strategy during the war on communism and especially during the global war on terrorism. The 9/11 Report and the World Bank recommendations calling for shared prosperity to reduce the demand for violence were largely ignored. The book looks at five civil wars and asks: Was American foreign policy militarized in these civil wars? Was the shared prosperity vision of Jean Monnet and George Marshall marginalized? When economic statecraft was applied, was the option of choice usually economic coercion instead of shared prosperity? Should more effort have been made to create viable free market economic strategies that fostered shared prosperity strategies inside and between nation states? The answer to these questions was almost always yes.

Chapter 2 looked at Iraq. In November 2016, the Iraqi government started to celebrate its military victory over the Islamic State of Iraq and Syria (ISIS). Investors were once again seeing reasons for optimism about Iraq's economic prospects. The stock market was on the on the upswing. Fitch gave the economy another vote of confidence in March when it upgraded

Iraq's economic outlook to stable, mostly based on the country's improving public finances. Iraq's GDP growth has also been booming. The defeat of ISIS prompted rare optimism that a window of opportunity would open for social inclusion and shared prosperity among all Iraqis.

But before long, that window of opportunity was squandered. Just eight months after Baghdad and the Western allies celebrated a hard-won victory over ISIS, the most serious anti-government protests in years swept across the country's oil-rich south. Baghdad struggled to contain the protests. Demonstrators laid siege to government buildings, ports and oil companies.

The demonstrators faced serious electricity and water shortages as well as high unemployment. They were fed up with their incompetent political leaders, and they demanded sweeping reform to disrupt the corruption and mismanagement that have crippled the Iraqi economy, despite the oil wealth. The protests undermined hopes that elections in May 2018 would be a turning point and put the embattled country on the road to social inclusion and shared prosperity after decades of conflict.

The Iraqi people have seen this "Big Build-up for the Big Let-down" movie before. Back in 2014, it also seemed like the best of times. The war was over in Iraq, and investors were pouring money into this country's economy. Corporate earnings were booming. International investors were confident that economic rewards in Iraq outweighed any possible risks.

Iraq's economy looked promising in so many ways. In February 2014, its oil production surged to its highest level in over 30 years, and Iraq's oil exports hit a post-2003 high. Iraq was one of the hottest commercial markets in the world. Asia Cell Communications had the biggest initial public offering (IPO) in the Middle East since 2008.

The future also looked bright. With the second-largest proven oil reserves in the Organization of the Petroleum Exporting Countries (OPEC), the International Energy Agency predicted that Iraq's oil output would double by the end of the decade. This was expected to grow by 600–700%. The Economist Intelligence Unit (EIU) predicted that Iraq's GDP growth would reach 8% in 2014 and almost 9% by 2020. No other country in the world had this kind of growth trajectory.

But this was all a false dawn. What did the optimists miss? US military doctrine says that civilian-led stabilization and reconstruction operations need to take place, like those successful efforts undertaken by the US in Germany after World War II. Hans Binnendijk and Stuart Johnson correctly argue that there has been a widening gap between the militarized phases of the US war plan (combat arms) and the shared prosperity phases of the US war plan (economic stabilization and reconstruction). Bad things happen in this gap. Even worse things happen when economics is marginalized, and America tries to kill its way out of Iraq. The absence of shared prosperity between Sunni and Shia was readily apparent, with continuous Shia government discrimination against Sunnis and a rising demand for violence.

140   *Conclusion*

Optimists thought that the fall of the divisive Prime Minister Maliki and the rise of a seemingly more inclusive Prime Minister Abadi was a hopeful sign. But it was too little, too late. Maliki's repression of the Sunnis was deep-rooted and contributed to the rapid expansionism of ISIS. The initial ISIS military success and the subsequent and belated military response of the US and its allies are now well known.

Chapter 3 looked at the war in Afghanistan. Did Washington learn anything about the dangers of militarizing this conflict and marginalizing economics? Washington officials did, at first, when General David Petraeus was the 4-star Commander at the US Central Command (or CENTCOM), from September 2011 to November 2012. Petraeus had previously studied economics at Princeton and taught economics at West Point, so, he was aware of the downside of simply militarizing the war in Afghanistan and marginalizing economics.

Petraeus and his tiger team at CENTCOM created an inclusive New Silk Road strategy, with plans for regional economic integration that would go through Afghanistan, and turn enemies into friends and aid into trade. All of this would promote shared prosperity and collective security. Then Secretary of State Hillary Clinton gave a speech in Chennai, India, embracing CENTCOM's New Silk Road Initiative. But implementation of the New Silk Road Initiative was always to be done by the more operational CENTCOM.

But behind the scenes, American foreign policy in Afghanistan started to change. Despite rhetoric about America militarizing American foreign policy too much, President Obama never supported America's New Silk Road Initiative at CENTCOM. In fact, he demoted Petraeus and sent him to Afghanistan to handle tactical military matters. Obama replaced Petraeus with "Mad Dog" James Mattis. No Hollywood producer would ever have miscast these two generals this way. The New Silk Road Initiative required a military man with a doctoral-level knowledge and experience in economics as well as military matters. Petraeus was the obvious choice. As stated earlier, Petraeus studied economics while getting his PhD in International Relations at Princeton. He also taught economics at West Point.

In contrast, "Mad Dog" Mattis was a Marine's Marine who was trained in using lethal force on the battlefield. His troops loved him. But economics was not his thing. Not surprisingly, he zeroed out the funding for the New Silk Road Initiative at CENTCOM. Most importantly, there was no objection from Obama when Mattis did so. Once again, Mattis would re-militarize the war in Afghanistan. Once again, there was a dangerous gap between the combat arms phase of the US war plan and dismissing economic stabilization and reconstruction as unimportant. Not surprisingly, America has tried to kill its way out of Afghanistan for 18 years without success.

China turned the tables on America by filling this economic gap with its own version of the New Silk Road, the "Belt and Road Initiative" (BRI). In contrast to America waving the economic white flag, Beijing was serious. China committed itself to an estimated 8 trillion dollars. To finance this commitment, it created a New Silk Road Bank and an Asian Infrastructure Investment Bank. Chinese President Xi Jinping calls the BRI his most important foreign policy initiative. In stark contrast to President Trump's "America First" nationalism, Xi's BRI is far more promising because it is socially inclusive and fosters shared prosperity.

How was China so successful in turning the tables on America? And why is America so reluctant to implement its version of the New Silk Road plan? The short answer is that China understands how to connect economics and security in its foreign policy. In contrast, American foreign policy keeps economics and security in separate silos. For the most part, too many US officials simply wave a virtual economic white flag and expect to kill their way out of Afghanistan.

Arab Spring protests in Yemen caught Washington off-guard. Since 9/11, America's foreign policy in this country had been like a one-trick pony. Washington was content to use autocratic Yemeni President Saleh as a willing conduit to let the US military use drones to attack al Qaeda targets in Yemen. In return, Washington implicitly turned a blind eye to Saleh's autocratic ways.

That one-trick pony may have played well at the Obama White House, but it was ill-advised and shortsighted American foreign policy. Not only did America have no moral high ground in Yemen, but this quid pro quo, "drones for autocracy" deal was soon overtaken by events. Arab Spring and Change Square in Yemen were grass-roots protests against US backed autocratic strongmen across the Middle East.

But the mindset at the White House was "better late than never." US diplomats went to work at the 11th hour to quickly "rebrand" Saleh and try to salvage their man. US diplomats put pressure on him to make "bold" concessions in a disingenuous attempt to placate long-suffering protesters at Change Square sites all around Yemen. Not surprisingly, the protesters didn't buy this US hypocrisy. The protesters had long lost faith in Saleh. They simply did not trust him to follow through and implement any of the "shake and bake," made in America, political and economic reforms he had never supported in the past.

In addition, the political wind in Yemen was blowing in a radically new direction. Saleh was losing support on multiple fronts. President Obama – who had been woefully behind on the economic and political power curve in Yemen – finally got the picture. It was now too late for Saleh to reform, so it was time for a policy turnaround and "regime change."

What are the lessons learned for American foreign policy? Don't pursue a militarized foreign policy which opts for narrow counterterrorism tactics in Yemen and turns a blind eye to negative economic and political conditions in the country. Hoping for the best is not a strategy. Don't think you can "rebrand" someone like Saleh, with a laundry list of economic and political reforms, at the 11th hour. It's hypocrisy. Don't force regime change when shake and bake reforms for Saleh don't click. The people in Yemen don't buy 180-degree changes in "drive by" US morality.

142   *Conclusion*

Remember what Roland Paris, author of *At War's End*, says. Political and economic shock therapy simply intensifies competition, which quickly turns into conflict and civil war. Instead, America needs to take the long view and work hard to facilitate political and economic liberalization in Yemen over decades rather than media cycles.

Finally, stop saying that America does not foster nation building. Rebalance American foreign policy in Yemen with diplomatic and economic actions rather than a one-trick pony approach of massive arms sales to an autocratic Saudi Arabia. Narrow US counterterrorism tactics against al Qaeda targets in Yemen are no substitute for fostering responsible nation building. The longer the war goes on, the longer the risk that deep resentment against the US will radicalize and lead to a rise in violent extremism. The massive US arms sales to Saudi Arabia put US lives in jeopardy. The rising anti-Americanism plays right into the hands of al Qaeda propaganda and the recruitment of more and more anti-US terrorists.

Henry Kissinger once said, "Opportunities cannot be hoarded; once past they are usually irretrievable." In Syria, the opportunity for shared prosperity instead of war came in 2009. Before then, the international community had reacted negatively to one wave of domestic repression after another in Syria. The first wave started in 2001, and the second one started in 2006. After each wave of repression, the international community treated Syria as a pariah. And whenever Syria feels threatened by a hostile external environment, it almost always becomes intolerant of domestic dissent and cracks down with a vengeance.

Thus, the Syrian domestic situation had changed. President Bashar al-Assad was pursuing economic reforms at home and abroad. Syrian free market reforms created a strategic opportunity for America to reward Damascus with economic interdependence and shared prosperity. If the Syrian people were happy with job creation and rising incomes as a result of Western trade and investment in Syria, hope and opportunity would replace the anger and fear of Arab Spring. Therefore, there would be no incentive for President Assad to crack down on muted political dissent at home. Assad would think twice before throwing away shared prosperity with America and the West.

Current US Secretary of Defense James Mattis recently said, "You don't want to miss an opportunity because you were not alert to the opportunity. So, you need to have that door open." Unfortunately, neither President Bush nor the Obama administration were alert to the opportunity or had a door open to support Syria's movement toward a free market economy. Why did they squander this strategic opportunity? President Bush militarized American foreign policy after 9/11. Syrian President Assad refused to support Bush's Iraq War (2003–2011), which was based on the fiction that there were weapons of mass destruction (WMD) in Iraq.

Earlier, we cited Henry Kissinger, who said, "opportunities cannot be hoarded; once past they are usually irretrievable." Not surprisingly,

America's decision to squander that creative economic opportunity with Syria led directly to Syrian resentment and civil war. The point is that President Assad arguably would have been more relaxed toward dissent at home when a more peaceful version of Arab Spring happened, had America pursued serious economic interdependence and shared prosperity with Syria.

Analysts tend to look back at the ideological, religious or political factors in the run-up to the Syrian civil war. What is too often overlooked is Syria's mismanagement of its natural resources, especially irresponsible irrigation and the depletion of water as an underlying root cause of the initial uprising and ensuing civil war. That Syrian unwillingness to build resiliency programs made its people extremely vulnerable to the 2006–2011 drought. Syrians from the northeast faced severe food insecurity and migrated to cities.

The trigger for the unrest was Assad's indifference to the hardship of his own people. The US Embassy in Damascus, as well as the Syrian government, warned Washington and the rest of the world that the Syrian government could not handle the social unrest, which could turn into violence. International security analysts argued that Syria was stable and immune to an Arab Spring one day before the revolt. Why did they miss the triggers? They were dismissing the longstanding deterioration of Syrian natural resources. The US had also signed and then ignored the UN responsibility to protect (R2P) vulnerable people only a few months earlier.

The Syrian government is struggling to recover and has requested help. It's time for the US to respond. Forget politics. Dr. Colin Kelley and his researchers predict an increasingly dry and hot future (i.e. extreme drought) for Syria and the surrounding Fertile Crescent. Therefore, outside intervention needs to happen as soon as possible to create resiliency programs and hereby prevent another humanitarian disaster and civil war, which would devastate even more Syrians.

The last civil war we discuss is the Israeli war against Hamas in Gaza. This chapter asked the following questions: Does Israeli coercion work? Do Israeli operational military actions get Hamas to cave in and surrender? Does it make Hamas submissive? Does it win over the Palestinians in Gaza?

The answer is no. Hamas will not become more submissive and less violent, and Israeli tactics do not win over the Palestinian people. The reason is simple. Hamas gets its political legitimacy from the Palestinians in Gaza by satisfying their socio-economic needs. While Israel has a legitimate right to curb the buildup of a Hamas weapons arsenal, destroying Gaza's economy has caused Israel to further lose the war for the hearts and minds of the Palestinians in Gaza and many countries and populations around the world, and has strengthened Hamas as the protector of Palestinian people in Gaza.

So, what kinds of wars was Israel fighting? The Israeli government viewed these wars against Hamas as narrow military campaigns against a conventional military enemy. So, Israel aimed to destroy as many Hamas targets as possible and reduce its military capability to launch more rocket attacks in the future. In this way, Israeli leaders argued that they were protecting the

144   *Conclusion*

Israeli people from Hamas terrorism. However, Israel was only addressing the supply side of war. It focused on destroying weapons. Hamas rocket attacks on Israelis show that replacing old rockets with new ones can occur almost overnight. At best, such a narrow operational approach to war as Israel's can only bring temporary gains.

In addition, the Israelis targeted Hamas "terrorists" wherever they could find them. Inevitably, this meant killing a handful of Hamas terrorists living amongst a multitude of Palestinian civilians. That accounts for why over half the deaths in the 50-Day War were those of Palestinian civilians. This toll in civilian casualties tends to turn their family members and friends into anti-Israeli Hamas "terrorists." Instead of changing tactics, the Israelis double down and become determined to bomb all these "new terrorists." This vicious circle of new terrorists produces an almost permanent state of conflict against the Palestinian people rather than Hamas. After a while, the Israelis desensitize themselves and wrongly dismiss the deaths as "collateral damage." Their thinking was short-sighted, ill-advised and conceptually flawed.

Why is Israeli economic and military coercion a counter-productive strategy toward Hamas? While it's always dangerous to over-generalize, Hamas certainly has its share of "true believers." These true believers feel they do not fit into their societies. They quickly become frustrated and feel they deserve far better. Israeli coercion often fails because it feeds this Hamas frustration and confirms their very sense that they deserve better.

Israeli-launched wars may sometimes be able to control Hamas, but violence will never eliminate it. If the extremist ideas of Hamas are to wane, they will do so only at the hands of more attractive ideas, which the current Israeli leadership seems temperamentally incapable of creating. Thus, it appears that Israel doesn't focus enough on how to shape a web of economic integration and shared prosperity into durable peace and security for all concerned. It logically follows that Israeli leaders have a one-dimensional view of economics. It fears that Hamas economic power will invariably generate military power to reach military goals. In a similar way, the Israeli government sees Hamas as a terrorist group that will never change its tactics. Therefore, the Israelis make no attempt to use serious diplomacy to address Hamas resentment or reduce the Hamas demand for counter-violence.

Finally, Israel dismisses the importance of the information war. No attempt is made to win hearts and minds. Not surprisingly, therefore, Israel lost this all-important information war. It is difficult to exaggerate the damage that has been done to Israel's reputation. The international community increasingly sees it more as a war on the Palestinians in Gaza than a campaign against Hamas.

The next chapter on Iran moves away from kinetic war and looks at war by other means. At first glance, the decade of sanctions against Iran appeared to work. Iran finally came to the negotiating table and signed a nuclear agreement with then US Secretary of State John Kerrey and his amazing team of negotiators. That said, the agreement is really a compromise, freezing the development of nuclear weapons for a decade in return for shared prosperity.

But then Donald Trump became president. That changed everything. He called the nuclear agreement with Iran a disaster. He claimed that Iran had been engaged in an "aggressive and expansionistic foreign policy" since its Islamic Revolution. Since the nuclear agreement ultimately provided Iran with at least $100 billion in unfrozen assets, he argued that Iran would be "emboldened" to support even more instability across the region. Apparently, Trump believes it's a foregone conclusion that Iran will use this money to escalate its funding for Houthi rebels in Yemen, President Assad in Syria, Hezbollah in Lebanon and sectarian militia in Iraq.

However, President Trump was ill-advised. He forgets that the purpose of the sanctions are to coerce Iran to negotiate. This economic squeeze worked. Iran agreed to roll back its nuclear program. But then Trump killed the nuclear deal and "tightened the sanctions" in hopes of getting "a better deal."

That won't work. First, Trump threw away a ten-year agreement that froze the Iranian nuclear program and received no viable alternative agreement in return. Trump is left wishing and hoping that more sanctions and economic coercion will somehow force Iran to totally give up nuclear weapons. But guess again. Wishing and hoping is not a strategy. To make matters worse, Trump has undermined Rouhani, who trusted the US to honor its side of the agreement.

Instead, Trump's withdrawal from the nuclear agreement and his re-imposition of severe sanctions will almost certainly backfire by strengthening the hand of the hard-liners in Iran, who argue that you can't trust America to honor an international commitment. America will just find another excuse to bully you with economic coercion. In short, America will betray you.

The hard-liners in Iran will likely gain the upper hand to Rouhani and the reformers. At home, the hard-liners will stifle political and economic reform. White House threats of regime change in Iran will raise concerns among the Iranian hard-liners of confrontation with the US, Israel and Saudi Arabia. In response, the hard-liners in Tehran will shore up support for its regional proxy forces as a form of deterrence. This will increase tensions between Iran and Saudi Arabia and raise the risk of conflict between Iran and Israel in southern Syria.

Much of the chapter reviewed how the previous round of economic coercion hurt the economy. Trump's "severe economic sanctions," which will begin in November 2018, will also hurt the Iranian economy. They will also arguably backfire and hurt the global oil market and security in the Middle East.

On the Iranian economic front, the US withdrawal from JCPOA and the re-imposition of sanctions will reduce oil export earnings. This kind of economic coercion will also deprive the economy of much-needed Western capital, technology and managerial skills, all of which are necessary to make

146   Conclusion

the transition to a free market economic model successful. Instead, Trump's severe sanctions will force the supreme leader to implement his "resistance economy." This will entrench an inward, nationalistic, socialistic economic model, protecting the militant Islamic Revolutionary Guard Corps (IRGC) and religious businesses in Iran at the expense of foreign (Western) investors. Trump is also learning that sanctions are a double-edged sword and are already backfiring and hurting the US and global economy.

The only good news is that the other P5 plus 1 members want to honor the nuclear agreement with Iran. They are willing to develop their own financial agreement with Iran which does not require US banks or Trump's agreement. The bad news is that Trump's rejection of the nuclear agreement drives one more wedge between America and its post-World War II allies.

Trump looked at Iran with historic determinism. He argued that it was "inevitable" that Iran would use the "lion share" of its $100 billion in unfrozen assets to fund instability. But the past does not have to be a precedent for the future. In fact, Iran has a choice: Choose option 1, and use the money to finance more instability, or choose option 2, and use the money to rebuild its infrastructure and revive its economy.

Iran's support of instability is not inevitable; it can choose re-entry into the global economy. The US is not a helpless bystander. If Trump loses in 2020, a new US president could work with the US private sector and shape Iran's decision to benefit from a web of economic interdependence as a responsible stakeholder. The US and its allies could tilt the playing field and shape's Iran's decision to pursue option two. But instead of wishing for Iran to choose option 2, a new US president would need to work for this with the Iranians. Iran should consider using the $100 billion in unfrozen assets from the nuclear deal to recapitalize a restructured banking sector.

In a broader sense, the new US president needs to work closely with US oil companies, US carmakers, etc. to boost investment and trade with Iran. When this happens, a web of economic interdependence occurs. In this case, Iran develops a stake in shared prosperity. Once it becomes a responsible stakeholder, it would think twice before it did anything blatant to destabilize the region and throw that all away.

This does not mean that the US and Iran will always see the world the same way. Their interests and policies may often diverge. But when US and Iranian interests largely converge, as they did in Iraq against ISIS, the US should not cave into political correctness. It should cooperate with Iran to maximize our chances of success against terrorist groups like ISIS in Syria.

The quartet's embargo against Qatar is a classic case study of why shared prosperity is invariably a better strategy than economic coercion. The quartet's economic coercion of Qatar was only successful in the short run. The boycott/embargo began in June 2017, and Qatar's economy bounced back with imports and GDP growth, returning to pre-crisis levels by October 2017. Qatar also projected long-term confidence by doubling its liquid natural gas (LNG) capacity during its crisis management. It also reached a new energy partnership with Shell.

The case study is also useful in explaining why the embargo did not last long. Qatar had an impressive resiliency plan. For starters, it had robust financial buffers. Thanks to over $300 billion in its sovereign wealth fund and $40 billion in foreign reserves, the central bank had 6.7 months of import cover in its foreign reserves in September – far more than 3 months. Thus, Doha could sell foreign reserves to prop up the riyal when the peg to the dollar was under pressure. It also diversified its supply chain with lots of new countries.

On the military front, Qatar bought dozens of new fighter jets from the US, the UK and France. As a result, it was able to either deter an attack from the quartet or fight in the sky. And if the quartet did invade, the fighter jets helped Qatar secure diplomatic ties with the US, the UK and France.

The quartet also learned that economic coercion is a double-edged sword. The embargo also backfired. Take the UAE. Before the crisis, its Jebel Ali was the busiest port in the region. Not anymore. Qatar opened Hamad, a $7.4 billion new port 40 km south of Doha, to circumvent the blockade.

What the quartet probably still does not understand is why Sunni Qatar and Shia Iran get along so well. The short answer is that this has nothing to do with religion or culture. What's important is the fact that Qatar and Iran share ownership of the South Pars/North Dome natural gas field, by far the largest in the world. Thus, shared prosperity between Qatar and Iran far outweighs the economic coercion of the quartet.

The case study also highlighted differences in Washington. Then Secretary of State Rex Tillerson showed he was the adult in the room by stopping the quartet's plan to invade Qatar. But why didn't Trump stop the embargo against Qatar?

One thing is for sure. America had a golden opportunity to broker an agreement. That's because the US has cross-cutting loyalties and access to all the players. On the one hand, Al Udeid Air Base near Doha in Qatar is the largest US Air Force base in the Middle East. The forward headquarters of the US Central Command (or CENTCOM) is located on the base, along with 10,000 US troops. Qatar also buys fighter jets from America, the UK and the French.

On the other hand, America also has strong political and military equities with the quartet. The Fifth Fleet is in Bahrain, and the US military has strong military assistance programs with all four countries in the quartet.

What was missing was Donald Trump's political will to broker a deal between Qatar and the quartet. Trump does not understand a positive sum game in which all countries can win with shared prosperity. In his mind, what matters is the $110 billion military assistance deal he signed with Saudi Arabia. That far outweighs whatever the US has going with Qatar. In this sense, he sees everything as a zero-sum game. Saudi Arabia is a "big time" winner. Qatar is "small time" and a loser. The Saudi monarchy think the same way as Trump. That's why Qatar ran rings around him and the quartet.

Not long ago, American foreign policymakers celebrated democracies around the world having free elections. On 6 May 2018, Lebanon had its first

148 *Conclusion*

parliamentary election in nine years. So, one might think that the Trump administration would welcome this democratic event. But guess again.

Forget the democratic process. Forget the will of the Lebanese people, who work hard to have a socially inclusive country. Forget the fact that Hezbollah is popular because it is also a social movement which supports health care and education for downtrodden Shia in Lebanon and throughout the Middle East. Forget the fact that its militia fought against the ISIS terrorist group when America did virtually nothing in Lebanon. Forget the fact that Hezbollah has its own military, which stands up to the Israeli army and protects the country. The Trump White House didn't like the results.

The parliamentary election saw Hezbollah gain ground. Hezbollah, a Shia group, and its allies (which include the predominantly Christian Free Patriotic Movement (FPM) of President Michel Aoun) now have a slight majority in parliament, having secured at least 67 of the 128 seats. Prime Minister Saad Hariri, who leads the Future Movement, a Sunni party, has emerged as the biggest loser from the election. Since Hezbollah is a Shia group with good relations with Shia Iran, Trump has come down hard against it.

The Trump administration announced sanctions on seven Lebanese companies for providing material support to Hezbollah amid renewed US threats to target any government ministries that were allocated to the party. The democratically elected Lebanese government does not appreciate this kind of economic coercion from Donald Trump. It is trying to influence Trump to limit the impact of the new sanctions that reportedly target the allies of Hezbollah.

Turkey's economy appeared to be on a roll. But in economics, things can and often do change quickly. The country is now headed for recession. To make matters worse, US sanctions were about to slam Turkey's economy in November 2018 because it bought oil from Iran, a country whose nuclear agreement with the international community Trump had just wrecked.

The timing of this US economic coercion against Turkey was not helpful to a NATO country struggling to keep its economy afloat. It was just a matter of time before the vulnerable Turkish economy fell into financial turmoil. In particular, the Turkish lira was vulnerable to shifts in foreign investor confidence. August 2018 was the month of reckoning. The Turkish lira fell 20% against a US dollar, which was getting stronger because the Federal Reserve (Fed) was tightening US monetary policy to offset super loose US fiscal policy due to a huge US tax cut, soaring budget deficits and a trillion dollars more to be added to the national debt. In Turkey, inflation rose following the currency slide. This forced its central bank to raise interest rates to 24% on 13 September 2018. Turkish President Erdogan was unhappy because high interest rates would send the economy into a recession.

As stated earlier, there were five economic reasons for the currency crisis. First, due to a structurally low national savings rate. The current account deficit was 5.6% of GDP in 2017. This made the lira vulnerable to a tightening in global liquidity due to rising interest rates in the US.

Conclusion   149

Second, the Turkish corporations cited earlier were highly indebted in foreign currency. Many were unable to service these debts. This triggered investor panic, capital flight and downward pressure on the lira.

Third, President Erdogan was implementing his executive presidency. Investors feared that he would politicize the central bank and be less willing to tighten monetary policy to offset Turkey's loose fiscal policy.

Fourth, Turkish tensions with Donald Trump were rising. In August, the US imposed sanctions on Turkish individuals, and Donald Trump announced that US tariffs would double on Turkish steel and aluminum exports to the US. US tariffs on Turkish steel would be 50%, and US tariffs on Turkish aluminum would rise to 30%.

Finally, Donald Trump also re-imposed sanctions on Iran. He wanted to curb Iranian oil exports to countries like Turkey. Trump would enforce this embargo with severe fines on any Turkish bank or company which used US dollars to finance purchases of Iranian oil. These US threats to punish Turkish banks or corporations caused Iranian bankers to be cautious about buying oil from Iran.

But because of Turkey's severe economic problems, as cited above, Erdogan needed to find ways to circumvent US sanctions and import Iranian oil. Therefore, Turkey considered at least four ways of getting around the US sanctions. First, it could use euros or other local currencies, instead of the US dollar, to finance purchases of Iranian oil. Second, it could try to arrange some barter deals that would offer Turkish goods instead of dollars in return for Iranian oil. Third, it could buy oil from the Turkish private sector on the Turkish stock exchange. Fourth, it could use "ghost tankers" in an effort to avoid the US tracking system.

President Trump blames China for "stealing" American jobs. In an effort to bring these jobs back, in July 2018, President Trump launched a trade war against the Chinese. As expected, his high tariffs and China's retaliation have hurt US workers, farmers and consumers.

George Will says that President Trump would like to "make America 1953 again," which means a 30% market share of global manufacturing. But thankfully, in 1953, America had statesmen like George Marshall who had bigger things in mind – like internalizing the lessons learned from the punitive economic coercion of the Treaty of Versailles, which ended World War I and led to the rise of a vindictive Adolf Hitler and World War II. America helped Germany rebuild its factories, and US market shares fell to 20%. But Germany is now in a positive web of economic interdependence and shared prosperity with America.

Like George Marshall, the scholars at the World Bank were impressive in connecting economics to global security. In their definitive 2003 study "Breaking the Conflict Trap: Civil War and Development Policy," they used statistical evidence to reveal a striking pattern: Civil war does not occur randomly around the world. Instead, it is heavily concentrated in the poorest countries. An important reason for this is that poverty increases

150   *Conclusion*

the likelihood of civil war. Thus, the World Bank study concludes that the root cause of conflict is the failure of economic development. More recently, scholars at the United Nations (UN) have highlighted the importance of free trade to counter this rising demand for violence. The UN finds that free trade across the world has cut the extreme global poverty rate in half since 1990.

In contrast, if Trump's protectionism and economic nationalism were to incite a global trend that rolled back this progress in free trade, he would also reverse this impressive decline in global poverty. That, in turn, would provide fertile ground for an even greater rise in the demand for violent extremism. The rising demand for violence would also lead to putting the brave men and women of the US military needlessly in harm's way repeatedly.

President Trump is stuck on blaming China for US unemployment in the rust belt and says that his trade war is designed to "bring back American jobs." The problem is that there is nowhere to bring the manufacturing jobs back from. Most US manufacturing jobs were lost to technology, not trade.

Along the way, President Trump missed this transformation in global manufacturing. In the old days when he says America was "great," manufacturing was one-dimensional. Victor Fung notes that it was done "in-house ... in one factory, under one roof, and in one country ... before that product was exported and sold in another country." But things changed, and products have become increasingly dispersed across different factories in different countries and have thus become globalized. Because of this dispersion of global production, countries previously omitted from manufacturing can now participate by performing just one or two pieces of the supply chain. Fung calls this the "democratization of the global production system." Dispersion also benefits American consumers because it reduces costs and makes products more affordable.

So, when Trump criticizes China for its rising trade surplus with the US, there are simple reasons for this development. As it turns out, many Chinese exports are put together from parts produced elsewhere. With the dispersion of global production, China became a final assembly point for goods that the US previously imported from companies based in Japan, South Korea and Taiwan. As the final leg of the supply chain shifted to China, US imports from China rose as the US imported less from the rest of Asia. In other words, there is nothing evil about China's last leg in this dispersion of global production.

President Trump also accuses China of stealing American jobs by manipulating its foreign exchange rate. If China wanted a low foreign exchange rate to underprice US products, why did its foreign exchange rate rise so much against the US dollar? In fact, it rose from 8 renminbi (RMB) to $1 in the mid-2000s to 6.3 RMB to $1 in 2015.

Instead of blaming China, President Trump needs an economist to tell him that his policies end up strengthening the US dollar and therefore overpricing US exports.[1] His huge $1.5 trillion tax cut increased public spending, a large percentage of which goes into imports. As imports grow faster than exports, the trade deficit rises. America must offset this with a surplus in the capital account (financial flows) in the balance of payments. To attract capital inflow, the Fed must tighten monetary policy by increasing interest rates. Rising interest rates strengthen the demand for the US dollar, and a stronger US dollar overprices US exports, worsens US trade and current account deficits, and throws Americans out of work in export industries.

Instead of blaming China for America's high trade deficit with China, President Trump's policies are counterproductive. His huge $1.5 trillion tax cut has caused the budget deficit and national debt to soar. The federal budget deficit is headed back towards at least 7% of the Gross Domestic Product (GDP) over the next 10 years. That's over two times worse than the 3% of GDP level that an EU Maastricht criterion says is financially unstable.

Similarly, the non-partisan US Congressional Budget Office (CBO) said that President Trump's public debt would hit 78% of GDP by the end of 2018, the highest level since 1950. The long-term projections are even worse. CBO says that the debt to GDP ratio is on track to hit 100% of GDP by 2030 and 152% by 2048. That's a far cry from the 60% of GDP level that another EU Maastricht criterion says is financially unstable.

Unfortunately, the national savings rate fell to just 2.4% of GDP in mid-2018. The problem is that President Trump keeps getting it wrong. His 1.5% tax cut will send the already dangerously low national savings rate into negative territory.

Trump officials are critical of Chinese economic initiatives in developing countries. They accuse China of "predatory" lending policies. They say that its five-year-old BRI is dangerous because it gets developing countries hooked on excessive debt. That criticism is ill-advised for several reasons. First, such patronizing advice to developing countries is hypocritical. The officials ignore the fact that no country in the world is as highly indebted to China as the US. The US government owes China over a trillion dollars. This debt is getting far worse because the Trump administration's tax cut for millionaires and billionaires is increasing the national debt by over a trillion dollars. Perhaps Trump should have hired former Admiral Michael Mullen, Chairman of the US Joint Chiefs of Staff, who said, "the most significant threat to our (America's) national security is our debt."

In addition, America is no role model when it comes to building modern infrastructure. The Trump administration has done virtually nothing to rebuild America's collapsing infrastructure. One of the biggest critics of China's BRI is Trump's Secretary of Defense James Mattis, yet it was James Mattis who waved the economic white flag and zeroed out the funding for the New Silk Road Initiative which General Petraeus had wisely started before him at CENTCOM. Second, America is still offering the same developing countries virtually nothing in contrast to China's trillion-dollar initiative.

In the 1980s, Taiwan's competitiveness was falling. Wages were too high, and unemployment was rising. Then, Taiwan's businessmen brought their capital, technology and managerial skills to Mainland China. Taiwan's trade and investments with the Mainland soared. Taiwan and Mainland China businessmen saw the cross-strait economic ties as a blessing. On the political front, in 1992, the Kuomintang Party in Taiwan and Mainland

152 *Conclusion*

China signed a consensus which basically said that both sides enjoyed shared prosperity and believed in "one China."

The problem is that not everyone on Taiwan sees rising cross-strait economic ties with the Mainland as such a good thing. The other major political party in Taiwan – the Democratic Progressive Party (or DPP) – says that it has become too dependent on the Mainland economy. A survey said that over half the residents in Taiwan regard themselves as exclusively Taiwanese, 37% said they were both Taiwanese and Chinese, and only 4% considered themselves only Chinese.

The fear on the Mainland is that the trend towards Taiwanese identity could lead to political independence, a redline for China to attack Taiwan militarily.

Although Taiwanese identity has obviously been rising since 1992, there has been no parallel change in attitudes towards unification and independence have remained the same. The Election Study Center finds that over half the Taiwan population still support the status quo.

Another survey, by Taiwan Brains Trust in 2016, finds that almost 80% of respondents said they would like to see the status quo continue. If so, Washington should be pleased to know that political independence for Taiwan and a China-Taiwan war are not inevitable. The status quo can theoretically hold, but it arguably cannot do so if Washington is a helpless bystander. The ongoing US-China trade war is also not helpful if President Trump wants to avoid such a war.

In addition, some folks on Taiwan have accused Beijing of economic coercion against Taiwan. Is Beijing guilty of such economic coercion? There is not much evidence of this.

First, the definition of coercion is to force someone to do something they would ordinarily not do. Is Beijing forcing Taiwan investors to invest on the Mainland? There is no evidence of this. Quite the contrary. Is Beijing forcing Taiwanese importers and exporters to engage in international trade? No. The trade is entirely voluntary.

Taiwanese also accuse the Mainland of creating economic ties that are "too tight" and forcing Taiwan to surrender its sovereignty. But what if China suddenly cut off all economic relations with Taiwan? What if it suddenly refused to trade with Taiwan and said that all future Taiwanese investment on the Mainland would be illegal? Wouldn't this PRC economic nationalism be a bigger threat to Taiwan? Wouldn't this be more provocative?

The coercion school seems to think that China has all the economic cards and can use them to coerce Taiwan to surrender and accept unification on Chinese terms. This school has created the image of China as an omnipotent economic superpower capable of coercing Taiwan as a helpless victim. Is China's economy really this strong? Quite the contrary. Yes, China has impressive economic strengths, but it also has its own economic problems. China is in a trade war with America in 2018. Domestic economic demand is softening. Investors have been pricing in these economic headwinds, with

Conclusion 153

a 20% fall in the stock market between January 2018 and July 2018. Added to these concerns has been downward pressure on the renminbi. After strengthening against the US dollar in 2017, the currency lost momentum in early 2018, with the renminbi falling 3.2% against the US dollar in June 2018 in its largest recorded monthly fall up to that point.

These Chinese economic weaknesses are a potential vulnerability to the PRC. Therefore, if China was ill advised enough to attempt to use its economic relationship with Taiwan to "coerce" it, Taipei could use the same "coercive" tactics to exploit China's serious economic and financial vulnerabilities.

Finally, the coercion school generally sees economics as a zero-sum game. Admittedly, economics can be a zero-sum game at the microeconomic level of head-to-head business competition, but that's the free market at work, not coercion. At the macroeconomic level, economics is also a positive sum game. Taiwan is not losing from international trade with the PRC, and China is not winning at Taiwan's expense. The Taiwan-Chinese economic relationship is not a struggle over which side is more economically independent or dependent on the other side. It is a mutually beneficial relationship and reflects economic interdependence. Both sides gain from their trade and Taiwan's investment on the Mainland. This economic relationship is positive and fosters shared prosperity.

That said, there's no question that cross-strait relations between China and Taiwan have worsened since Taiwanese President Tsai Ing-wen came into power in 2016. Instead of moving closer to One China, her rejection of the 1992 Consensus means she is moving closer to political independence, a redline which would trigger a Chinese attack on the island and a possible US-Chinese naval confrontation in the Taiwan Strait.

On the other hand, not everyone sees China's economic trajectory as such a bad thing. In fact, many people in Asia and around the world are benefiting from its commercial success. They see it as a blessing rather than a threat, a partner rather than an enemy. As China's economy grows, its appetite for imports also rises. Asian exporters benefit from the Chinese importing capital goods for their factories. As China's middle class grows, they travel more and spend tourism dollars around the world. US and Asian consumers benefit from high-quality, low-cost Chinese products. Thus, China and Taiwan enjoy mutual gains from free trade, economic interdependence and shared prosperity. Even those who don't currently benefit from China's success story stand to benefit in the future as new commercial opportunities develop with the Chinese.

Can China's economic interdependence with Taiwan reduce its incentives to use military force? There is obviously no easy answer to this question, but an increasing number of Chinese and Taiwanese businessmen on the Mainland are becoming vested in the cross-strait economic relationship. This, in turn, creates a growing force within China for moderating tensions with Taiwan. These economic benefits may become an increasingly important component of Beijing's political calculations, should the economic

154 *Conclusion*

relationship continue to grow. In other words, China has a vested stake in economic interdependence and shared prosperity.

Put another way, if Beijing had no significant economic relationship with Taiwan, the chances of a PRC attack would be much higher since it "would have nothing to lose." Perhaps Thomas Friedman puts it best when he says that strong economic ties between Mainland China and Taiwan greatly reduce the possibility of military conflict between the two sides since such a development would cause "mutual assured economic destruction."

What if Taiwan decides to pursue economic nationalism and the kind of protectionism that effectively locks China out of the global economic system? The Chinese would arguably become more dangerous as they would logically conclude that only military force would enable them to reach their economic objectives.

That said, in a crisis, China may still choose to use military force, as a member of the global economic system. Still, they will at least think twice before they throw away all they've gained from their amazing economic success story. As the Chinese think twice, US and other Asian leaders will arguably have more time to pursue a settlement with them.

To move away from the brink of a war in the Taiwan Strait, Washington needs to make it clear that China and Taiwan have a strong stake in shared prosperity and financial and economic interdependence. China and Taiwan should not throw away all this progress. The current political and military tensions in cross-strait relations are serious threats to peace and stability. Every effort must be made to de-escalate the military and political tension, and work toward even closer economic and financial integration of China and Taiwan.

Donald Trump likes to criticize China for unfair trade practices. If this were accurate, we would expect to see China cheating to maintain or increase its market shares in the cut-throat global garment industry. To test out this hypothesis, we turned the clock back to 2005 and looked at over a decade (2005–2016) of Bangladeshi efforts to compete with China in this industry.

The garment trade in Bangladesh was possible because of the 30-year-old Multi-Fiber Arrangement (MFA) which gave Bangladesh and other poor countries preferential access to important markets in the EU and America. So, when the MFA rules governing garment exports to rich countries were changed at the start of 2005, Bangladesh faced a time bomb. It feared huge jobs losses because of the potential collapse of its garment industry. Bangladeshi garment makers were afraid they couldn't compete against China. Why? For a six-year period – 1998 to 2004 – China had price deflation in textiles and other low-end manufacturing. The Chinese price seemed more and more unbeatable.

Optimists said it would take China a long time to capture new market shares after MFA expired on 01 January 2005. Well, guess again. China enjoyed virtually overnight success. In the first quarter of 2005, its cotton shirt sales in the US market rose 1,250% from the same period in 2004. China's cotton trouser sales in the US market rose 1,500% from the same period. As a result, unemployment in Bangladesh could soar.

Conclusion 155

To make matters worse, Bangladesh – a poor, overpopulated, corrupt country with rising income disparity – was always fertile ground for extremism. Now, the extremists had an issue they could exploit. They blamed the US for globalization and the end of MFA, and planned to exploit this ill-advised but pervasive perception of social and economic injustice.

This connection between the economy and violence contributed to a "great debate" in the country. Given the specter of rising unemployment, would terrorism break out in Bangladesh? One "supply" school of thought said that the Bangladeshi government had beefed up its "capacity" (or supply of intelligence and counter-violence) to combat terrorism. A competing "demand" school of thought said that capacity building – while necessary – was not enough. This school said that the socio-economic demand for violence was rising. Frustrated people were at risk of buying the propaganda line of violent extremists. Who was right? Was the terrorist threat up or down? In August 2005, the worst fears of the demand school played out. Five hundred bombings occurred in Bangladesh in just one month.

But at a time when things looked especially bleak, things were changing in the Chinese countryside that would reverberate in every nook and cranny of the international garment industry. These developments would also reduce the demand for violent extremism in Bangladesh.

Social unrest was rising in the Chinese countryside. In 2005, there were 87,000 public disturbances in China. That's a 13% rise over 2004. Frustrated Chinese farmers were pouring into Chinese coastal cities looking for work in the garment factories. An oversupply of Chinese workers in the cities pushed Chinese wages below those of Bangladesh. Most of these ex-farm workers stayed in the cities. If the great American singer Eddie Cantor were still alive and visited China at this time, he might have sung, "How you gonna keep 'em down on the farm after they've seen Shanghai?"

Then everything changed. In September 2005 – one month after 500 bombings in Bangladesh – Beijing announced that the agricultural tax – which dates back over 2,000 years – would be eliminated. What was the impact of abolishing this tax in China? At first glance, eliminating it seemed like a good idea to Beijing. It was more affordable for Chinese farmers to stay on the farm now that their taxes were gone. This also reduced at least some of the social unrest in the countryside.

But be careful what you wish for. There were unintended consequences for Beijing. Improving life in the rural areas of China meant fewer migrant workers leaving the countryside looking for work in urban garment factories along the PRC coast.

So, imagine you're running a garment factory in Shanghai. You now have a shortfall of workers knocking on your door. How are you going to attract more workers? You must boost wages. In 2005, there was a double-digit rise in Chinese wages. That didn't just happen in the textile industry. It happened across the board in Chinese low-end manufacturing. As a result, China's manufacturing competitiveness fell in 2005. It was no longer the low-cost producer.

156 *Conclusion*

Who benefited from rising prices in China? This was a godsend for the garment factories in Bangladesh. Back then, garment workers in Dhaka earned 39 US cents an hour, while the hourly wage for sewing and stitching in coastal China rose to 88 cents. In Bangladesh, garment factory orders started to soar. Thanks to China's rising prices, Bangladeshi garment exports rose by $500 million in 2005 over those in 2004. UN fears of a million Bangladesh garment workers being laid off never came to pass.

Bangladesh nearly doubled its garment exports between 2004 and 2009. China's garment workers made about $117 to $147 a month in 2010, while Bangladesh workers made about half that. This spurred production in Bangladesh. The production of Walmart and Liz Claiborne products there rose 20% in 2010, while China's production for the same two companies fell 5%.

If we fast forward to 2015, we discover that China's rising production costs (particularly for labor and land) allowed Bangladesh and other rival producers to eat into its market share. In fact, China's wages in the garment industry have doubled in recent years, while those in Bangladesh have remained relatively flat. Over the first eight months of 2015, US garment imports from China fell by 7.7% year on year. Those who most clearly benefitted from China's decline were Bangladesh, Vietnam and India. EU imports from China fell by 9.7% year on year from January–July 2016, while those of Bangladesh and Vietnam surged by 6.3% and 8.8%, respectively.

News flash to Trump officials – that doesn't sound like China cheats. Far from it. In fact, it deserves three cheers for fostering shared prosperity with Bangladesh. In the past, Bangladesh suffered from unreliable energy utilities and inadequate logistics infrastructure. Beijing is committed to helping it overcome these challenges. China's government will contribute to the ability of Bangladesh to cope with the rapid growth in shipment volumes by providing it with finances for port and power infrastructure upgrades under the Belt and Road Initiative (BRI).

The point is that China believes in shared prosperity in the region, even when its own percentage of the garment pie declines. BRI is all about a rising tide lifting all ships of state. This Chinese positive sum game and support for shared prosperity stands in sharp contrast to Trump's zero-sum game of "America First" economic nationalism.

Now, imagine you're a recruiter for a violent extremist group in Bangladesh. Bashing globalization has lost its punch. China's shared prosperity has reduced the demand for violence. Jobs and incomes at Bangladeshi textile factories are rising. Globalization is wonderful. The free market has marginalized you. The demand for violent extremism has therefore fallen. Nobody believes your propaganda.

Note

1 See Stephen Roach, "US-China Trade Deficit Is Set to Keep Rising", CNBC. com, 26 March 2018; and Stephen Roach, "The Current Account Counts", *Project Syndicate*, 27 August 2018.

Index

Note: Page numbers followed by "n" denote endnotes.

Abadi, Haider al 12–14, 140
Abbas, Mahmoud 72
Abdul-Mahdi, Adel 18, 20
Afghan conflict: economic development
  and 35–6; poverty related indicators
  37; root cause of 37
Afghan East-West Road Corridor 28
Afghanistan: brain drain 36; challenge
  of reconciliation 32–4; failure of
  economic development 35–6; fiscal
  revenue costs 36; Gross Domestic
  Product (GDP) 26; overview 25–7;
  public infrastructure 28; reducing
  post-conflict risk 34–5; root cause of
  Afghan conflict 37; unemployment in
  29; weak trade diversification 27–32
Afghan North-South Road Corridor 28
Afghan Ring Road 28
Ahmadinejad, Mahmoud 80
Ahmed, Ismail Ould Cheikh 49
Al Jazeera 89
Allen, John 28, 68
Allen, Mel 35
Allied Powers 4
al Qaeda: anti-Americanism and 46,
  50, 142; Saleh and 43, 49, 141; US
  counterterrorism tactics against
  50, 142
"America First" (or America Alone)
  economic nationalism 7, 136, 141, 156
American Enterprise Institute (AEI) 60
American foreign policy: in Afghanistan
  140; Bush and 56, 142; economics
  and security in separate silos in 141;
  elevating economics in 2; in Middle
  East 56; militarization of 8, 42–3,
  46–7, 50, 56, 138, 140–2; Obama

administration and 2–3, 42–3, 46, 56,
  68, 141; rebalancing 2–3, 50, 56, 141;
  Trump and 42, 46
Aoun, Michel 96, 148
Arab Spring: America and 49; Bahrain
  and 89; Iraq and 14; oil prices during
  14; Syria and 6, 55–7, 63, 142–3;
  Yemen and 42–4, 49, 141
Arab Studies Institute 63
Armitage, Richard 1
Army National Guard and Reserves 3
ASEAN 25
Asia Cell Communications 11, 139
Asian Infrastructure Investment Bank
  (AIIB) 29, 32, 130, 141
al-Assad, Bashar 6, 55
At War's End (Paris) 5, 50, 142
Austin, Lloyd 31, 58
Aynak Copper Mine 28

Bahrain 7, 89–91, 147
Ball State University 114
Bangladesh 133–6; bombings in 134–5,
  155; China and 133–6, 156; garment
  exports 135, 156; garment trade in
  133–6, 154; Multi-Fiber Arrangement
  (MFA) 133–4, 154–5; terrorism and
  134, 155; unemployment in 134, 154;
  violent extremism in 134, 155
Bank of China (Hong Kong) 121
Basindwa, Mohammed Salim 44
Basra Gas Company 17, 20
Belt and Road Initiative (BRI) 6, 25, 32,
  117, 130, 133, 136, 140–1, 151, 156
Binnendijk, Hans 12, 26, 139
Blackwill, Robert D. 1
borrowing costs 29

158 *Index*

Brafman, Ori 4
brain drain: Afghanistan 36; Syria 54
"Breaking the Conflict Trap: Civil War and Development Policy" 112, 149
"Breaking the Impasse" group 74
Bureau of Conflict and Stabilization (CSO) 32
Bush, George W. 2, 56, 142

Campbell, John 3
Cantor, Eddie 134, 155
Carter, Jimmy 113, 126
CENTCOM 3, 6, 8, 9n21, 27–9, 31–2, 58, 67n40, 90, 118, 140, 147, 151
Central Asia-South Asia Electricity Project (CASA 1000) 28
Change Square protests 43–5, 141
Chen, Charles I-hsin 129–30
Chen Shui-bian 123
Chevrolet 79
Chevron 80, 82–3
China: Bangladesh and 133–6, 156; as biggest export market to Taiwan 121; coercion strategy 127; economic coercion 8, 127, 152; economic weaknesses 128; Gross Domestic Product (GDP) 120; One Belt, One Road Initiative (BRI) 6, 25, 117, 130, 133, 136, 140–1, 151, 156; Taiwan's exports to 123; Taiwan's imports from 123; tourism to Taiwan 126; and Trump, Donald 111–18, 135–6, 141; Trump and 111–18
Chiu Chui-cheng 126
Christian Free Patriotic Movement (FPM) 96, 148
Cisco Systems 80, 122
civil war 3; Afghan 34–7; political center on 8n5; political left on 8n5; political right on 8n5; in Yemen 42, 46–50
Clausewitz, Carl von 70
Clemenceau, George 4, 56, 138
Clinton, Hillary 84, 101, 140; "New Silk Road" speech 25, 31
Coca-Cola 79
Cold War 1
"collateral damage" 71
Collier, Paul 34
communism: global war against 1, 138
Conoco 82
ConocoPhillips 82
costs: borrowing 29; fiscal revenue 36; real interest 30

Daghir, Ahmed bin 49
Daly, Patricia 114
Dassault 93
Democratic Progressive Party (DPP) 125, 127, 152
democratization 5, 114, 150
Dempsey, Martin 2, 4
Deng Xiaoping 120
Deni, John R. 2, 56
Descalzi, Claudio 83
Dickens, Charles 78

East Timor 26
economic coercion 138; China 8, 127, 152; Clemenceau and 4, 56, 138; Israeli 6, 68–9, 73, 75; of Qatar 89, 93, 147; Saudi-led, of Houthis 48; short-sighted 4; US 3–5, 7, 56, 78, 80–1, 84–5, 90, 97–8, 101, 103–4, 109, 113, 138, 145–9
"economic coercion theory" 127
economic development: Afghanistan 35–6; failure of 35–6
economic sanctions 59–60; Iran under severe 59–60, 85, 145; JCPOA and 78; by US against Lebanon's Jammal Trust Bank 96
The Economist 68
Economist Intelligence Unit (EIU) 12, 100
Egypt 7; blockade imposed on Gaza by 72, 74; Gulf-backed military coup in 105; Saudi Arabia subsidizing energy supplies to 19; Turkey's exports to 105
Eisenhower, Dwight D. 34
Elbinger, Lewis 27, 28
electricity: Iraq 11, 16–22; most critical challenge 16–22
Eni 81–3
Erdogan, Recep Tayyip 103, 104, 107–9, 148–9
European Coal and Steel Community (ECSC) 3–5, 74, 90, 138
European Union (EU) 13, 44, 133; Maastricht criterion 99–100
European University Institute 4
Exxon Mobil 82

Fahim, Kareem 46
Fallon, William "Fox" 31
Farhadi, Adib 28
Fatah (party) 72–3, 75
Federal Reserve (Fed) 115, 148

Index 159

Femia, Francisco 63
Fiber Optic Ring telecom project 28
50 Day Gaza War (8 July 2014–26 August 2014) 70–2, 74, 144
Financial Times 81
fiscal revenue costs and Afghan War 36
Fitch 11, 91, 138
food insecurity, in Syria 62–3, 143
Ford, Robert 57
Ford Motor 122
Formosa Plastics 124
France: diplomatic ties with Qatar 147; and Germany 4, 9n14; and Qatar 147
Franco-German Friendship 4, 9n14
Friedman, Thomas 129, 154
Fung, Victor 114, 150
Future Movement (Sunni party) 96, 148

garment industry: in Bangladesh 133–5, 156; China's wages in 156; global 8, 154
Gaza 68–75; American foreign policy and 68; "Breaking the Impasse" and 74; economic coercion and 68–9, 75; economic recovery in 72, 75; 50 Day Gaza War 70–1; international aid to power sector in 72–3; international organizations and 70; rebuilding of 73; 3-Week Gaza War 69; wars between Hamas and Israel 69
Gaza Strip 69, 73
GE 19, 80
"geo-economics" 1
Germany 4, 9n14, 28, 74, 78–9, 105, 112, 117, 120, 138–9, 149
Gfoeller, Michael 27, 28
Ghani, Ashraf 32
Gleick, P.H. 63
global garment industry 8, 154
global war against communism 1
Great Depression 26, 78, 113
Greater China 8, 120–1
Griffiths, Martin 48–50
Gross Domestic Product (GDP): Afghan 26; China 120; Iraq 11; Lebanon 98; Qatar 90; Syria 54
Grossman, Marc 31, 38n20
Gulf Cooperation Council (GCC) 19, 43, 57, 97

Haas, Richard 57
Hadi, Abdu Rabbu Mansour 44–6, 49
Hajigak Iron Ore Mine 28

Haley, Nikki 68
Hamas 68–73, 75, 143–4
Hanratty, Martin 28
Hariri, Saad 96–7, 148
Harley, Jeffrey 28
Harris, Jennifer M. 1
"hereditary enmity" 4
Hezbollah 57, 84, 96–7, 101n4, 145, 148
Hitler, Adolf 4, 56, 112, 138, 149
Hodgson, Ted 28
Holbrooke, Richard 28
Hoover, Herbert 113; Smoot-Hawley Act 113
Houthis 44–50
humanitarian crises 3
Hussein, Saddam 16, 89

"institutions before liberalization" (IBL) 5
internally displaced people (IDP) 12, 35–6
International Atomic Energy Agency (IAEA) 7, 80
International Criminal Court (ICC) 73
International Energy Agency 12, 139
International Monetary Fund (IMF) 12–14, 27, 29–30, 36–7, 39n29, 54, 65, 97–101, 106, 109
International Security Assistance Force (ISAF) 25
Iran 78–86; banking sector 80; Chinese oil companies and 84; economic sanctions 59–60; under economic sanctions 59–60, 85, 104, 108, 144–5, 148–9; energy industry in 81–3; foreign direct investment (FDI) in 81–2; Houthis and 46–7; international community's nuclear agreement with 7, 33, 79, 83–4, 144–5; IRGC hard-liners in 85, 145–6; oil and gas reserves 79; Qatar and 89–92; Syria and 57–60
Iran Deal 7
Iranian Petroleum Contract 83
Iranian Revolutionary Guard (IRG) 60
Iranian Revolutionary Guard Corps (IRGC) 83–5, 146
Iraq 5–6; Arab Spring 14; "Big Build-up for the Big Let-down" 139; electricity in 11, 16–22; financing budget deficit 13–14; gold holdings in 13; Gross Domestic Product (GDP) 11; IMF and 12–14; Iraqi reconstruction 14–16; ISIS and 11–16, 20; LNG 20;

160 *Index*

oil Sector in 16; as "one trick pony" economy 13; overview 11–14; power sector in 17–18; replacing Iranian imports 18–19; World Bank and 15, 17, 22
Iraqi reconstruction 14–16
Iraq War (2003–2011) 56
Irwin, Douglas 113
Islamic Revolution 84
Islamic Revolutionary Guard Corps (IRGC) 146
Islamic State of Iraq and Syria (ISIS) 5, 11–16, 20, 26, 33, 57–8, 86, 96–7, 100–1, 104–5, 138–40, 146, 148
Islamic State of Iraq and the Levant (ISIL) 23n14

Jadaliyya 63
Jammal Trust Bank 96
Japan 28, 82, 115–17, 120–1, 150
Johnson, Stuart 12, 26, 139
Joint Comprehensive Plan of Action (JCPOA) 78, 84–5, 86n1, 145

Kabul-Jalalabad-Peshawar Expressway 28
Kandemir, Asli 107
Karman, Tawakkol 43
Kelley, Colin P. 64, 143
Kerrey, John 144
Khalilzad, Zalmay 33
Khashoggi, Jamal 42
Kirkuk-Ceyhan pipeline 12
Kissinger, Henry 22, 53, 56, 142
Krotz, Ulrich 4, 9n14
Krugman, Paul 116
Kuomintang Party (KMT) 125
Kurdish oil fields 12
Kurdish Regional Government (KRG) 13
Kurdistan 23n14
Kurds 14
Kushner, Jared 73

Lebanon 96–101; Consumer Confidence Index 98; first parliamentary election in 7, 96, 147–8; Gross Domestic Product (GDP) 98; impact of conflict on weak labor market 99; ISIS and 97, 100–1; Lebanese diaspora population 100–1; poverty and high unemployment in 99; remittance inflows 100–1; Syrian Civil War and

97–8; Syrian refugees in 99; tourism and 97–8; Trump praising 97; Trump's economic coercion against 97; unemployment in 98–9
Lee Teng-Hui 123
liberalization 5, 50, 142
"liberal market economies" 5
"liberal peace thesis" 5
Liz Claiborne (brand) 135
Locke, John 5
Lovelace, Douglas 2
Lu, Annette 128

"Make America Great Again" 111
al-Maliki, Nouri 12, 140
Mao Zedong 126
Marshall, George 4–5, 26, 81, 89, 112, 138, 149
Marshall Plan 3, 5, 112, 138
Mattis, James 25, 31, 55, 117, 140, 142, 151
Ma Ying-jeou 125
Meacham, Jon 4
Middle East 7, 11, 43, 58, 60, 63, 73, 79, 85, 90, 96, 98, 139, 141, 145, 147–8
migration: forced, in Afghanistan 35; Syria 62; US agriculture strategists and 9n24
al-Mikhlafi, Abdul Malik 49
Miliband, David 48
Mitsubishi 17
Monnet, Jean 4, 74, 89, 138
Moslem Brotherhood 105
Motorola 122
Mullen, Michael 2, 117, 151
Multi-Fiber Arrangement (MFA) 133–4, 154–5
Murphy, Chris 42, 46–7
Museveni, Yoweri 65

Nabhan, Gary 61
National Chenghi University 125
National Dialogue Conference (NDC), Yemen 44
National Security Strategy documents 2
natural resources: Syrian mismanagement of 60–1, 63, 65, 143
Near East Quarterly 62
Netanyahu, Benjamin 60, 68, 73
New Silk Road 6, 25–9, 31, 32
New Silk Road Bank 141
New Silk Road Initiative 6, 9n21, 28, 67n40, 117, 140–1, 151

Index 161

Niarchos, Nicolas 46
9/11 Commission 1–2
9/11 Commission Report 2
Nokia 122
North American Free Trade Agreement (NAFTA) 101
North Atlantic Treaty Organization (NATO) 7, 103–4, 112, 138, 148
Northern Rail Corridor 28
North Korea 116
Norwegian Refugee Council (NRC) 6–7

Obama, Barack 2, 6; Afghanistan and 26; American foreign policy and 2, 42, 46, 56–7; New Silk Road initiative and 31, 140; Syria and 56–8; took office in 2009 2; Yemen and 43, 46–7
One Belt, One Road Initiative (BRI) 6, 25, 32, 117, 130, 133, 136, 140–1, 151, 156
Organization for Economic Co-operation and Development (OECD) 7, 104
Organization of the Petroleum Exporting Countries (OPEC) 12, 15, 139
Oxford Analytica 30

Palestinian Monetary Authority 69
Palestinians 6–7, 68–75, 143–4
Paris, Roland 5, 9n16, 50, 142
Patton, George 31
Perry, William 64
Peshmerga (Kurdish military) 23n14
Peterson Institute 113
Petraeus, David 3, 6, 25–26, 28, 31, 117, 140, 151
Policy Planning Council (US State Department) 27, 31–2, 38n16
political center 8n5
political left 8n5
political right 8n5
political unrest: at Deirez-Zour 63; at Hama 63; Syria 63
Pollack, Ken 60
Pompeo, Mike 48
Ponzio, Richard 28
post-conflict risk: reducing, in Afghanistan 34–5
Pouyanne, Patrick 80
Powell, Colin 32
President Enterprises 124

protectionism 111; negative aspects of 114; Taiwan and 129, 154; Trump's 112–14, 136, 150
Putin, Vladimir 59

Qatar 7, 89–93; aid to the Palestinians 72; diplomatic ties with US, UK and France 147; economic coercion of 89, 93, 146; financial buffers of 92; Gross Domestic Product (GDP) 90; Saudi-led boycott of 7
Qatar Air Force 93
Qatar Airways 91
Qatar Petroleum (QP) 93

Rachman, Gideon 80–1
Radical Inclusion: What the Post-9/11 World Should Have Taught us About Leadership (Dempsey and Brafman) 4
Rand, Dafna H. 46
real interest costs 30
reconciliation: Afghanistan 32–4; challenge of 32–4
Responsibility to Protect (R2P) 64, 143
Riedel, Bruce 46
Roosevelt, Franklin 46
Rostow, Walt 26
Rouhani, Hassan 80, 84–5, 145
Royal Dutch Shell 81, 93
Ruckstuhl, Sandra 65
Russia 79; Assad receiving military support from 57–8; Iran's nuclear agreement with 78; ISIS and 104; Syrian civil war and 57–60

Sach, Jeffrey 5
al-Sadr, Muqtada 20
Salameh, Riad 96
Salang Tunnel 28
Saleeby, Suzanne 63
Saleh, Ali Abdullah 42–6, 48–50, 141
Salman, Mohammed bin 42
Sarkozy, Nicolas 55
Saudi Arabia 7; American foreign policy and 42; Houthis and 45, 48; Iraq and 15, 18–21; Lebanon and 98; Obama and 46–7; Qatar and 89, 91; Turkey's exports to 105; US arms sales to 142
"Save and Win" campaign 96
September 11, 2001 terrorist attack 1
Sheberghan Gas Fired Thermal Power Facility 28

162 *Index*

Shell 17, 82
Shia 14, 58–60, 89, 96, 139, 148
Shia militia 58–60
Siemens 19
Smoot-Hawley Act 113
social inclusion 4, 7, 11, 65, 68, 74–5, 81, 97–8, 139
"social market economy" 54
Sony 122
The Soul of America (Meacham) 4
South Korea 82, 113, 115–16, 150
South Pars gas field 80
Soviet Union 60, 79
Starr, Fred 27
Starr, Stephen 62
"statistical illusion" 116
Summers, Larry 28–30, 65
Sunni revanchism 57
Sunnis 12, 14, 139–40
Syria: Arab Spring 6, 55–7, 63, 142–6; brain drain 54; decade of lost chances 60; food insecurity 62; Gross Domestic Product (GDP) 54; migration 62; mismanagement of natural resources 60–1; overview 53–60; political unrest 63; start recovery 64–5; unemployment in 54; US Embassy and Syrian government warnings 63–4; water depletion 61–2
Syria: A Decade of Lost Chances (Wieland) 60
Syrian Air Force 58–9
Syrian Ba'ath party 53
Syrian Civil War 6, 56–60, 64–5, 97–100, 105, 143
Syrian socialism 53

Taiwan 116, 120–30; Board of Trade (BOFT) 123; business community of 122–3, 130n13, 151–2; China as biggest export market to 121; Chinese tourism to 126; economic coercion in 8; exports to China 123; imports from China 123; investment on Mainland China 123–5, 130n13, 153–4; "New Southbound Policy" 125; social and economic interactions between Mainland China and 122; unemployment in 122, 151
Taiwan Brains Trust 126
The Taiwan-China Connection: Democracy and Development across the Taiwan Strait (Tse-Kang Leng) 127
Taiwan Relations Act (TRA) 126

Taiwan Strait crisis of 1995–1996 123
A Tale of Two Cities (Dickens) 78
Taliban 6, 32–6
Task Force for Business & Stability Operations (TF/BSO) 32
terrorism: Bangladesh and 134, 155; global war on 1, 138; Hamas 70, 144; Iranian Revolutionary Guard Corps (IRGC) and 83
3-Week Gaza War 69
Tiananmen Square massacre 123
Tillerson, Rex 89–90, 147
Tishrin Dam, Syrian construction of 66n16
Total 80, 81
trade diversification: weak, in Afghanistan 27–32
Transfeld, Mareike 46–7, 51n27
Treaty of Versailles 4, 112, 138
Truman, Harry S. 4, 113
Trump, Donald 2, 6, 32; "America First" (or America Alone) economic nationalism 7, 81; arms sales to Saudi Arabia and 42, 46; and China 111–18, 135–6, 141; Iran and 78, 80–2, 84–6, 145–9; Israeli-Palestinian issue and 68, 74–5; Lebanon and 96–8; militarized American foreign policy under 46; protectionism and 112–14, 136, 150; Turkish tensions with 103–4, 108–9
Tsai Ing-wen 125–6, 128, 153
Tse-Kang Leng 127
Turkey 103–9; currency crisis of 104; current account deficit 105–6; domestic savings rate of 109; external financial vulnerabilities of 109; severe economic problems 104–9, 148–9; Trump and 103–4, 108–9; US economic coercion against 103; US sanctions on 7, 103–4, 108–9
Turkmenistan, Afghanistan, Pakistan and India (TAPI) gas pipeline 28
"two-state theory" 123

unemployment: in Afghanistan 29; in Bangladesh 134, 154; in Lebanon 98–9; in Syria 54; in Taiwan 122, 151; US 114, 150
United Arab Emirates (UAE) 7, 22, 46, 48, 72, 89, 91–3, 98, 105, 147
United Kingdom (UK): diplomatic ties with Qatar 147; Syrian civil war and 57
United Nations (UN) 26, 44; Food and Agriculture Organization (FAO) 62–4,

67n30; Responsibility to Protect (R2P) 64, 143; Security Council 48, 68
United Nations Relief and Works Agency 70
United Nations Relief and Works Agency for Palestinian Refugees (UNRWA) 72
United States (US): counterinsurgency doctrine 3; counterterrorism tactics 142; diplomatic ties with Qatar 147; economic coercion 3–5, 7, 56, 78, 80–1, 84–5, 90, 97–8, 101, 103–4, 109, 113, 138, 145–9; Great Depression 26, 78, 113; New Silk Road Initiative 6, 9n21, 67n40, 117, 140–1, 151; unemployment 114, 150
US Agency for International Development (USAID) 32, 47, 96
US Air Force 46, 90, 147
US Army Corps of Engineers 64
US Army War College 2, 8
US Central Command (CENTCOM) 3, 6, 8, 9n21, 25, 27–9, 31–2, 58, 67n40, 90, 118, 140, 147, 151
US Congress 58, 126
US Congressional Budget Office (CBO) 116–7, 151
US Department of Agriculture 64
US Department of Defense (DOD) 48
US Embassy and Syrian government warnings 63–4
US Energy Information Agency (EIA) 15
US Geological Survey 26
US Pacific Command (PACOM) 3, 8
US State Department 25, 27, 31–2
US Treasury Department 26, 96

Van Dam, Nikolaos 56
violent extremism 1–3, 46, 50, 75, 97, 112, 134, 136, 142, 150, 155–6

Walmart 135
Ward, Christopher 65
Washington Post 42, 46
water depletion: Syria 61–2
Watson Brown Foundation 35
weak trade diversification: Afghanistan 27–32
weapons of mass destruction (WMD) 56, 142
Western Europe 4, 105
Wieland, Carsten 60
Will, George 112
Wilson, Woodrow 5
World Bank 1, 2, 17, 22; Logistics Performance Index (LPI) 27
World Food Program (WFP) 47
World Trade Center attack 1
World Trade Organization (WTO) 111, 121
World War I 4, 56, 112, 138
World War II 3, 4, 56, 74, 112, 138

Xi Jinping 126, 141

Yehia, Abdullah bin 63
Yemen 42–50; America's militarized foreign policy toward 47, 50, 141–2; Arab Spring 42–4, 49, 141; domestic oil production 42; Houthi rebels in 84, 145; National Dialogue Conference (NDC) 44; Obama and 43

Zedillo, Ernesto 101
Zoellick, Robert 1

Printed in the United States
By Bookmasters